Politics in Africa:
The Former British Territories

COMPARATIVE MODERN GOVERNMENTS

General Editor: Max Beloff

Gladstone Professor of Government and Public Administration,
University of Oxford

India's Democracy   A. H. HANSON AND JANET DOUGLAS

The One and Indivisible French Republic   JACK HAYWARD

Politics in Africa: The Former British Territories
   J. F. MAITLAND-JONES

Italy—Republic Without Government?   P. A. ALLUM

Further Titles to Be Announced

Politics in Africa

The Former British Territories

J. F. MAITLAND-JONES

W·W·NORTON & COMPANY·INC·

NEW YORK

Copyright © 1973 by J. F. Maitland-Jones

Library of Congress Cataloging in Publication Data

Maitland-Jones, J   F
  Politics in Africa.

  (Comparative modern governments series)
  London ed. (Weidenfeld & Nicolson) has title: Poli-
tics in ex-British Africa.
  Bibliography: p.
  1. Africa—Politics—1960-   2. Comparative
government. I. Title.
JQ1883 1973.M34   320.9′6′03   73-20361
ISBN 0-393-05516-7
ISBN 0-393-09305-0 (pbk.)

Contents

Tables

Abbreviations

AA	Anglo-American Group
AATUF	All-African Trade Union Federation
AG	Action Group
ANC	African National Congress
AP	Associated Press
APC	African Peoples' Congress
ASP	Afro-Shirazi Party
BBP	Bechuana Peoples' Party
BCP	Basutoland Congress Party
BDP	Bechuanaland Democratic Party
BIP	Botswana Independence Party
BN	Basotho National Party
BNF	Botswana National Front
BSACO	British South Africa Company
CAST	Consolidated African Selection Trust
CIA	Central Intelligence Agency
CPP	Convention Peoples' Party
CSO	Central Selling Organization
DCSL	Diamond Corporation of Sierra Leone
DICORWAF	Diamond Corporation of West Africa Ltd
DP	Dominion Party
EACSO	East African Common Services Organization
ECOSOC	Economic and Social Council
EEC	European Economic Community
Exec. Co.	Executive Council
FLN	Front de Libération Nationale
GATT	General Agreement on Tariffs and Trade
GDO	Government Diamond Office

IBEAC	Imperial British East Africa Company
ICFTU	International Confederation of Free Trade Unions
ICU	Industrial and Commercial Workers' Union of Africa
INM	Imbokodvo National Movement
KADU	Kenya African Democratic Union
KANU	Kenya African National Union
KPU	Kenya Peoples' Union
KY	Kabaka Yekka Party
Leg. Co.	Legislative Council
MCP	Malawi Congress Party
MFN	Most Favoured Nation
NCNC	National Convention of Nigerian Citizens
NLC	National Liberation Council
NNA	Nigerian National Alliance
NNDP	Nigerian National Democratic Party
NNLC	Ngwana National Liberatory Congress
NP	National Party
NPC	Northern Peoples' Congress
NRC	National Redemption Council
NTUC	Nigerian Trade Union Congress
OAU	Organization of African Unity
PAC	Pan-African Congress
POGR	President's Own Guard Regiment
PPP	People's Progressive Party
RF	Rhodesia Front
RST	Rhodesia Selection Trust
SA	South Africa Party
SLPP	Sierra Leone People's Party
SLST	Sierra Leone Selection Trust
TANU	Tanganyika African National Union
TUC (N)	Trade Union Congress (Nigeria)
TUCSA	Trade Union Council of South Africa
UDI	Unilateral Declaration of Independence
UDP	United Democratic Party
UFP	United Federal Party

UPGA	United Progressive Grand Alliance
UNCTAD	United Nations Commission on Trade and Development
UNIP	United National Independence Party
UP	United Party
UPC	Uganda People's Conference
WFTU	World Federation of Trade Unions
ZANU	Zimbabwe African National Union
ZAPU	Zimbabwe African Peoples' Union
ZNP	Zanzibar Nationalist Party

Editor's Introduction

The series of which this is the first volume is intended as a contribution to the study of contemporary political institutions in a number of countries both in Europe and in the rest of the world, selected either for their intrinsic importance or because of the particular interest attaching to their form of government and the manner of its working. Although we expect that most readers of such a series will be students of politics in universities or other institutions of higher or further education, the approach is not wholly that of what is now technically styled 'political science'. Our aims have been at once more modest and more practical.

All study of government must be comparative, in that the questions one asks about one system will usually arise from one's knowledge of another, and although we hope that anyone who has read a number of these volumes will derive some valuable general ideas about political institutions, the notion that politics is a suitable subject for generalization and prediction is alien to the empirical spirit that animates the series.

The authors are concerned with government as an important practical activity which now impinges upon the life of the citizen in almost every sphere. They seek in each individual country to ask such questions as how laws are made and how enforced, who determines and in what manner the basic domestic and foreign policies of the country. They seek to estimate the role not only of elected persons, presidents, ministers, members of parliament and of lesser assemblies but also of the officials and members of the armed forces who play a vital role in different ways in the different societies.

But government is not something carried out for its own sake; ultimately the criterion of success and failure is to be found in its impact upon the lives of individual citizens. And here two further questions need to be asked : how does government conduct itself in regard to the citizen and what protection has he through the courts or in other ways against arbitrary action or mal-administration? The second question is how the citizen can in fact make his influence felt upon the course of government, since most of the countries that will be discussed in these volumes claim to be democratic in the broadest sense. And this inquiry leads on to a discussion of political parties and the various interest-groups or pressure-groups which in modern states form the normal vehicles for self-expression by citizens sharing a common interest or common opinions. To understand their working, some knowledge of the role of the press and other mass-media is clearly essential.

The study of such aspects of politics has recently been very fashionable and is sometimes styled the behavioural approach or the investigation of a political culture. But our authors have kept in mind the fact that while the nature of a country's formal institutions may be explained as the product of its political culture, the informal aspects of politics can only be understood if the legal and institutional framework is clearly kept in mind. In the end the decisions are made, except where anarchy or chaos prevails, by constituted authority.

We would like to feel that anyone suddenly required for official or business or cultural purposes to go to one of these countries hitherto unknown to him would find the relevant volume of immediate use in enabling him to find his way about its governmental structure and to understand the way in which it might impinge upon his own concerns. There is a great deal to be said for a guide-book even in politics.

Nevertheless no attempt has been made to impose uniformity of treatment upon these volumes. Each writer is an authority for his particular country or group of countries and will have a different set of priorities; none would wish to treat in the same way an old-established and highly integrated polity such as that of France or the United Kingdom, a vast and heterogeneous political society still searching for stability such as India, or a whole group of countries at very different stages of development but with a common factor in their previous allegiance to the British crown which is the subject of the present volume.

The editor wishes to thank Miss J. F. Maitland-Jones, the deputy editor, for much help in the planning of the series as a whole and in the presentation of the individual volumes.

Foreword

This book was begun when the first of the British territories in Africa to achieve full independence under indigenous rule, Ghana, had been independent for sixteen years, and when the last, Swaziland (always excepting Rhodesia, in a constitutional limbo since UDI in 1965) had been free for only four. Any book that tries to graft these two events on to the political developments of white-controlled Africa runs the risk of being thought either irrelevant, or presumptuous – perhaps both. Although it is customary to consider black Africa apart from white Africa because of the polarity of the political systems each has evolved, there is very good reason to attempt to combine the two into a single story. It is interesting to note the similarity of the challenges posed and the responses evoked by essentially the same political predicaments confronting both black- and white-controlled governments. It is worth remembering that the real problems of Africa are not those of race, but the intractables of poverty, social mobility and industrial development – expressed, maybe, in racial terms, because this is the easiest and most obvious way in which to do so.

Why write *now*, it may be asked, when the rate of change in Africa renders words out-of-date the day after they are written? It is precisely these rapid changes that make some sort of context for them essential if the Africans themselves, let alone the British and Americans looking in on them from the outside, are to understand events as part of a wider pattern. Decolonization is now complete, so that we can begin to grasp what the mainstream of political progress has been since independence; yet the whole affair is not so remote in time for us to be unable to draw conclusions and put them to good use. Finally, the further we progress in time, the more tenuous will become the links of the ex-British countries with each other and with Britain herself, the less striking the British heritage, and the more difficult to discern a common starting point for individual development. To the British themselves the evolution of their former territories offers a pungent comment on the quality of their own civilization which they bequeathed to their successor states, and forms an important component of national pride; the sooner we have the wherewithal to judge our prowess as empire-builders, the sooner we can purge our pride or guilt or contempt and move on to fill other roles, more fitting, perhaps, for our relative strength and willpower in today's world.

Practical politics has to do with power, the persons who wield it, and the means at their disposal for ensuring their survival. It has also to do with the measures they adopt to overcome the challenges – real or fancied – with which they are confronted, and to perpetuate their rule. Politics in Africa today is a grassroots affair of a sort of which the western world may have a little book knowledge but next to no practical experience. The politics of Britain is Buggins' turn; that of African states is a test of personal physical survival. Ignorance, poverty, ambition, corruption and the consciousness of a kind of manifest destiny to carve out a fair place for the black man in today's world all inflame the issues facing African governments. The issues themselves are clear enough. To create and maintain conditions in which peace, prosperity, stable government, personal opportunity and freedom can flourish are the aims of African, as of other, countries' governments. To achieve these aims is more difficult, involving as it does an amalgam of the experience of other and older societies with indigenous formulae. It is not that there are no answers to the African predicament; there are, rather, too many. The problem is not what to include but what to leave out.

This book had something of the same problem. Africa, even just those parts that were once British, is an enormous canvas and the treatment therefore had to be impressionistic rather than exhaustive. In isolating those subjects and trends that seemed important others had to be left out or, perhaps, treated less fully than might be expected. An attempt has been made to highlight the continuing problems that have a reasonably universal application over the continent, without dwelling on the most evocative subjects – such as race relations – which attract much coverage elsewhere.

My thanks are due to the library staff at the Royal Institute of International Affairs, where some of my research was done, and in particular to Mr R. Townsend, librarian at the Institute of Commonwealth Studies, Oxford, for his help and the speed with which he laid hands on the material I needed. I am also deeply grateful to the general editor of this series, Professor Max Beloff, for giving me the opportunity to write this book; and to the publishers, for their patience.

London, December 1972

J.F.M-J.

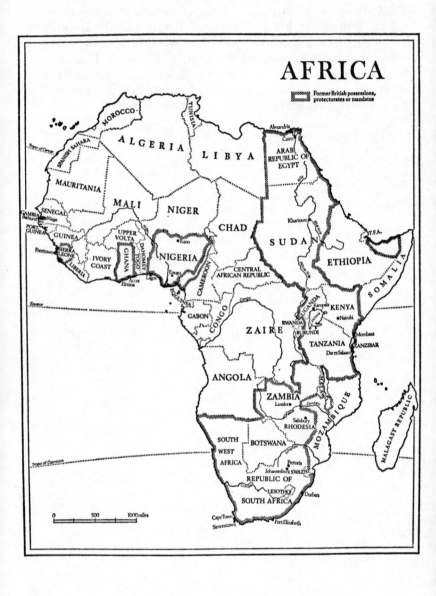

AFFRICA

Former British possessions, protectorates or mandates

Politics in Africa:
The Former British Territories

1 Historical Background

British Africa was a century and a half in the making, a mere decade or so in the losing.

It is true that the earliest British contacts with sub-Saharan Africa took place on the west coast from the seventeenth century onwards. Exploratory to begin with, they developed slaving bases from which the slaves so necessary to West Indian and American economies could be shipped; and in turn the slaving bases developed to handle the commercial trade in commodities and consumer goods that grew out of the slave trade. It was after the slave trade had been forbidden to British nationals in 1807, however, that British strongholds were set up on the West African coast to encourage the development of legitimate trade; bases were founded in Sierra Leone in 1808, in the Gambia in 1816 and in the then Gold Coast in 1821.

By the middle of the century the success of the palm oil traders in the Niger delta was ensuring continued British interest in, and control over, the area that is now Nigeria. British influence in South and Central Africa began with the establishment of Cape Colony in 1805 to guard the route to India, and spread northwards to include the three protectorates of Bechuanaland, Basutoland and Swaziland as well as what is now Rhodesia, Malawi and Zambia. In East Africa, the spread of British interest through Zanzibar from the 1820s onwards was inspired by the wish to rid the east coast of slavery. By 1886 an Anglo-German agreement ensured that what is now Uganda and Kenya would fall within the British sphere of influence; Tanganyika itself became a British mandated territory at the end of the First World War.

West Africa

Of the four British territories – the Gambia, Sierra Leone, Ghana

1

and Nigeria – the first two listed were the first to become formally British. Fort James on the Gambia river had been a trading
settlement from 1661, and belonged to the Royal African Company, an English joint-stock trading company formed in 1672
with a royal charter. Originally it held a slaving monopoly, but
when this proved to be unprofitable the company declined and
finally lost its charter in 1750. Fort James was then merged with
the colonial possessions in the area captured from the French in
1758, and the new colony called Senegambia thus formed was
given a constitution by act of the British parliament in 1765.
This lasted only until 1783, when the former French territories
were returned to French control and Fort James reverted to rule
by the English merchant company, the Company of Merchants
Trading to Africa. In 1894 a British protectorate was declared
over its hinterland as a result of the colonial horse-trading of the
time among the British, French, Germans and Belgians, and the
territory assumed its present geographical extent.

Sierra Leone's first settlement dated from 1787, when it was
used as a refuge for slaves liberated in England; very soon afterwards it was destroyed by local indigenous Africans, and thereafter interest centred on the town of Freetown, which was settled
first in 1791 and administered by a chartered company which
hoped to combine money-making by legitimate trade with
humanitarian care for liberated slaves. In this it was disappointed,
for it never prospered and by 1808 could no longer afford to
continue trading. In the same year Freetown became a crown
colony, its status as a refuge for liberated slaves ensuring that the
humanitarian lobby in England would insist on it remaining
British territory. In later years it became a centre for naval
patrols seeking to eliminate slaving, and in 1896 the British declared a protectorate over the hinterland – again, as in the case
of the Gambia, a result of European negotiations to carve up the
remaining African territories into spheres of influence.

Ghana, early known as the Gold Coast, had like the Gambia
been the site of operations by the Royal African Company, whose
main headquarters was at Cape Coast Castle. Again, slaving was
the main activity, but this together with legitimate trade was
unprofitable and in 1750 the company gave up its charter and
rid itself of its responsibility for administering the area. The
company's premises were then controlled by the Company of

Merchants Trading to Africa until 1821, when finances became disastrous and the area reverted to crown colony status, and from 1828 to 1874 the bases were administered under the over-all control of the Governor of Sierra Leone. British power in the coastal area expanded in 1850 with the acquisition of forts pre-viously held by the Danes, and in 1872 the Dutch relinquished Elmina. When Ashantiland and the Northern Territories in the interior of the Cape Coast were constituted a protectorate in 1901, the area that is modern Ghana was virtually completed as a British possession; Togoland, which was joined with Ghana at independence in 1957, was taken from Germany during the First World War.

The giant of the West African coast, Nigeria, was the latest in time to pass under British rule. Lagos was acquired only in 1861, but British trading interests in the area – which after the abolition of slavery had come to be centred on the export of palm oil and the import of consumer goods – were of much longer standing. By the 1880s Britain was in competition par-ticularly with France over colonies in West Africa, and by 1885 had declared the Oil Rivers area, which stretched from Lagos eastwards for 400 miles to the Cameroons and extended inland for about 250 miles, a protectorate so as to nullify French claims to the area. Further north and higher up the Niger river the British presence depended on yet another chartered company, the Royal Niger Company, and the extent to which it could beat the French in negotiating treaties with the indigenous rulers and establish effective occupation as a prelude to official British rule. By 1898 further French expansion in what is now northern Nigeria had been blocked, and in 1903 a protectorate over the territory was announced. A policy of centralization and unifica-tion was now followed with the various parts of Nigeria, with the result that in 1906 the colony of Lagos was united for ad-ministrative purposes with the protectorate of the Oil Rivers and in 1914 the northern and southern areas of the country were united; thus did modern Nigeria assume her presentday boundaries.

South and Central Africa

The British presence at the Cape dated from 1785, when a

3

British force defeated the Dutch and French Huguenot settlers there and assumed control of the base to protect the safety of the route to India. Once established, British humanitarian motives operated to protect the natives from exploitation by the settlers, and this resulted in continual pressure on the Boers to escape British power by moving northwards; and this in turn conflicted with the movement southwards of the Bantu peoples fleeing the Zulus, at that time an expansionary element in Central Africa. In 1842 the British formally occupied Natal, and by 1848 had claimed authority over the other Boer settlements in southern Africa; but recognized the Transvaal in 1852, and the Orange Free State in 1854, as independent sovereign states. In 1877 the Transvaal was again annexed by Britain, but after stiff and successful Boer resistance independence was regained in 1881.

Meanwhile, other, commercial, motives were taking the place of the strategic and humanitarian ones that had first led the British on in southern Africa. The diamonds discovered in Griqaland West in 1870, and the gold first turned up on the Rand in 1886, were to load the stakes for those playing for the territories of southern Africa and sharpened the conflict between Boer and Briton which developed into open war in 1899. The military defeat of the Boers was followed by peace in 1902, and the Union of South Africa, formed by the merging of Cape Colony, Natal, the Transvaal and the Orange Free State in 1909, appeared to offer the best hope of a unified Anglo-Boer nation.

There had meanwhile been other moves northwards, spurred on by Cecil Rhodes and his financial interests and by his dreams for a Cape to Cairo railroad and the paramountcy of British interests over those of the Boers as well as those of the other European powers taking a hand in the partition of Africa. Rhodes obtained a royal charter for his company in 1889, and after bringing pressure to bear on British officials and government members had, by 1893, obtained financial and administrative responsibility over the whole of the Rhodesias. Company rule continued until 1923, when Northern Rhodesia (later independent as Zambia) reverted to protectorate status, and Southern Rhodesia by a referendum conducted among the white population voted to remain apart from South Africa, becoming a crown colony enjoying a special near-dominion status of its own.

Nyasaland, later to become Malawi at independence, was

above all the product of missionary endeavour and humanitarian sentiment. The African Lakes Company had originated in 1878 with its object to substitute commerce for the slave trade, but its financial resources were slender. It had demanded, but been refused, the establishment of a British protectorate over the territory in 1885, and by 1888, confronted by Arab slavers as well as by Portuguese expeditions from the east, it was again importuning the Foreign Office. Salisbury again refused to establish a protectorate over the area, on the grounds that it would incur expense and the odium of the British taxpayer; but by 1889 the pressure was upon him from Rhodes, who wished to secure a clear commercial field to the north of the Boer republics, and who accordingly offered to pay for administering Nyasaland and to buy the African Lakes Company. This move was frustrated by the pressures in London of representatives of the Scots missions in Nyasaland, but Rhodes' interest in and stated readiness to pay for Nyasaland enhanced the territory's value in British official eyes, and eventually the cabinet bowed to pressure from the missions and public opinion and declared Nyasaland a British protectorate in May 1891.

The three territories of Bechuanaland, Basutoland (after independence known respectively as Botswana and Lesotho) and Swaziland, embedded as they are in South African territory, owe their independence to an accident of history. Each at one time was closely connected with some constituent part of the later Republic of South Africa. Bechuanaland was declared a British protectorate in 1885, ostensibly to protect its natives from the incursion of Boer freebooters from the Transvaal but also, in reality, so as to contain and suppress a suspected plot by Germany and the Transvaal to establish themselves in control of southern Africa. While the southern part of Bechuanaland was incorporated into Cape Colony, and thus became part of the Union of South Africa in 1909, the northern part remained a protectorate and today forms the independent country of Botswana.

Basutoland's earliest connection lay with the Orange Free State. At the time of the great trek northwards of the Boers to escape the British in 1836 increasing numbers sought land in areas dominated by Basuto tribesmen. Friction arose, and despite efforts to compose matters by demarcating land boundaries, fighting broke out in 1858 and again in 1865. In 1866 the Governor of Cape Colony, wishing to prevent the Orange Free State gaining control of Basutoland, urged the annexation of the territory on the government of Cape Colony, and in 1871 this took place. The Basuto continued, however, to resist and refused to be disarmed, and in 1884, following a preference indicated by Basuto chiefs for living under the direct rule of the Queen of England they reverted again to British control.

Swaziland, meanwhile, had come under the rule of the Transvaal. Its agricultural land was coveted by the Boers and in 1875 a commando was despatched to crush a conflict that arose over the disputed succession to the paramount chieftaincy; once in, the Boers remained. During the negotiations of the Convention of Pretoria in 1881, which ended the First Boer War, Natal held out successfully for the independence of Swaziland from the Transvaal; and although Britain conducted a convention with the Transvaal in 1894 which gave that government rights of protection over Swaziland, this fell far short of complete sovereignty.

When the Second Boer War broke out in 1899, none of the three territories was directly involved, but control over them was assumed by the British. At the peace talks it was agreed that their future should await settlement later, as it was clear that the former Boer republics were reluctant to grant them the limited form of the franchise exercised in Cape Colony that the British government felt was their due. The settlement was never achieved. To South African insistence that the incorporation of the territories in the Union, later the Republic, had been promised by Britain, the British government countered with the reminder that it had pledged itself to consult the inhabitants of the territories concerned before handing them over; and so the three territories have remained formally independent of South Africa.

The four East African territories of Zanzibar, Kenya, Uganda and Tanganyika were the last to come under British control in the continent. Both strategically and commercially the area held little attraction for Britain in the early years of the nineteenth century, and her need to protect the route to India was adequately met by control at the Cape. Nevertheless, the East African coastline came within the purview of British survey and patrol ships despatched from India, and from February 1824 to October 1826 a Royal Navy contingent performed a peacekeeping role in separating the warring Mazrui, rulers of Mombasa, from the Omani Arabs of Zanzibar who were then in a state of imperialist expansion. Formal British influence and representation in the area was not resumed until 1841 when Consul Hamerton, the British representative in Muscat (the Omanis' capital), followed the Omani sultan in establishing his headquarters in Zanzibar; and from 1870 Consul Kirk used the political vulnerability of the new Sultan Burghash in securing British influence in all spheres of Zanzibari rule.

The nature of this informal British presence, almost devoid as it was of military backing and official interest, was now to change with the growth of European commercial pressures, missionary activity and international rivalries. From 1877 onwards Mackinnon was attempting to secure a royal charter for a company to develop the mainland, along the lines of the old East India Company; and although he too ran foul of Salisbury at the Foreign Office in London a growing body of British opinion came to favour setting up rule by chartered company, which offered the dual advantages of expanding legitimate trade and exercising sovereignty at no (or so it was argued) cost to the British taxpayer. By the late 1880s an overriding consideration in the British official mind was the necessity to gain control over as much of Africa as possible, if only to deny it to other nations, and in 1886 the German and British governments had agreed on the extent of their spheres of influence in East Africa. Mackinnon obtained a royal charter in 1888 for his Imperial British East Africa Company to trade with and administer what is now Kenya and Uganda from a British government which was preoccupied with events in Egypt and deeply concerned to prevent any other European power from obtaining a foothold near the headwaters of the Nile.

Following hard on the heels of all this came developments in Uganda that called for immediate British official intervention there. In October 1889 the kabaka (chief of the principal tribe, the Baganda) was deposed in circumstances that seemed about to lead to intense religious strife between Christians and Muslims. The Christian missions in the country were deeply split themselves as between Catholic and Protestant factions. In March 1890 a German expedition to restore order set out, to be followed in April by a British expedition under the command of Lugard on behalf of Mackinnon's IBEAC. Militarily the expedition was a success, but financially the Company was nearly bankrupt and by 1892 was in desperate straits, inspiring cabinet discussion and public dissension in England as to whether the government should intervene to retain Uganda when the Company was forced to retire. In April 1894 the report of the commissioner, Portal, a convinced imperialist who had been despatched to report on the situation on the spot, was published; it called for the retention of Uganda under British control, and for the building of a railroad from the coast to the interior to assist administration and to lay the groundwork for economic development. Two days after the report appeared the government, spurred on by vigorous public lobbying and fear of other European dabblings in the area, declared Uganda a protectorate.

Elsewhere in East Africa the late 1880s and the decade of the 1890s saw the establishment of formal British rule to replace the informal system of control by personal influence that had previously existed. The establishment of a protectorate over Zanzibar in 1890 reflected the changed British attitudes toward the feasibility of exerting indirect control through and on behalf of the sultan, in the altered and now very competitive conditions posed by the interest taken in the area by the other European powers. In July 1895 British official control, as distinct from that formerly exercised by the now-defunct IBEAC, was formalized over the Kenya area with the announcement of the establishment of the East African Protectorate. In 1902 Uganda's Eastern Province was transferred to Kenya, and from that date onwards their boundaries remained intact and their administrations separate from each other during the fifty years or so of British rule. Tanganyika came under British rule at the end of the First World War, when this former German colony was granted to Great Britain as a class C mandate to govern. Thereafter her administration, although technically of a different status to those of the other East African countries, in practice followed the same principles.

To include a chapter on historical background in what is essentially an overcrowded book on modern politics demands at least the justification that it is relevant to the central theme; in this case, that the nature of the historical process of colonization affected subsequent political development. In considering whether this is true, and, if so, to what extent, we need to assess some of the elements of the imperial era.

No one should forget that all the African countries possessed very considerable pre-colonial histories, and the fact that many of these are fragmentary in nature and documented poorly (if at all) should not encourage us to forget their existence or to discount their influence over events today. The outward trappings of civilization are scanty over most of the continent and the sophisticated political veneer is laid very thin indeed, so that any government that can justly claim popular backing must rely as much on traditional appeals as on modern creeds and electoral manipulations. If it should be wondered why the African countries of their own free will chose to graft their politics on to the Westminster model, the answer probably lies in the multiplicity of local organizations; to have selected one out of the many domestic choices available would have been invidious. Westminster was a convenience rather than a conviction, and if we look to it to survive we must expect it to undergo mutations.

African history and political development, then, did not start with the colonizers; nor was British imperialism the only imperialism to overtake African peoples. We should note the part played by local imperialisms, such as that which caused the Zulu nation to thrust outwards disturbing the Matabele, who in turn came up against the Dutch trekking northwards from the Cape, who were in their turn attempting to escape the imperialism of the British. The nature of the Zulu wars, as well as the organization of the more structured tribes such as the Baganda, played a major part in influencing the course and timing of the colonial incursion. Above all one should not overlook the incidence of Arab nationalism; the Fulani Empire in northern Nigeria, pressures from the Sudan both northwards towards Egypt and southwards into Uganda and the Congo, and the activities of the Omani Arabs along the north-east coast and in the Horn of Africa seem now to be but the local spasms of a more generalized Arab nationalism located more customarily in Cairo, Baghdad and Damascus. British imperialism overcame for a short while these other, older imperialisms, but had it never existed the same responses it evoked would have been called forth from Africa by other alien movements.

The motives of the imperialists have long fascinated the historian as well as the modern politician. They can be regarded as seven in number. The strategists in the Foreign Office who were concerned to ensure the safety of the imperial route to India could count on support from those who thus early adhered to the domino theory, that to secure law and order elsewhere it was essential to police yet one more tract of primitive Africa; and both these could join forces with those who saw the world's stage as Europe, where the diplomats took what they could for their own countries and denied all they could to their opponents. The unofficial pressures towards colonization stemmed from the humanitarians who were concerned to abolish slavery and instal legitimate trade in its place, from the religious who sensed a territory and a people ripe for guidance and salvation, and from the city gentlemen who saw in Africa a source of raw materials and a destination for manufactured goods. Interwoven with all of this was the White Man's Burden theory, that White was Right or more narrowly that British was Best and that a duty lay upon the white man to dispense civilization and in particular the British version of it.

The fact that many of these motives appear today to be contradictory, and those who held them hypocritical, does not mean that they were not genuinely and tenaciously held at the time and it would seem reasonable to expect them to have left their mark on posterity – although it would of course be expecting too much that these ideals would have resulted in the formation of utopian societies. There are two ways of looking at this. One is, so to speak, from the outside in, from the standpoint of Britain or America or Outer Mongolia. It tends to assume that imperialism is either admirable or abysmal – depending upon which segment of the political spectrum one inhabits – and by extension, that imperialism either elevated or depraved the imperial power. Anyone may argue either case quite convincingly, but to do so overlooks perhaps the more important issue and the one that is certainly more relevant to the Africans themselves, looking at the colonial experience from the inside, outwards. What *do* these high ideals mean to those at the receiving end of them? The more cynical regard them as a piece of self-deception aimed at fooling the rest of the world; some no doubt are led to measure the extent to which performance fell short of promises; and in many they induce a huge lack of self-confidence in their own capabilities that finds an outlet in truculence on the world stage. If the outsiders tend to regard Africa as the scales for weighing the deficiencies or the validity of their own way of life, the Africans themselves glimpse the urgent necessity to forge societies that are rooted in their own history and answer their own needs rather than ape the procedures of elsewhere.

One can argue, then, that the British imperial era achieved nothing that would not have happened anyway; Africa, one can guess, would have been violated by the outside world whether or not Britannia ruled the waves in the nineteenth century. There might have been differences in time, place, personnel, method and motive, but the end result would have been the same. But when we come to the effects of British imperialism upon the inter-relationships of the African states and peoples, it seems highly likely that here the British did indeed manage a unique contribution to the subsequent development of Africa. British notions of an official hierarchy, of the responsibility of rulers for the ruled, of a pecking-order in civilian society and an incorruptible, painstaking administration based on individual initiative, are all notions that have not necessarily survived unscathed, but have nevertheless left an indelible mark in the *mores* of the ex-British territories. Again, British wariness towards the other European powers induced a reserve towards their colonies, so that if pan-Africanism appears today as far away as ever this could be because the offshore island that is Britain bequeathed separatism to her African colonies. If the whole imperial process was inevitable, the manner of its approach was not, and it is this that justifies an historical background to a political story because it has affected subsequent political developments.

2 Constitutions: The Setting-up

The decade that began in 1957 is customarily regarded as the decade of African independence. No less than thirteen of the fifteen countries with which this book is concerned assumed formal independence of Britain during this time.

Table 1

Chronology of African Independence

South Africa	30 May	1910
Ghana (+ Togoland)	6 Mar.	1957
Nigeria (+ N. Cameroons)	1 Oct.	1960
Sierra Leone	27 Apr.	1961
Tanganyika	9 Dec.	1961
Uganda	9 Oct.	1962
Zanzibar	10 Dec.	1963
Kenya	12 Dec.	1963
Malawi	6 Jul.	1964
Zambia	24 Oct.	1964
The Gambia	18 Feb.	1965
Rhodesia (UDI)	11 Nov.	1965
Botswana	30 Sep.	1966
Lesotho	4 Oct.	1966
Swaziland	6 Sep.	1968

Included here for *de facto* reasons is Rhodesia, because, whatever the outcome of UDI and the findings of the Pearce Commission, at the time of writing it seems most unlikely that the country will ever revert to a status of dependence upon Britain. Not included are British Somaliland, which merged to become part of

the Somali Republic, nor Southern Cameroons, which joined
the Cameroon Republic at independence.

The odd man out is South Africa, independent as a dominion
at a distance in time and under totally different auspices from the
other African countries. These latter fall into four distinct groupings. The West African countries of Ghana, Nigeria, Sierra
Leone and the Gambia were virtually assured of independence
soon after the Second World War, when growing unrest and discontent in Ghana erupted into violence and, by 1951, established
Nkrumah as first prime minister and so set a pattern for self-rule.
The next group to stake a claim to independence was the East
African countries of Uganda, Kenya, Tanganyika and Zanzibar,
always assumed by the British government to form a geographic
and economic entity; these by the end of the 1950s appeared to
have won their case for independence, and the February 1960
Lancaster House conference on the constitutional progress of
Kenya served to confirm that independence would be granted
even if it were to the detriment of the interests of the sizable
white minority there. The third group to attain independence
was that of the Central African states of Malawi, Zambia and
Rhodesia, following the breakup of the Central African Federation with the secession of Malawi (then Nyasaland) in 1962. The
fourth group comprised the three states embedded in, and wholly
dependent economically upon, the Republic of South Africa;
Botswana, Lesotho and Swaziland, whose independence was
assured from 1966 onwards.

This chronology of events is significant. It shows that the
attainment of African independence was by no means the hasty
affair that is sometimes assumed by the detractors of the process;
from the time when independence first became an attainable
target to the moment when it was a demonstrable fact, some
twenty years – or a generation in time – elapsed. It also shows
that what mattered in the achievement of independence was not
the readiness or otherwise of the territory concerned, nor yet the
development of any logical progression of thought or ideology by
the British government, but rather the successive crumbling away
of layers of British mental and psychological resistance to African
independence. The case of Ghana proved that Africans, as well
as Indians, could be allowed to rule themselves; Kenya proved
that even the kith-and-kin claims of the settler community could

be disregarded; Malawi and the Gambia disproved the arguments that economic viability was a prerequisite to political stature; Botswana, Lesotho and Swaziland – the hostage states – showed that long-cherished South African claims to their territory could be refuted; and finally the case of Rhodesia shows that the time when the British government was prepared to intervene in force to discharge its responsibilities had long since passed. For something like twenty years British policy towards Africa assumed the character of a series of *ad hoc* responses to individual crises, in logical succession to the previous wish to let sleeping dogs lie.

In contrast, the nature of the independence constitutions under which the African territories began their separate careers resemble well-charted trade routes; the principles of navigation are followed faithfully, and the only things that differ are the actual ports of call. It was assumed that the Westminster model of parliamentary democracy should be bequeathed, with its emphasis on one-man, one-vote, the notion of government and a loyal opposition, and its identification with the western democracies. There was a near-universal tendency to attempt to limit the sovereignty of these parliaments by writing entrenched clauses into the constitutions, in an attempt to guarantee the liberties of those – minorities, or majorities – whose powers and duties seemed precarious. And there was, perhaps, an over-emphasis on the outward trappings of democracy, an unjustified assumption that Mr Speaker's mace, judicial wigs and the swagger-stick on parade could somehow achieve that independence of politics so characteristic of the judiciary, the military and the civil service in Britain. The wonder is not that the 'Westminster model' has failed, but that it was called that in the first place.

It is sometimes alleged that the Westminster civil servants framed constitutions that were unsuited to the new nations. In their reliance on outward forms, entrenched clauses to the derogation of parliamentary sovereignty, and the power of the written word, it might more justly be thought that the framers of the constitutions were ignorant of the realities of the exercise of ruling power behind the facade of Westminster. They understood many of the difficulties that were to confront the leaders of the new nations, but they were unable to translate Westminster into Africana.

The inheritance

When the Westminster model was finally promulgated in Africa, however, it did not fall as a bolt from the blue of an otherwise untroubled sky. All the independence constitutions had their genesis in the past and in the slow and jerky progress towards representative and responsible government that British Africa had made. Two quite different aims had been pursued, which had become so interlocked in the growth of constitutional usage as to suggest that a single process had been followed; but one needs to distinguish between them here because the degree to which either or both had been achieved by the time of independence, and the manner of their coming about, almost certainly influenced political developments after independence. There are also differences in timing in the processes, as between one country and another, which could well be significant factors in subsequent events – particularly if a rather narrow time definition of political maturity is held; that is to say, can one seriously argue that because a country has experienced a measure of self-rule for ten years or twenty, or for twice as long as another country, that it is therefore twice as mature and as capable of total self-rule as that other country? And if not, what is to become of the argument held by many of the ex-colonialists that independence came too early and should have been held back by an unspecified number of years?

REPRESENTATIVE GOVERNMENT: The achievement of representative government was one of the ideals held by all colonial officials, partly because it fulfilled the liberal notions of many of the English ruling class and partly because to associate local people in government appeared to be the only way in which to secure that other ideal of the Colonial Office in London, quiet government. The most popular colonial governor was he whose despatches landed least often on Colonial Office desks.

Governors of colonies were appointed to ensure law and order and what was thought of as 'good government'; that is, one which levied taxation fairly and spent it parsimoniously on essential public works and administration, and eschewed bribery and corruption. In his colony the governor might be god to those he ruled, but he remained the handmaid of the Colonial Office (or, it might be, the Foreign Office) in London which in general only interfered where it seemed likely that heavy-handed administration would lead to serious unrest which might get reported, and stir up parliamentary questions or the activities of the pressure groups in the United Kingdom.

But the governor was not left alone to govern; around him he gathered a small group of colonial civil servants (the 'officials') to advise him and to execute certain of the functions of government, and increasingly he turned to those of the local population (the 'unofficials') who by reason of their position or occupation he wished to associate with the business of government. Governor, officials and unofficials met in Legislative Council (Leg. Co.) to debate measures of government, and in Executive Council (Exec. Co.) to put the measures into effect. Exec. Co. comprised the men in charge of government departments, such as the Treasury and the Ministry of Public Works, and was later to develop into a cabinet responsible to the parliament that had evolved from Leg. Co.

While the governor might (and certainly if he was wise he would) temper his policies to meet the criticisms of his councils, he remained in absolute control of all aspects of government and solely responsible to London for his colony until a few months before independence. Even then he retained some reserve powers over newly formed governments. This system not unnaturally frustrated those, particularly the unofficials, who felt their advice went unheeded; and so various voting systems and mini-constitutions for Leg. and Exec. Cos were devised, to enable votes to be cast and some semblance of proper government-by-vote to emerge. This was a long, slow and uncertain process of constitutional growth, involving as it did the gradual transfer of legislative responsibility from the governor to the legislature and the curtailment of the overriding powers of the governor. His troubles started when the unofficials in government outnumbered the officials and could use their voices and votes to criticize, delay or delete proposed legislation, and they mounted in direct ratio to the number of strong-willed, interested parties on his councils. The weaker governors of Kenya, for instance, must have felt the game hardly worth the candle when confronted by some of the wild men among the settlers.

Nevertheless, this was the start of a form of democratic, as opposed to totally autocratic, colonial government. It should be remembered, however, that the unofficials of Leg. and Exec. Co. in no way acted as representatives of the people at large; they represented themselves or their class (e.g. chiefs) or their occupation (e.g. trade and commerce), and the job of safeguarding the interests of ordinary people was vested either in the governor himself and his government collectively, or in some individual whom he might select for the task. Occasionally it came about that certain classes of people or races could wrest from governor and Colonial Office the right to select for themselves those whom they wished to represent them on Leg. Co., but this forerunner of the later style of community representation was rarely exercised, and then only in special situations – as, for instance, in Kenya, where both the white settler and the Asian immigrant communities, locked in conflict with each other and with successive governors, demanded the right to choose their own representatives.

Representative government, then, while it undoubtedly introduced able indigenous men to some of the detailed craft and administration associated with modern governing processes, did not until the few years immediately preceding independence confer the vote on any large number of people, nor did it attempt to associate the masses of the people with government. It counted upon tacit consent to the governing process rather than active participation in it on the part of the majority of people, and where tacit consent no longer existed it argued that the people had been misled by demagogues into taking sides against their own best interests. It also injected two other lasting elements into the body politic. The paternalism of the ruling power, which arrogated to itself the judgment as to other people's best interests, has spilled over into some of the attitudes still to be found in modern African ruling circles, where it is often expressed as a contempt for the opinions of rural and unlettered voters. And although politics is always contentious, it seems that the frustrations of the representative government system – as well as those inherent in the colonial situation – have fathered a special breed of politician successor to those clamorous classes who first obtained seats on Leg. Co., men who cling to power without sharing it turn and turn about with an opposition. Neither did the colonial governments alternate power with an opposition.

RESPONSIBLE GOVERNMENT: The growth of forms of representative government brought with them the pressures towards responsible government. This had been envisaged as the end-product of the uncertain colonial process ever since the American colonies had revolted and cut the apron strings for good; responsible, that is, in the sense that those politicians operating the governmental process were ultimately responsible for their actions not to a colonial governor and his council, nor to a far-off Colonial Office located in an alien land, but to a bunch of local electors. Responsible government involved much more than merely the culmination of an irregular progress towards one-man one-vote. It demanded the adoption of a set of basic attitudes towards one's fellow men; of their fitness to rule not just themselves, but people of different colours and creeds. It also demanded the resolution of the representative government wrangle; just how representative should government be to justify the granting by the imperial power of the right to fully responsible government, enshrined in the concept of full sovereignty?

The answer to this question has depended upon when it has been asked. In 1910 the South Africans obtained responsible government on the strength of a franchise loaded in favour of Afrikaner farmers *vis-à-vis* the British; the racial question then was taken in terms of the two white races and consideration was barely given to the future needs of the black majority. Since then the nigglings of conscience have grown, to culminate in the granting of responsible government at the time of independence to the East and Central African countries with sizable white populations which are controlled by the majority of Africans. In Rhodesia the achievement of responsible government has been forcibly assumed by a government that depends on a majority of votes cast by a predominantly white minority. It is unlikely to be relinquished.

It is clear that responsible government has usually but not invariably been achieved at the end of a series of constitutional shifts leading to the establishment of fully representative government on the basis of a democratic voting system. Less usually it has been usurped by a minority acting on behalf of all the people. While it seems that the development of true representative government must lead via the devolution of power to responsible government, the converse is clearly not true; that is, we can see that responsible government does not necessarily rest upon a basis of fully representative government. We must, then, be careful to separate these two processes as we look at the chronology of constitutional development. If one tends to be hypercritical of the assumption and exercise of responsible government this is probably because its meaning has changed so profoundly within the last half-century or so. When South Africa attained fully responsible government in 1910, for instance, a lasting relationship with crown, empire and British people was envisaged; now, the advent of responsible, independent government brings to mind the inevitable cutting of ties with the imperial power. Surely a paradox, this, in an era when debate no longer exists as to whether dominion status and/or independence and membership of the Commonwealth implies dependent status. Whether the explanation of this lies in the advent of militant African nationalism, or in the status game that is international relations, or in the timing and pressures that led to the growth of representative and responsible government, it is not easy to be certain.

Constitutional progress

The West African countries (Ghana, Nigeria, Sierra Leone and the Gambia) experienced the longest run-in to independence of all the ex-British territories in Africa. The accompanying table shows that about a hundred years elapsed between the establishment of Legislative and Executive Councils, and the moment when independent, fully responsible government was achieved. During that century the successive stages of constitutional development can be discerned. First came the moment when Africans were nominated by the governor to serve on either, or both, Leg. Co. and Exec. Co.; at a later stage a form of indirect election of Africans took place, whereby, for instance, a member of an urban council or of a grouping of chiefs was elected by his peers to serve on the governor's Councils; at a still later stage this election became direct, in that members of the general public were enfranchised to elect to the Councils direct, without any intervening medium or nomination process. Meanwhile, the official or colonial civil servant element on the Councils was being outnumbered by the unofficial membership, comprised of local Africans together with, probably, representatives of trading

Table 2

Constitutional Developments in West Africa

Dates of first:

1 formation of Legislative and Executive Councils
2 nominated indigenous representatives on Councils
3 indirectly elected indigenous representatives on Councils
4 directly elected indigenous representatives on Councils
5 majority of unofficials on Councils
6 indigenous representatives on Executive Councils
7 designation of Executive Council as cabinet

	1	2	3	4	5	6	7
Ghana	1850	1886	1925	1925	1946	1942	1952
Nigeria	1861	1914	1922	1922	1946	1951	1960
Sierra Leone	1863	1863	1924	1924	1951	1943	1960
The Gambia	1888	1946	1946	1954	1954	1954	1962

and commercial interests. Exec. Co. was becoming the nucleus of the later cabinet as those civil servants who had headed government departments were displaced by indigenous Africans, who thus combined a civil service function together with that of a politician. The final stage was reached when Exec. Co. was designated a cabinet, members of which accepted joint responsibility for government policy and were culled from the majority party in Leg. Co. (by now probably known as the House of Representatives, or parliament).

It is probably a true generalization to say that the timing of this process depended on wars, the surges of commodity prices and the activities of the Fabian Society in London. Africans who served with the armed forces during the European wars had their horizons rudely enlarged, and those who saw the quality of the Africans' service were more inclined to concede their fitness and moral right to development. The vagaries of international trade conditioned the amount of money available for development of all kinds, including education and travel overseas; and Africans who came up against the political theorists in the mother country soon learned to compare their own constitutional development with that postulated by the politically aware élite in England. It is noteworthy that the period just after the Second World War, when African agitation for self-rule came to a head, saw not only the independence of India in 1947 but also the conjunction of a Labour government (strongly committed to Fabian principles of colonial development) in England with a remarkable rise in commodity prices occasioned by the Korean War. Those who look for the yellow peril in Africa today may be interested in this early instance of the indirect effect of Chinese foreign relations upon the continent of Africa.

Post-Second World War political agitations, then, resulted in the rash of constitutions with which the British attempted to pacify the demands of African nationalism. In Ghana the Burns constitution of 1946 and the Coussey constitution of 1951 preceded the designation of Nkrumah as prime minister in 1952 and the development of full cabinet government in the same year. General elections held in 1951, 1954 and 1956 confirmed the charisma of Nkrumah and the strength of his popular appeal, and when independence came in 1957 he accordingly assumed full responsibility for his government. In Nigeria, progress was complicated by the need to accommodate the Muslim north within the country as a whole; the Richards constitution of 1946 and the Macpherson constitution of 1951 provided for a federal framework for the country, which was confirmed by the adoption of the Lyttelton constitution in 1954. In 1957 the east and the west regions became self-governing, and in 1959 the northern region followed suit; in 1960 the independence constitution provided for a federation whose division of powers sowed the seeds of the Biafran Civil War. In Sierra Leone the Stevenson constitution of 1951 led to African majorities in both Leg. Co. and Exec. Co.; general elections held in 1952 and 1957 confirmed Sir Milton Margai's Sierra Leone People's Party (SLPP) in power, and in 1961 Margai led his country to independence. In the Gambia, alterations to the make-up of Leg. and Exec. Co. took place in 1946, 1951 and 1954, with the effect of broadening their membership and increasing African participation and power. A general election in 1960 led to the formation of a coalition government until the emergence of Pierre N'Jie, the leader of the United Party (UP), as chief minister with the backing of the chiefs. Further changes in Leg. and Exec. Co. and another election in 1962 resulted in the establishment of parliamentary-style government under Jawara of the People's Progressive Party (PPP), internal self-government in 1963, and full independence in 1965 with Jawara as prime minister and the head of the majority party in parliament.

Meanwhile, in East Africa, in Kenya, Uganda, Tanganyika and Zanzibar, the constitutional process was both more hurried and more complicated, mainly because of the interplay of the minority groups there (the Asians and the Europeans) both of whom regarded themselves as having made a permanent home in Africa, but were considered by the Africans, with some justice, as alien intruders. So far as the Colonial Office was concerned this was 'white' Africa, that is, the area was envisaged as one of permanent European settlement which, it was widely assumed, would lead to the eventual establishment of another great imperial dominion. These basic attitudes meant that the political history of Kenya, for instance (which was white settlerdom at its apogee), was chequered with demands from Europeans for representative, leading to responsible, government in white hands; from the Asians for parity of representation with the Europeans; from both, occasionally, for self-government free from Colonial Office interference; from a few Africans and rather more European missionaries for greater consideration for African needs; and later in time from the African nationalists, demands for common-roll representative elections. Over all, at all times, there loomed the two most intractable questions of all, those of land ownership and of the closer union of the territories.

Kenya's Leg. and Exec. Councils dated from 1907 when, also, the principle of Asian and non-white participation was conceded with the appointment of an Asian to Leg. Co. The white settlers gained elective representation for their community in 1923, and although the Asians at the same time were denied parity of membership of Leg. Co., the principle of communal electorates for Asians as well as Europeans was laid down. Responsible government (loudly demanded by the Europeans) was firmly repudiated by the Colonial Office for many years to come, and African interests in the country were declared to be paramount; the whole might be taken as falling far short of European desires. In 1924 the first representative for African interests was appointed to Leg. Co. in the person of a European missionary. In 1931 the vexed question of closer union of the East African territories was laid to rest by the Colonial Office, to the dismay of the white settler interests of Kenya, and throughout the 1930s the political wranglings continued – mainly concerning the parity question, and whether or not non-whites should be permitted to own land in the Highlands area (not permitted from 1939 onwards). In 1944 the first African was appointed to Leg. Co. to represent his community's interests. 1948 saw the enlargement of Leg. Co. to accommodate an unofficial majority, and at the same time European interests were threatened with the adoption of the parity of other races' representation. In May 1951 the first African was appointed to Exec. Co., and by 1952 the unofficials had achieved a majority in Leg. Co., but the frustrations and tensions were affecting the Africans as well as the other races, and the outbreak of the Mau Mau emergency later in the same year froze the play of normal (by Kenya standards) politics.

Successive colonial secretaries then took the view that a military solution to the uprising must be paralleled by positive African political advance. The 1954 Lyttelton constitution made provision for a ministerial form of government to include two Asian, one African and three European ministers, in an attempt to achieve some form of multi-racialism. In 1957 the Coutts report on African representation resulted in the first, qualified, African franchise and the consequent election of eight African members of Leg. Co. In March 1958 the Lennox-Boyd constitution produced elections for six more African members of Leg. Co., an equality of African with communally elected Europeans, and an attempt to secure multi-racialism by the special election of twelve members by Leg. Co. sitting as an electoral college. An African boycott of legislative proposals led to the 1960 Lancaster House Constitutional Conference in London, at which African majority representation and political control were clearly foreshadowed. A general election in 1961, the release of Kenyatta (on whom had been pinned responsibility for Mau Mau) from detention, a further constitutional conference in London in February 1962 and the birth of an independence constitution which enshrined regionalism, led up to the June 1963 election which installed Kenyatta as first prime minister, and to independence later the same year.

Uganda's constitutional progress was less lurid than that of Kenya, partly because the white settler problem did not exist and partly because African political aspirations could find an outlet in the tribal institutions. The land issue caused no friction because in 1923 a policy of African peasant production, rather than the growth of huge foreign-owned plantations, was enunciated by the Colonial Office. Leg. Co. was set up in 1921 with five officials and two Europeans and one Asian member as unofficials; in 1934 parity of representation for the two immigrant communities was established. The Council never, however, became an adequate forum for discussion of executive action because of the lack of weight of the communities represented on it, and also because of the absence of African participation. The main tribe, the Baganda (under their chief or kabaka), refused to take part in Leg. Co. because they realized that it would reduce their own assembly, the Lukiko, to a mere talking-shop; this divorce of one of the mainstreams of African life from the administration was to sow the seeds of many future difficulties. After the Second World War the pace of constitutional advance quickened, and sharpened with the loss of African confidence in the administration. In 1945 the first African was admitted to Leg. Co. (although the Baganda Lukiko maintained its boycott until 1955), in 1946 the first unofficial entered Exec. Co., in 1950 the unofficials in Leg. Co. were doubled to sixteen of whom eight were African, and in 1953 unofficials numbered twenty-eight with half of them being Africans. There were as yet no direct elections, however, membership being by nomination by the governor or by selection by African district councils, and the main reforms took place at local government, rather than central government level.

The Buganda crisis of 1953–5, which in its essentials concerned the relationship of the kingdom to the whole country of Uganda, but was formulated in terms of a dispute between the kabaka and the British government, then intervened and led to attempted reform at the centre. In 1955 a ministerial system of government was instituted, with three Africans, one European, and one Asian as unofficial ministers out of a total of eleven ministers; in Leg. Co. the number of Africans indirectly elected was raised to eighteen, while European and Asian membership was reduced to six each. This greatly enhanced the importance of Leg. Co. and therefore gave rise to demands for the holding of direct elections, but this in turn led to renewed Baganda fears as to the role of the Lukiko and the status of their kingdom within the country and resulted in their withdrawal, again, from Leg. Co. Elections were held in 1958 which brought directly elected Africans into both Exec. Co. and Leg. Co., but the Baganda boycott continued and in the March 1961 elections this resulted in power passing to Kiwanuka's Democratic Party (DP). In July 1961 the Uganda Relationships Committee, set up to define the status of Buganda, recommended a federal relationship and the September 1961 constitutional conference in London confirmed this; internal self-government was set for April 1962, and full independence for October of the same year. Before this happened, however, another election in April 1962 had ousted Kiwanuka's DP and put into power the Uganda People's Congress (UPC) headed by Milton Obote; Obote, therefore, with qualified support from Buganda, headed the independence government.

Tanganyika, as already indicated, came into the British orbit following the peacemaking after the First World War, as a class B mandate for whom independence seemed totally remote. The terms of the mandate were mainly protective in character, and there is little evidence that the existence of the mandate materially affected the conduct of the British authorities there. The medium of African administration was indirect rule through such chiefs as could be plucked out of the disintegrated tribal system, and atop this, Legislative and Executive Councils had been established by 1926 to aid the governor, Sir Donald Cameron. A preponderance of officials characterized the Councils, and although Asians were admitted to membership the majority between the wars was always European and English in origin, no Africans being admitted.

After the war Tanganyika's constitutional progress remained slow. Two chiefs in 1945, and one more in 1946, were nominated to Leg. Co. which contained fifteen officials and fourteen unofficials. During the war unofficial Europeans had joined Exec. Co. and in 1952 officials in Exec. Co. took responsibility for government departments as a forerunner of cabinet evolution in the Council. In 1951 the first African had joined Exec. Co. and in 1954 the principle of racial parity there amongst unofficials was conceded with the appointment of two Europeans, two Asians and two Africans. Later the same year African unofficial membership was increased to three. In April 1955 Leg. Co. was enlarged to contain nine nominated representatives of each race for nine constituency areas, and one of each race on the unofficial side. In 1957 members of Exec. Co. in charge of government departments were styled ministers, and six unofficial assistant ministers – four African, one Asian and one European – were appointed to sit in Leg. Co. Elections held in September 1958 and February 1959, proposed by the constitutional commissioner, W. J. M. Mackenzie, resulted in an overwhelming victory for the Tanganyika African National Union (TANU) headed by Nyerere, whose chief platform was an insistence not on multiracialism but on non-racialism under majority rule. Thereafter, the close personal friendship and regard that developed between Nyerere and the governor, Sir Richard Turnbull, speeded the progress of self-rule. A Council of Ministers established in July 1959 with five unofficial ministries became the main executive body of government; in December the same year it was announced that responsible government would be inaugurated in 1960 following a general election in August. Again, Nyerere's TANU won the overwhelming majority of votes to form the government. Full internal self-rule was achieved in May 1961, and independence followed in December the same year.

Zanzibar's formal constitutional development began in 1926 when Executive and Legislative Councils were set up. The sultan sat on Exec. Co. together with the British resident and other officials, and Leg. Co. contained also the resident and various official members and a minority of six unofficials of whom three were Arab, two Asian and one European. In 1946 the first African was appointed, and in 1947 the second. Little stirred in politics until the 1950s, however, when racial demands for concessions in representation were heard. The constitutional changes in 1957 included the setting up of a privy council to advise the sultan, and the expansion of Exec. Co. to take in three unofficials – one Arab, one Asian and one African – nominated by the governor to associate themselves with the workings of government departments. Leg. Co., meanwhile, was to be increased to thirteen officials and twelve unofficials, of whom six were to be directly elected. This gave rise to party dissension between the Zanzibar Nationalist Party (ZNP), the tool of the ruling Arab élite of landowners and wealthy traders, and the Afro-Shirazi Party (ASP), identified with the large mass of deprived and impoverished African labourers; it was the latter which gained the most seats, and a two-year period of party manoeuvrings developed. In 1959 two more unofficials were absorbed into Exec. Co. and the number of elected members was increased to eight, four still being nominated; a widening of the franchise was also provided for, with women to receive the vote. In August 1960 the report of the constitutional adviser, Sir Hilary Blood, was accepted by the British resident; this allowed for a large measure of elected membership of Leg. Co. and for the phasing-out of official members.

Meanwhile, immediately prior to independence, there had taken place a significant shift in political allegiance of the Shirazis in Pemba; originally attracted to the ZNP because it appealed to their Muslim religion and affiliations with the Arabs who led the party, they now tended towards the ASP which had softened its anti-Muslim, anti-Arab line and stressed its ethnic bonds with the Shirazis of Pemba. At both the elections of June 1961 and July 1963, the latter held immediately before independence and hence destined to provide the government, the ZNP of the Arabs and wealthy interests had triumphed over the ASP; but on the second occasion at least the arrangement of electoral districts and absence of proportional representation had allowed the victory to the ZNP instead of to the numerically-superior mass party of the ASP, which had in fact managed to obtain 54.3 per cent of the total votes cast in the elections. When, therefore, independence came on 10 December 1963 the sultan headed a government which did not fairly represent the majority of the people of Zanzibar.

So far, we have charted the constitutional progress of the West African countries where white settlement was never mooted, and of the countries in East Africa where, although it was assumed that white settlement would predominate, the interests of the Africans were never quite relinquished in favour of the Europeans. In Central and southern Africa, however, the story has been very different. In South Africa itself white domination has rarely been questioned, let alone seriously challenged. Independence came easily and swiftly to the three former High Commission territories whose existence, far from challenging the validity of South African racial policies, merely serves to point up the physical strength and ideological persistence of *apartheid* policies. In the history of the Rhodesias and Nyasaland, and particularly in the rise and decline of the Central African Federa-

27

tion, we see the establishment and then the breakdown of white dominance – and its accession again in Rhodesia at UDI.

As we have seen earlier, the history of the Rhodesias and Nyasaland was intimately bound up with the British South Africa Company (the Chartered Company); in 1923, however, the Charter was rescinded because of the Company's financial troubles, and Northern Rhodesia and Nyasaland as protectorates, and Southern Rhodesia as a crown colony anomalously enjoying self-government, assumed individual status within the British Empire. The nature and extent of the British connection and the powers of parliament at Westminster to initiate or assent to Rhodesian legislation remained ill-defined; broadly speaking in the two protectorates Britain retained, and exercised, the right to regulate affairs touching on African interests but in Southern Rhodesia the convention existed that whatever Westminster's theoretical or actual powers might be, they would not be exercised save with the advice and consent of the Southern Rhodesian government. This convention played a prime part in the development of other British colonies to dominion status, and its application to Southern Rhodesia merely put her upon the same path already trodden by Canada, Australia, South Africa and Ireland. The constitution introduced in Southern Rhodesia in 1923 allowed for a non-racial franchise, but in practice the qualifications for exercising the vote were pitched so high as to exclude all but Europeans, a few Asians and some coloureds, and a handful of Africans from the vote. By 1950, indeed, only 419 Africans were listed on the voters' roll.

Nyasaland, on the other hand, whose Leg. Co. dated from as early as 1908, was spared many of the strains of racial politics by reason of the tiny number of whites in the country and the lack of economic conflict between their interests and those of the body of Africans. It was in Northern Rhodesia, where the tensions of progress existed yet had not been embalmed in the early grant of internal self-government, that one can best see the play of the constitutional processes leading up to Federation.

Northern Rhodesia had enjoyed a measure of settler rule since the granting of an Advisory Council by the Chartered Company in 1918, while 1924 saw the setting up of its first Leg. Co., consisting of nine officials and five unofficial elected members, and an Exec. Co. entirely composed of officials. In 1929 an increase in the number of unofficials in Leg. Co. appeared to indicate progress towards responsible government, but between 1930 and 1934 a series of wrangles (similar to those in Kenya, but without all the difficulties posed by the existence of the Asian community) as to whether African interests were to be paramount in the territory led to a loss of confidence among both Europeans and Africans. In consequence, Europeans tended to look towards some form of union with Southern Rhodesia to reinforce their position, while African suspicions of the motives both of the settlers and of the Colonial Office mounted. During the period leading up to the Second World War political developments tended along two lines; towards amalgamation with Southern Rhodesia, and towards a greater measure of self-rule. By 1938 the number of unofficials in Leg. Co. was equal to that of the officials, and by 1939 elected unofficials had entered Exec. Co. for the first time.

In 1945 the end of the war saw eight elected unofficial Europeans in a majority of thirteen to nine over the officials of Leg. Co.; but in Exec. Co. the unofficials in a minority of three to five were awarded no responsibilities for running government departments. In 1946, however, the new constitution that extended the life of Leg. Co. from three to five years replaced, also, the governor's function in the Council by that of an elected speaker; the elected unofficials and the officials each had ten seats in the chamber, and the nominated unofficials (all of whom represented African interests) were reduced from five to four with the important addition, for the first time, of two nominated Africans to represent their own people. Official control was retained over Exec. Co., with four out of its eleven seats being allocated to elected unofficials and one to a nominated representative African. In 1948 the important convention was conceded that, in practice, the governor would not overrule the unanimous advice of the elected unofficials; this, and the fact that in 1949 two of the elected unofficials in Exec. Co. were given portfolios, signalized an immense development in the status of the unofficial members of the Councils.

Federation, when it came about in October 1953, was the product of long agitation by the whites of the two Rhodesias to entrench their vulnerable position in southern Africa; one receives the impression that Nyasaland was tacked on to the Federation because no one knew how else to dispose of her. With the wisdom of hindsight one can see that the mixture of local autonomy with overrule from Westminster, coupled with the very uneven constitutional development of the three territories, betokened trouble in the sense that without absolute devolution of power the competition from those who felt themselves entitled to increase their share of its exercise was bound to lead to clashes. For the first three years of Federation the intense African opposition to it was quietened; then, two pieces of federal legislation that became law in 1957 inflamed African fears. Together, the Constitutional Amendment Bill and the Federal Franchise Bill were seen to devalue African representation in the Federal Assembly; and the fact that they were not disallowed by the British government reinforced Africans in their belief that their rights were being whittled away with no hope of redress. And the federal elections of 1958, where those Africans returned to the Federal Assembly remained dependent upon support from European voters, bore these fears out.

It was by now clear that the earlier European drive for federation had been succeeded by a bid for complete independence, to remove all vestiges of British government responsibility from the arena. The attempt by the Governor of Northern Rhodesia, Sir Arthur Benson, to establish a new constitution in 1959 that would join the line of battle along party, rather than racial, lines, failed to offer the African nationalists what they wanted. The election remained, in the words of a recent historian of Zambia, 'essentially a contest among Europeans';[1] the nationalists' boycott of registration of African voters, resulted, in urban areas, in only some 20 per cent of those entitled to register actually doing so. Meanwhile the return of Dr Hastings Banda to the Nyasaland political scene from England in July 1958 had preceded the outbreak of disturbances which resulted in the setting up of a state of emergency there in March 1959. All three territories experienced disorders. In July 1959 the publication of the Devlin report on the Nyasaland disturbances indicated severe criticisms of what was stigmatized a police state, and led to the appointment in November 1959 of the Monckton commission to investigate the workings of the Federation as a whole. Its report which appeared in October 1960 heralded the break-up of the Federation. It called not only for a greater number of Africans in the

Federal Assembly – a majority of the commission urged parity as between Africans and Europeans – and for a widening of the franchise, but for the first time officially cast doubt upon the Federation's continued existence.

The African nationalists' point of attack on the Federation lay, according to Mulford, in Northern Rhodesia; for Nyasaland was too small and weak, and Southern Rhodesia too well entrenched in its self-governing powers, for the concept of Federation to be overturned by action in either country; and the means of attack lay through territorial, not federal, constitutional developments. And one should not forget the strength of a new factor, namely the growing awareness in British official circles that the Europeans of the Federation had been given their opportunity to construct a genuine partnership with the Africans, and had muffed it by attempting to maintain white hegemony. Successive colonial secretaries were less than sympathetic to the blusterings of white politicians, and it was Iain MacLeod's willingness to accede to African demands that led to the introduction of a two-tier franchise for the Northern Rhodesian elections in October 1962. A successful drive for registration took place, and no less than 7,321 Africans, well over twice as many as previous government estimates, qualified for the upper voting roll – some 20 per cent of the total. For the lower roll, 91,941 Africans qualified, thus gaining the right to exercise their vote. The result of the election was the formation of Northern Rhodesia's first African-headed government, composed of a coalition between the two main African parties of the United National Independence Party (UNIP) of Kenneth Kaunda and the African National Congress (ANC) of Harry Nkumbula and including in it a substantial portion of European voting strength. This led in turn to the pre-independence election of January 1964, which confirmed Kaunda's UNIP in power with fifty-five of the sixty-five seats in parliament for which voting on the main roll took place. Independence came about the following October.

The story of the Federation is really the history of its breakup, in which the constitutional development of Northern Rhodesia played the major part. Nevertheless one should not overlook the part played by Banda, the Nyasaland leader, whose determination to break the Federation was rewarded in 1962 when Nyasaland seceded. But whereas Northern Rhodesia (independent as

Zambia) and Nyasaland (independent as Malawi) embarked on African majority rule, Rhodesia has reverted to the European rule to which Federation represented but an intrusion. The new Rhodesian constitution of 1962 on the breakup of the Federation was the forerunner of UDI in 1965, just as it was the descendent of the crown colony government established at the demise of the Charter in 1923. The convention that enshrined British non-interference in internal affairs proved too powerful to be broken.

3 Constitutions of East and West Africa: The Breaking-down

Despite the radically differing circumstances of their formation the independence constitutions of the African countries had much in common with each other, although they fell far short of being carbon copies either of each other or of the (unwritten) British constitution on which they were based. To avoid undue repetition it is worth summarizing the main points that were common to most of them before proceeding to note on a country by country basis the main constitutional changes that subsequently took place.

The constitutional norm

First of all, and arising from the fact that the African constitutions owed so much to the constitutional practice evolved over many centuries in England, there was a common set of basic assumptions as to the proper functioning of government. It was taken for granted that the head of state would be largely ceremonial and almost wholly non-executive; the position of the constitutional monarch in England was the model for the post of governor-general, and the real power was envisaged to lie in the hands of a prime minister, who occupied the position of head of the political party which commanded the support of the majority in a popularly elected, representative legislature. The prime minister and his cabinet were responsible to parliament for the advice tendered to the head of state, in whose name the country was ruled, and if they failed to retain the confidence of parliament in their advice and actions they would resign. The British concept of a loyal opposition as an essential ingredient in a two-party political system permeated the constitutions, as did the concept of the sovereignty of parliament; that is, in accordance with British practice it was parliament and not the courts of law that was competent to pronounce on the constitutionality or otherwise of parliamentary Acts, the courts merely interpreting the will of parliament as expressed in the Acts on the statute book. There was a basic faith in democracy as the means of ascertaining the people's wishes and ensuring their best interests, and, hence, the assumption that one-man, one-vote parliamentary elections were the desirable means to this end. At the same time it had to be admitted that the traditional elements in society, for example chiefly authorities, deserved some part in government and some means of ensuring that their voice was heard, so that a recurrent pattern in the African constitutions shows in the establishment of the second houses in the parliamentary system that bore considerable resemblance to the role played in Britain by the House of Lords. It was, also, a fundamental tenet of faith in the endurance and relevance of the British parliamentary system that assumed the independence of the judiciary, the civil service and the armed forces from the wiles and machinations of the politicians.

These principles, then – of constitutional monarchy, the prime ministerial and cabinet system of responsible parliamentary government, the sovereignty of parliament, democracy, and the independence and impartiality of the judiciary, civil service and the armed forces – animated the draftsmen of the constitutions of the African countries. It is the attempts to formulate these principles into guidelines of practice that make up the substance of these written constitutions.

THE HEADS OF STATE: These were, in almost every case, the Queen of England represented by the person of the governor-general, who was almost invariably the man who had been governor during the final few years of the colonial regime, and who therefore imparted an element of continuity to the new regime, although he would soon be replaced by a locally-born person as governor-general or, if a republic were established, as president. (In the choice of governor-general the African countries were following the precedent set by the older self-governing countries of the Commonwealth, such as Australia and Canada, whose governors-general are now customarily indigenous.)

The duty of the governor-general was to act as a constitutional monarch, in that he was bound to accept the advice of his prime minister and to act upon it – following the precedent set by British constitutional practice. His freedom of action was closely circumscribed. He might prorogue parliament, but otherwise his powers were very closely detailed and confined to what was laid down by the constitution. It was his duty to appoint the prime minister, for example, but this was to be the man who headed the party which appeared to enjoy the majority support in parliament; it was also his duty to remove the prime minister, but he could only do so if it were apparent that the latter no longer enjoyed parliamentary support, and then it was his duty to appoint as the new prime minister another member of parliament who, it appeared, could muster the required support.

It was also one of the governor-general's duties to dissolve parliament, but this he could only do on the advice of his prime minister – or, in exceptional circumstances, he could and constitutionally should act to do so on his own initiative if it appeared to him that the prime minister was remiss in not so advising him; in practice this could only happen if the prime minister had either forfeited his own parliamentary majority, or failed to carry out the requirements of the constitution to hold a general election. It was the governor-general's duty to appoint members of the cabinet and certain members of the public service and the judiciary, but in doing this he was bound to be guided by, and to accept, the advice of the prime minister concerning the individual appointed.

The governor-general, in short, acted as constitutional monarch in his dealings with his prime minister, in that he was bound to accept the latter's advice; and his exercise of his supreme powers was tempered by the limitations laid down in the constitution. The written constitutions of the African countries merely put on paper the unwritten constitutional usage that has grown up around the functions of the monarchy through the centuries in England.

PRIME MINISTER AND CABINET : As mentioned above, the real political power was assumed to reside in the prime minister who, as in England, was the leader of the political party which enjoyed the most support in Parliament and who could count on obtaining a parliamentary majority to ensure the passage of legislation.

He chose his own ministers to run departments of state, and from among them a cabinet, composed of elected members of parliament and collectively responsible to parliament and through that to the people for government policy. Occasionally and very exceptionally, cabinet and ordinary ministers could be non-parliamentarians (so as to enable the smallest and least viable countries to maintain the necessary standards of ability in public office).

PARLIAMENT : Parliament was normally bicameral, consisting of a chamber of popularly elected representatives and, usually, an upper chamber of people having either hereditary or occupational claims to a part in the governing process. There was universal manhood suffrage (except in the case of the Muslim northern Nigeria, where women did not receive the vote); there was usually an age limit, of twenty-one or twenty-five, below which the vote might not be exercised, and frequently an age qualification of thirty or forty years of age for membership of an upper house. Neither property, nor education (both of which had sometimes figured as qualifications for voting or representation in parliament under British rule) was used as a qualifying standard under the independent governments. One necessary qualification, however, was that of language; it was almost invariably stipulated that a candidate for election should command enough English to enable him to understand the proceedings of parliament, a necessary condition in circumstances where tribal multiplicity made it impossible to select a tongue other than English which might be understood by all yet offend none.

Members of parliament usually had certain limitations placed on their theoretical ability to legislate. Invariably, and as mentioned earlier, British parliamentary practice and the development of the powers of the House of Commons *vis-à-vis* the House of Lords set the precedent for limiting the powers of the upper houses; in general they might neither initiate money bills, nor could they delay assent to legislation already passed by the lower houses for more than six months. Another disability which is taken straight from British parliamentary practice was that backbenchers of the lower houses were usually disallowed from introducing legislation to increase taxation or expenditure unless it were certified as acceptable legislation by a minister in the government.

ELECTORAL COMMISSION: The constitution-makers realized that the prop and stay of the whole parliamentary system depended upon the fair working of the electoral process; provision had to be made for the regular holding of general elections, for the reasonable demarcation of electoral constituency boundaries drawn as far as possible to secure constituencies of a roughly similar size, and for the adequate supervision of elections. Most of the constitutions attempted to secure these conditions by writing-in a limit for the lifetime of a parliament (usually five years from the date of the previous general election) and specifying that if the prime minister had not advised his governor-general to dissolve parliament within this time, then the governor-general should act on his own initiative to do so. Provision was frequently made for the establishment of an electoral commission, whose duty was to demarcate constituencies by reviewing their shape and size and to act generally to supervise elections and the operation of a fair and secret ballot.

Great care was exercised in the composition of electoral commissions; usually they would be headed by a non-partisan public figure, for example the speaker of a house of representatives or, perhaps, the head of the public service commission, supported by three or perhaps five other members who should be neither MPs nor public servants. Usually the commission was appointed by the governor-general acting on the advice of the prime minister, and its members could only be dismissed by the same procedure and then only for misconduct, disability to hold office, or at the end of a specified term of office (usually five, seven, or eight years).

THE JUDICIARY : The most detailed care was expended on defining and safeguarding the judiciary, a reflection of the fact that those who drafted the constitutions were closely advised by English constitutional lawyers, and of the emphasis placed upon the rule of law in the operations of the British constitution. The guiding principle was the separation of the judiciary from the whims of the political world, to ensure an unbiased and non-partisan judiciary; but a peculiar difficulty existed in that, although the English judges remain aloof from politics, they are appointed by the prime minister of the day or the lord chancellor and the lord chancellor himself, the head of the legal system, is an intensely political appointment – although in the everyday administration of the law, party political considerations never intrude. It was clearly appreciated that these anomalies would prove extremely difficult to resolve in the circumstances of the newly established African countries, faced as they were with the need to make their own constitutions work and to forge new and reliable relationships within government.

The constitution-makers therefore tried to ensure the independence of the judiciary by a series of detailed provisions written-in to the constitutions; thus the chief justices should be appointed by the governors-general on the advice of the prime minister, while other justices of the high court should be appointed by the governors-general acting on the advice of a judicial service commission (see below, pp. 88ff). To get rid of any of the justices was difficult indeed, and could only be attempted if they were alleged to be unable to function by reason of mental or physical disability, or to have misconducted themselves. In some cases a justice could only be removed after the case for doing so had been brought to the privy council in London; in other cases the procedure was hedged about with such safeguards as the necessity for his brother justices to concur in his removal, or for the matter to be referred to a special tribunal composed partly of judges, partly of public servants and operating independently of the prime minister and the political party currently enjoying power.

THE LAW OFFICERS : Here, too, it was attempted to secure the independence of the legal system, by separating the political functions of the law officers from their purely legal activities, or by specifying, for instance, that the attorney-general should be designated a public servant even though he should function as the government's chief legal adviser. It was frequently emphasized that the director of public prosecutions, responsible as he was for initiating and pursuing civil and criminal suits, should not be responsible to or moved by the opinions or actions of anybody else in the execution of his duty; frequently he was defined as a public officer, always it was extremely difficult to remove him except as the culmination of a lengthy process involving politically neutral elements in some form of supervising judgment. Occasionally the constitutions provided for the post of director of public prosecutions, a public office, only to become effective when that of attorney-general had changed from a public office to a political one; frequently, in an attempt to sustain the legal and professional standing of the holders of these posts, it was stipulated that they should only be held by those of, say, ten years' standing in practice before a superior court. Occasionally the attorney-general would be permitted to fill a ministerial post in the government without necessarily being an elected member of the legislature. In general, the pattern to emerge was that of an attempt to secure the independence and professional competence of the law officers, by the separation of judicial from political functions and by the detailing of the professional standards required of office-holders.

THE PUBLIC SERVICE : There was detailed provision for that other prop of the British constitutional monarchy, a non-political public service, in the African independence constitutions. It was expected that the civil servants themselves should be politically neutral and their careers based on merit rather than on nepotism and some local version of the old school tie; to this end a public service commission was instituted, or, where it already existed before independence, its provisions were extended. This commission would consist of three or perhaps five men prominent in public life, whose selection and tenure of office were hedged about with the same sort of conditions as governed the choice of members of the electoral commission or, for that matter, of the judicial service commission. There was considerable overlapping of membership of these commissions, with, for instance, the head of the public service commission frequently being a member also of the judicial service commission; and infinite care was expended on ensuring that appointments, while appearing to be under the control of the political head of the government (i.e. the prime minister), in fact remained subservient either to the non-political head of state (i.e. the governor-general) or to persons other than the prime minister. It was the duty of this commission to vet those put forward to fill senior appointments, and, significantly, to act as a kind of judicial forum when dismissals were put forward.

Another body found enshrined in most of the independence constitutions was the police service commission, whose membership and duties bore a close resemblance to those enumerated above for the public service commission.

Constitutional developments

It is as easy to see as it has become trite to say, that what chiefly distinguishes these constitutions so laboriously constructed is the ease with which they have been dismantled. Not one of the fifteen is today the same as when it was promulgated; most suffered very considerable and far-reaching change within one year of coming into force. Is this the fault of the constitutions themselves, one wonders, or is the reason to be found mainly within the context in which they had to operate? These and other questions are not easy to answer, partly, no doubt, because there is no single answer; to arrive somewhere near the truth we have to take account of many strands of action. First we should look at what actual changes and upheavals have taken place in the various countries since they gained their independence and assumed responsibility for their own constitutional progress; later, we can attempt to trace the general pattern of events, to enable us to define what has been happening with a view to projecting future developments.

GHANA: The 1957 independence constitution differed from most of the other constitutions in that the central legislature was unicameral, consisting only of a National Assembly; at the regional level, however, provision was made for a bicameral structure by the establishment of elective regional assemblies, with houses of chiefs in each of the five regions to be set up within twelve months of independence. This was a compromise between the highly centralist policy of Nkrumah and his Convention Peoples' Party (CPP), and the demands of the traditional chiefly authorities in the regions whose interests were safeguarded by the entrenched clauses in the constitution. Thus, constitutional modification or amendment required a two-thirds majority of the members of the National Assembly on a bill's third reading, while amendments affecting chiefly or regional matters required in addition the approval of two-thirds of the regional assemblies. While Nkrumah's CPP held seventy-two out of the 104 seats in the National Assembly, and hence dominated affairs there, they held only eight of the twenty-one seats in Ashanti Region and eleven out of twenty-six in the Northern Territories and were not, therefore, fully in command of the regions; to remedy this was Nkrumah's immediate ambition, and he achieved it in 1958 by the simple expedient of using the CPP's majority in the National Assembly to amend the constitution so as to abolish the two-third rule in the regional assemblies. The following year, 1959, saw the dissolution of the regional assemblies and the consequent centralizing of power in Accra.

1960 saw Ghana a republic, a measure achieved by popular plebiscite and the enactment of a new constitution by a constituent assembly which in all essentials was the same as the former National Assembly. The plebiscite called upon people to choose a president elect as well as to decide whether to set up a republic; in a 54 per cent vote, there was a majority of 1,008,724 to 131,425 in favour of the new constitution, and a majority of 1,026,076 to 124,623 in favour of Nkrumah over Dr Danquah as first president of the new republic. It should be noted, first that the whole procedure was characterized by the utmost care to preserve legality; and secondly, that the constitution which was finally enacted by the constituent assembly later in 1960 differed in several important ways from the draft constitution on which the plebiscite had been held, in particular in the extensive powers conferred on the president.

The 1960 republican constitution indicated the pattern along which politics in Ghana were moving. It stressed the common people as the source of power, recognized African unity as a prime goal of statecraft, and emphasized the use of the referendum as a tool of politics. Certain elements in the old independence constitution remained, as, for instance, the institutional survival of the unicameral legislature. Other facets of the new constitution, however, indicated the revolutionary (rather than evolutionary) nature of the changes made and the means by which they were carried out. But its main feature was the immense power wielded by Nkrumah, which was augmented in 1964 following another referendum and the passing of the Constitution Amendment Act; Nkrumah, who was already entitled to dismiss the chief justice, was now also empowered to dismiss judges of the Supreme or High Courts, 'at any time for reasons which to him appear sufficient'. By the same enactment, Ghana became a one-party state.

On 24 February 1966 Nkrumah was ousted from power and the government was vested in the National Liberation Council (NLC), dominated by the military who ruled by decree while a constitutional commission was set up to determine the future form of government. In December 1968 a constituent assembly met, and following its deliberations the NLC transferred power in September 1969 following elections to a civilian government headed by Dr K. Busia as prime minister. For a while the military influence was continued by a three-man presidential commission headed by Brigadier A. A. Afrifa, but this was dissolved in August 1970 and the former chief justice, Sir Edward Akufo-Ado, was elected president by an electoral college composed of the National Assembly and twenty-four chiefs. In January 1972 the civil regime was ousted again, following another military coup led by Colonel I. K. Acheampong who assumed the chairmanship of the National Redemption Council (NRC), the largely military body he had appointed to rule the country.

NIGERIA : Following independence, the main political problem in Nigeria – in contrast to Ghana, where it was that of the concentration of supreme power in the hands of one individual – has been that of the relationship of the regions to the central government. In 1960 Federal Nigeria consisted of three regions and the federal area of Lagos, and with the North greater in size than the other two regions put together the fundamental disequilibrium was clear. In July 1963 a referendum approved the creation of a new state, the Mid-West, following majority decisions in the Federal Assembly and all the regional assemblies.

The independence constitution was both complicated and lengthy, in an attempt to demarcate possibly conflicting areas of interest. A bicameral legislative structure at both centre and regional levels was set up, and detailed lists of concurrent and exclusive legislation drawn up with the residue of powers remaining with the federal government, a tendency that was to continue. On 1 October 1963 Nigeria became a republic within the Commonwealth, with a president elected by an electoral college of members of the Federal Senate and House of Representatives. The federal government was then to consist of the president, a council of ministers presided over by the prime minister, a Senate composed of equal numbers of representatives from all the regions, and a House of Representatives of 312 popularly elected members. At the regional level, the bicameral legislatures remained.

In the immediate post-independence stage, party politics were vivid and conflicting. In the north, the Northern Peoples' Congress (NPC) ruled supreme and by virtue of its strength dominated also the federal government; this was the party of the Muslim emirs, whose political leader, Sir Ahmadu Bello, Sardauna of Sokoto, preserved his northern power base and deputed Sir Abubakar Tafawa Belawa to assume the federal premiership. In the east the National Convention of Nigerian Citizens (NCNC) dominated regional politics; in the west it was the Action Group (AG) under the leadership of Awolowo, its chief protagonist at federal level, and Akintola, the party leader in the regional assembly that secured power. It is clear that it was these competing power areas that severely strained, eventually to rupture, federal cohesion.

The political strains came into the open in 1962, when Awolowo's attempts to augment his power at the federal centre and to lead an opposition party with a genuine alternative policy led him to adopt a policy of democratic socialism which did not accord with Akintola's regional leadership. This split the AG and Awolowo attempted to oust Akintola from the leadership, provoking thereby serious political rioting and a fight to the death in the Western Region assembly chamber. The federal government intervened to declare a state of emergency in the West (the legality or otherwise of this action is discussed later on), suspended the government and appointed an administrator to run the government in the meanwhile. Awolowo was arrested in September 1962 and was charged with conspiring to overthrow the government by force (see p. 92, for an account of the extradition of Chief Enaharo from England to stand trial with Awolowo), and a commission of enquiry was appointed to look into the disappearance of regional funds – quantities of which were subsequently divulged to have been diverted to AG purposes (*see* below, p. 107). Early in 1963 the state of emergency was lifted and Akintola, whose section of the AG had split off to form the UPC, became premier; the UPC joined with a section of the western group of the NCNC to form the Nigerian National Democratic Party (NNDP), while the rest of the western Yoruba of the old AG joined with Ibo from the east to form the United Progressive Grand Alliance (UPGA).

Meanwhile controversy raged elsewhere. The balance of power in the Federal Assembly depended upon regional population figures, on which representation was based, and the 1962 census gave the figures as 21.4 million in the north and 23.7 million in the south; these figures were rejected in the 1963 recount, which restored the superiority of the north by reckoning its population as 29.7 million and that of the south as 25.6 million. This restored the 54:46 ratio on which northern representation came to 174, and that of the south 138, in the assembly; and was inherently unbelievable, for it argued a 1962 population of over 55 million compared with 30.4 million when the census was last taken in 1953. The widespread realization of the falsity of these figures which rendered it impossible to abolish the power of the north, coupled with the unrest caused by the first Nigerian general strike which took place in 1964, greatly contributed to the sense of grievance and impending political disaster which dominated the political scene.

Indeed, the elections of end-1964 and 1965 demonstrated that regional jealousies, resulting in widespread rioting, intimidation and permanent political apathy, posed a very serious threat to the existence of the Federation. At the centre, the Nigerian National Alliance (NNA), composed of the NPC, NNDP, Mid-West Democratic Front and Dynamic Party, won control. For a week the president, Dr Azikiwe, refused to call upon the northern leaders to form a government; then, on an assurance that Balewa intended to form a broad-based ministry, he consented to do so. Despite this, bitterness at the power of the northern politicians increased during 1965. In October the delayed regional election was held in the West; when the results were known (NNDP seventy-four, UPGA seventeen) rioting, violence and murder broke out in the West, but this time the federal government refused to invoke a state of emergency.

It was probably the apparent inability of the federal government to intervene effectively, coupled with the overweening power of the northern politicians and a widespread sense that political graft and corruption had broken all bounds, rather than the existence of an Ibo plot as such that brought about the first of the military incursions into the government of Nigeria. On 15 January 1966 the young, mainly eastern-led officers' coup resulted in the murders of Sir Ahmadu Bello, Akintola, Balewa and the federal finance minister, Chief Festus Okotie-Eboh. On 17 January the federal cabinet called upon General Ironsi to rule, and the constitution was suspended in favour of rule by military government. Ironsi's apparent favouring of Ibo interests and his dismissal of regional considerations in his efforts to restore and centralize authority led in turn to his downfall, which took place at the end of July when northern troops mutinied and killed Ironsi and other Ibos. The northern, but Christian, General Gowon succeeded to power, and among his first acts were the rescinding of the decree that had abolished the regions and the release of Awolowo from prison.

Meanwhile, throughout August and September, great massacres of Ibos were taking place in the North, and the move of the Ibos back to their homeland in the east of the country had begun. The demands of the Ibo leader, Ojukwu, for the protection of the Ibo people, and their right to secede from the Federation, were not met. On 30 May 1967 the eastern government claimed to have seceded from the Federation, and the Biafran War was on. It did not end until 12 January 1970, when the Federation finally imposed its will.

Political parties had been banned in 1966, and the country was thereafter ruled by a Supreme Military Council which consisted of army leadership, and by a Federal Executive Council; it was dominated by the military, but also contained some of the pre-1966 politicians. Nevertheless, many of the old problems remained (and remain today). In April 1968 the military government had divided the country into twelve states, and proceeded to rule through the actions of political leaders designated commissioners of states; but the very act of further dividing the country, although it did much to break up the old power exercised by the North, roused suspicions by its action in dividing other cohesions, in particular that of the Yoruba tribe. It does

45

not seem even yet that the regional/centre issue has been satisfactorily resolved.

SIERRA LEONE : At indepedence Sierra Leone continued with a unicameral legislature, a House of Representatives and sixty-six elected members, twelve indirectly elected chiefs and a speaker; and initially the government formed was a coalition which united the SLPP, the membership of which predominantly reflected the Mende tribe under the leadership of the two Margai brothers, with the African Peoples' Congress (APC) supported by the Temne tribe and led by Siaka Stevens. The coalition soon broke up, however, and in elections held in 1962 the SLPP won twenty-eight seats outright and with support from Independent members and from many chiefs formed the government. In 1964 the elder Margai brother, Sir Milton, died and his successor, Sir Albert, pressed for the establishment of a republic.

It was the complexities of the adoption of a republican constitution that provided the vehicle for political unrest. By the independence constitution, the legislative requirements for setting up republican government were two majority votes in parliament, which had to be separated by a parliamentary dissolution and a general election. Margai obtained one such vote in 1967, but lost his majority in the election held in March and the governor-general accordingly called upon Stevens to form the government in his stead. On 20 March Brigadier David Lansana, whose sympathies lay with Margai, moved on State House, declared martial law and arrested both the governor-general and Stevens. On 23 March came a counter-coup by other army officers, who arrested Lansana and detained both Sir Albert Margai and Siaka Stevens; Brigadier Juxon-Smith assumed supreme power, set up a National Reformation Council to rule the country, suspended the offices of prime minister and governor-general, and abolished the House of Representatives and all political parties.

The NRC set up a commission of enquiry into the 1967 election, which concluded that the APC under Siaka Stevens had won fairly and recommended the resumption of civilian government. On 18 April 1968 discontent at the slowness with which the military was implementing the recommendation brought about the so-called NCO's rebellion; three NCOs mutinied, gained support from the rest of the army, formed the National Interim Council, and on

26 April caused Stevens to be sworn in at the head of an all-party government.

Again, this coalition government did not last long. In November 1968 clashes between Mende supporters of the SLPP and Temne of the APC resulted in the declaration of a state of emergency; this was lifted in February 1969, and in June of that year the national coalition gave way to an all-APC government led by Stevens. From now on he pursued his own schemes to bring about the establishment of a republic, and the growth of his personal power caused a split in the APC. Part of it broke away to form a new party, the United Democratic Party (UDP) under Dr John Karefa Smart, but in September 1970 another state of emergency was declared and Karefa Smart was imprisoned. In March 1971 came an unsuccessful army plot, which was beaten off by 200 paratroopers from Guinea, brought into the country under the defence agreement concluded with that country. In April 1971, following parliamentary legislation to amend the constitution so that a new constitution might be legal if it were passed through parliament with a two-thirds majority, Siaka Stevens secured his republic. He became its first executive president, with J. J. Karema, another APC member, the prime minister. In January 1971 the state of emergency had been extended, and the elections postponed for three and a half years. In this atmosphere it seems that pressures for the formation of a one-party state and for the disbandment of the army and its replacement by a militia, coupled with the dominance of the Temne in the civil service and professions, will further polarize politics between the two leading tribes in the country and result in further tensions.

THE GAMBIA: The Gambia became independent in February 1965 with a unicameral legislature, a House of Representatives composed of a speaker, thirty-two elected members, four categorized as chiefs' representative members and two nominated members (who were not entitled to vote in the House). The government was a coalition between the PPP led by David Jawara, which had obtained eighteen seats in the 1962 elections, and the UP whose head was P. N'Jie, with thirteen seats.

This coalition did not last long as N'Jie left the government soon after independence, when politics assumed a vivid party character. In November 1965 a referendum was held on the issue of declaring a republic, which failed by only 758 votes to get the two-thirds majority of the population needed to secure the measure. In May 1966 a general election resulted in the PPP winning twenty-four of the thirty-two directly elected seats in the House of Representatives, thus retaining Jawara in power, with a parliament that meets for some ten to twelve days a year. It does not, therefore, wield much influence in government, which is indeed dominated not so much by Jawara's ministers, who lack experience and calibre, as by the civil service which is still to a sizable extent staffed by Englishmen to counteract the dearth of trained manpower.

Political activity has been confined to two main issues: the declaration of a republic, and the possibility of a union with the neighbouring Senegal. In April 1970 another referendum was held, and a majority vote (84,968 to 35,638) in a total poll of 120,606 out of the 135,000 registered voters in the country decided in favour of a republic. The republican constitution provided for an executive presidency, the post to be filled by the then prime minister, Jawara, and for the judiciary to exercise a certain check on parliament if it should legislate beyond its given sphere.

If the republic was finally brought about, the prospects for union with Senegal have, if anything, receded since 1963 when a common budget was presented to concert development projects in The Gambia and Senegal. In April 1966 a treaty of association between the two countries was signed, but this has proved to be little more than a dead letter; little cooperation has developed, and the two countries have, if anything, drifted further apart in their relationship.

TANZANIA: Tanganyika was the first of the East African countries to gain independence, on 9 December 1961. Two months later the prime minister, Julius Nyerere, had resigned his post and returned to lead his political party, TANU, in the field, in an attempt to associate the grass-roots of his country's society with national politics. This concern to link the ordinary people with government through means other than solely through the exercise of voting power has remained an abiding thread in Nyerere's political leadership.

One year after independence the people voted for Tanganyika to become a republic with Nyerere, who a month previously had returned to active political life, the president; and a commission to explore the feasibility of establishing a one-party state was set up. In January 1964 came the revolutionary overthrow of the sultan's government in Zanzibar, followed a few days later by the mutiny of elements of the Tanganyika army. In April 1964 the United Republic of Tanganyika and Zanzibar, Tanzania, was set up with Nyerere as its president, the Zanzibari leader, Abeid Karume, as first vice-president, and the former Tanganyika prime minister, Rashid Kawawa, as second vice-president. Since that date the operation of the union has proved a fruitful source of dissension among outside observers as much as in Tanzanian ruling circles, for the considerable limitations on Zanzibari sovereignty that exist on paper in the Act of Union are far from being realized in day-to-day government. Notwithstanding anything to the contrary in the Act, Zanzibar pursues an active foreign policy of her own that is generally further to the left than that of the mainland, she calls upon the central government for development funds, but maintains control of her own receipts from foreign trade, she has followed an idiosyncratic and brutal internal policy dictated by Karume in known contravention of Nyerere's wishes, and has broken completely with the practice of law as followed on the mainland. There are two schools of thought as to the relationship between the two parts of the united republic; one, that Nyerere tempers the worst of the leftist elements and policies that might otherwise dominate the island, and second that Nyerere is a helpless fellow-traveller on the communist-driven train that is hurtling the united republic towards disaster. On the whole, particularly taking into account Nyerere's well publicized, coherent and original thinking on the political philosophy best suited to his country and his people, it is more reasonable to assume that the first of these schools of thought is the closer to the truth.

In March 1965 the commission on the one-party state published its report, and in September the first elections under the new constitution were held. Exercise of the suffrage was withdrawn from Zanzibaris, whose interests were protected by members nominated by Nyerere to serve in the national assembly on the mainland. Voters on the mainland, however, could choose between rival TANU supporters in their constituencies, and as a result two cabinet members, six junior ministers and many ordinary members of the previous parliament failed to gain re-election. Candidates had been proposed by ordinary constituency members, and a further process of selection exercised further up the TANU party hierarchy before a short-list was submitted back to constituencies. President Nyerere was re-elected on a basis of a 98 per cent favourable vote.

In February 1967 came the Arusha Declaration, a highly important document drawn up by Nyerere himself and reflecting his philosophy of creating a socialist society in Tanzania. It defined socialism as the essence of human equality, castigated exploitation, and urged the public control of the means of production. It called for national self-reliance and for development to begin at the lowest rural level, and it prohibited TANU and government leaders from such capitalistic practices as holding shares in private companies, receiving rent for houses, or drawing two salaries at the same time. Banks, insurance, and some import/export houses were nationalized, and government control assumed over some of the most important manufacturing businesses. Later, in September 1967, farming cooperatives were set up to develop agriculture.

The year for implementing the Arusha Declaration, 1968, saw considerable clashes between the president and a group of dissenting MPs which culminated in October in the expulsion of six of them from TANU and, *ipso facto*, from parliament also. TANU, and in particular its central committee, seems to have exercised a considerable amount of influence over developments and on occasion to have run counter to Nyerere's wishes, so that the mantle of both government and opposition fell on the political party outside, rather than inside, parliament.

In March 1969 Nyerere's socialist doctrine led to the publication of a new policy for the development of *ujamaa* (self-help, cooperative) villages. Preparations for the 1970 general election resulted in an increase in the number of parliamentary constituencies from 103 to 120. The election itself, held in November 1970, was the first since 1965, and resulted in the defeat of three ministers and a considerable number of MPs. The selection of candidates this time was altered so as to take place at district, rather than provincial or central, TANU level and it is thought that in fact the TANU selectors interfered very little with the previously ascertained popular choice of candidates. Nyerere received support at a meeting of ASP in Zanzibar as well as from TANU for his sole candidacy for president, although he is said to have refused a suggestion emanating from Zanzibar that he should be created life-president of the united republic. At the election he polled 3,456,573 votes in his favour compared with a vote against him of 109,828. In the parliamentary elections, two non-African former ministers (one Asian and one European) were remarkable for their large and increased majorities. Otherwise, the political year saw increased efforts to accustom the majority of the population to the spirit as well as the letter of the Arusha Declaration, and at the same time the emergence of a body of opinion that opposed it, much of it, it would seem, for personal/opportunist reasons. Further nationalization of the import/export and wholesale trades continued.

The principles of the Arusha Declaration have never received enthusiastic backing in Zanzibar, where stories of the personal and political corruption of Karume and his associates have abounded. The Revolutionary Council that came into power in January 1965 has always consisted mainly of ASP members with a few representatives of the Umma Party, a more extreme leftist party led by Babu. Plots, of which the chief took place in 1969 and 1972 (when Karume was murdered) are but outward signs of the tensions existing between those elements of the Revolutionary Council that were purely pro-Karume, those that were pro-Chinese (which included three members of the Umma Party), and those that were pro-East German and, hence, anti-Chinese. Cross-cutting these divisions are a number of Council members who are basically hostile to the union with Tanganyika. Foreign elements on the island have altered significantly. By 1970 the four hundred or so Chinese were the only appreciable communist influence left, the East Germans, it seems, having been repatriated; meanwhile, a few tenuous links with the west have been maintained, that with Great Britain being operative not through consular representation but evidenced in procurements by the Crown Agents. It would not, however, be correct to view this as incipient pro-westernism, but rather as evidence that Zanzibar, concerned to secure her own self-interest, is prepared to turn to quarters that suit her best. The murdered Karume was succeeded by his close associate Jumbe, who pledged himself to carry out his predecessor's policies as closely as possible.

UGANDA : In December 1962 Uganda became independent under the ruling party, UPC, led by Milton Obote, opposed by the DP led by Benedicto Kiwanuka. The form of government was a quasi-federation, the relationship between Buganda and the country of Uganda as a whole being critical – as it had been throughout the colonial period.

Buganda separatism had, earlier, demanded complete separation, but during 1961 the kabaka's following, the Kabaka Yekka (KY) Party, had merged with the UPC and, hence, achieved most of what it wanted. It had triumphed in the first direct elections to the Lukiko, held in February 1962, and on independence it allied with the UPC to form a coalition. A series of federal relationships between Uganda and the four kingdoms of Buganda, Ankole, Toro and Bunyoro was established, in which Buganda took pride of place; a head of state, styled president, was to be found from among the four rulers of the kingdoms, who should rule as a constitutional monarch.

Much of the interest in the original Uganda independence constitution centred upon the powers of the central government *vis-à-vis* those of the kingdoms/federal areas. The central government retained exclusive powers to legislate in the spheres of defence, external affairs, security, the penal and criminal codes, the public service, finance, taxation, health, and a series of miscellaneous areas. The legislature of Buganda had exclusive power to legislate concerning the kabakaship, its powers and duties, the kabaka's ministers and public service, the Lukiko, and certain types of taxation. The kabaka's government was to be supported by guaranteed payments from the central legislature. Legislatures of the other kingdoms retained power over their traditional interests similar to those enjoyed by Buganda, but to a more limited extent. Those powers that were not allocated exclusively either to the federal states or to the central government should be exercised, in the case of Buganda concurrently by the central and Buganda governments, in the case of the other kingdoms exclusively by the central Uganda government.

It would be true to summarize that, of the four kingdoms/federal areas, Buganda emerged very much as *primus inter pares*; the kabaka's unique position was recognized in the considerable powers granted him, but the constitution framers had, also, a very real sense of awareness of the need to prevent Buganda from imposing its interests over the whole of the country. The result was that the inevitable conflict between Buganda and the central government came to a head in the years following independence.

In October 1963 the republic was formed, with the kabaka as its first president and Obote his prime minister in a relationship intended to resemble that of the British constitutional monarchy. Wrangling over the funds for the kabaka's government broke out, however, and in August 1964 Obote broke with the KY and the UPC governed alone, but with the kabaka still titular president of the republic. In November 1964 came the episode of the referendum on the lost counties issue, whereby the occupants of disputed territory chose to belong to Bunyoro rather than to Buganda; the kabaka, acting as president of Uganda, refused to sign the parliamentary bill that enacted the move and Obote accordingly signed the bill himself.

Conflict thus joined was sharpened in 1965 and early 1966 by dissension within the UPC itself. In February 1966 parliament effectively passed a vote of no confidence in Obote, who retaliated on 22 February by removing five of his ministers from office for intriguing against him, suspending the constitution, and arrogating all power to himself. In May 1966 the Lukiko refused to pass the new constitution devised by Obote, and claimed to secede from Uganda. A state of emergency was declared, and on 23 May the kabaka's palace was bombarded and he fled into exile.

In June 1967 Obote put through a new constitution which abolished all the four kingdoms in favour of a unitary state, where executive power resided in the president (Obote himself) and, in a unicameral legislature of eighty-two members, direct election of MPs took place from all over the republic. Obote thenceforth ruled, it would seem, with the support of elements of the army and police to keep him in power; from 1968 onwards his policies veered to the left, perhaps to compensate for the stringent economic circumstances in which the country was placed. In November 1969 the kabaka died in London of alcoholic poisoning, but in Buganda it was asserted he had been murdered; on 19 December shots were fired at Obote, following which all opposition parties were banned, many people, including MPs, imprisoned, and procedures started to form a one-party state.

It was a military intervention that finally ended this fragile regime. During 1970 intrigues in the army as well as among politicians were rife, and in October of that year the powers of General Amin, a senior army officer, were curtailed; it appears that this led Amin to believe his own career would be cut short, and during Obote's absence from Uganda during the Commonwealth Conference at Singapore in January 1971 Amin assumed power. The circumstances of this coup remain in dispute, but they resulted in a radical change of regime headed by the military and in a considerable reversal of the leftist policy formerly promulgated by Obote.

KENYA : The independence constitution of Kenya provided for a bicameral central legislature, and for the establishment of seven regional assemblies. This was an attempt to placate the fears of the non-Kikuyu (the dominating tribe) who feared the influence of the former freedom fighters, and also those of the Europeans who saw regional influence acting to restrain the possible anti-European attitudes of the central government. In the pre-independence elections, the Kenya Africa National Union (KANU) which owed allegiance to Jomo Kenyatta had scored a large majority in the lower house, a small victory in the senate and majorities in three of the assemblies; but the Kenya African Democratic Union (KADU) had triumphed in three other of the assemblies, and at that time posed a real threat to KANU's domination. It was, therefore, an early target of the KANU-dominated government to remove all possible sources of a threat to its own dominance.

On 12 December 1964, a year to the day after independence, Kenya completed the legislation necessary for it to become a republic within the Commonwealth; and at the same time virtually abolished regional powers. The president, Jomo Kenyatta, the former prime minister, was to head an executive cabinet, and for the time being the two political parties were to merge to form a *de facto* all-party government. The former head of KADU, Oginga Odinga, became vice-president. This one-party system did not however last long, partly because of tribal animosities centring on Odinga's membership of the rival Luo tribe, and partly because Odinga, for reasons either of personal conviction or because he wished to formulate a meaningful opposition that stood a chance of gaining power, was evidently more leftist than the rest of the government. In the party elections of March 1966 Odinga was not re-elected to office, and he accordingly resigned from the government and became leader of the Kenya Peoples' Union (KPU), which formed the opposition.

In December 1966 the two houses of parliament merged to form a single-chamber national assembly. The play of politics now tested the ability of a two-party system with a formal opposition to survive. During 1967 the KPU was being accused of subversion and sedition, and in local government elections in August 1968 the mass of KPU-backed nominations were disqualified on the grounds that their electoral forms had not been filled out correctly (KANU-backed candidates did not experience the same difficulty). In September 1968 twenty of the KPU members in the national assembly crossed the floor to join KANU, and by December the KPU numbers in the assembly were so low (below seven) that it no longer enjoyed the speaker's recognition as a political party. It would not, therefore, be entitled to put up candidates in an election.

In July 1969 another eminent Luo, Tom Mboya, the union leader and a very strong member of the Kenyatta government, was murdered in somewhat obscure circumstances. This was but one incident in a year of turbulent politics, which saw the opposition KPU suppressed in October and its leaders detained and also the growth of significant factions within KANU itself and also the Kikuyu tribe. Factional fighting developed among politicians at the coast, and also in the west of the country. In December the primary elections for KANU parliamentary candidates were held, and in January 1970 the election (the first general election since December 1963) was held.

These election results were very significant. Enormous rivalry developed between members of KANU, so that a genuine degree of choice was offered to voters. The rule that candidates should have been members of KANU for at least six months was waived, so that two ex-members of the KPU could stand for election, about half the sitting MPs were defeated, as were five ministers and fourteen junior ministers, and it seems that a genuine shift of unpopular government personnel took place. Another most important development was the increase in power and influence noted among the provincial commissioners, who as civil servants enjoying the president's direct support have come to play a decisive part in administration.

The rest of 1970 saw attempts to reconcile the Luo tribe with the government system. By the end of the year all the detained KPU leaders, except for Odinga himself and five other ringleaders, had been released following revelations of KPU links with communist finance. Generally, power continued to be concentrated at the centre in Kenya. A major political problem continued to be that of the succession to Kenyatta, and this issue has encouraged factional in-fighting among possible candidates themselves, and also as between the Kikuyu, generally thought of as the dominant tribe with claims to the leadership, and the other tribes.

4 Constitutions of Central and Southern Africa: The Breaking-down

So far in these constitutional chapters we have indicated a few of the most important of the principles upon which the independence constitutions were based, and have then proceeded to summarize constitutional developments as they have occurred in each country. This chapter resumes the constitutional developments as they have occurred in Central and southern Africa, where, it will be recalled, the interest and influence of the European settlers were always the greatest – and where, in fact, they remain so today in South Africa and the three former high commission territories of Botswana, Lesotho and Swaziland, and in Rhodesia.

Malawi

The break-up of the Central African Federation, of which Malawi (the former Nyasaland) was a member, was inevitable from the time when the principle of secession by any of the three territories that comprised it was recognized by the British government, in March 1963. On 9 May the same year Malawi achieved internal self-government, and on 6 July 1964 she became an independent sovereign state under the leadership of that former scourge of the colonial power, the medical practitioner from Glasgow, Dr Hastings Banda. Legislative power lay with a parliament, a national assembly composed of fifty elected members and three to five (European) members who were nominated by Banda; the only party to function was the Malawi Congress Party (MCP). At the local level, the country was divided into three provinces and thence into twenty-three districts, each of which had a council and a president elected by universal suffrage.

Although Malawi suffers little from tribal strains as such, political controversy was joined as early as October 1964 and took the form of acute tension between Banda, whose personal and idiosyncratic style of government was already marked, and those of his ministers who felt that their claims to make as well as to execute policy should be respected. Banda himself resisted the more extreme claims of the pan-Africanists, preferring to align his country openly with the west and advocating cooperation with Rhodesia and Portugal, upon both of whom his land-locked country is dependent; in addition he showed himself markedly anti-Chinese, and was also reluctant to Africanize his civil service at the expense of efficiency. Undoubtedly by supporting moves to increase hospital fees and cut civil servants' emoluments he alienated a certain amount of support from what might be termed the middle classes of urban society, and Banda's chief antagonist, the minister of education, H. B. M. Chipembere, did in fact gain most of his support from intellectuals, civil servants and the middle strata of the people. Banda was supported by the masses, however, and he acted to stop the formation of an opposition party; meanwhile, the administrative capital of Zomba, which had virtually been shut down during an episode when revolution seemed imminent, saw business as usual carried on by the nine hundred or so British officials who remained in senior positions.

The matter was terminated for the time being with the dismissal of three of Banda's cabinet ministers, and the resignation of three others in protest at their treatment. Banda himself introduced legislation into parliament to enable him to detain anyone without trial in the interests of public safety and order, and also stipulated that MPs in the one-party state who ceased to represent their party should be dismissed from parliament. The affair also pointed up the very real dilemma presented to the white liberals who had sought to serve in an African government. Colin Cameron, the only white man in the cabinet (minister of works), and Peter Moxon had joined the MCP very early and had suffered criticism from other Europeans for their espousal of African causes since 1958, and these were two of the men who now left Banda's government in protest against the promulgation of preventive detention. On the other hand, Michael Blackwood, a

European MP who had long and openly supported the cause of the Central African Federation and had opposed majority rule, remained acceptable to Banda and stayed in office – perhaps because his views stood no chance of attracting any substantial support from numbers of people, and hence posed no threat to Banda's power – although Blackwood was later, in 1969, to be critical of the way in which the UK was handling the Rhodesia question.

The years after 1964 saw Banda consolidate his position. In July 1966 Malawi became a republic, with Banda its president and occupying the positions also of minister of defence, external affairs and supplies; at the same time the country became a formal one-party state, with the MCP supreme and an active if obstreperous youth wing. Banda has continued his somewhat puritanical policies as to mini-skirts (in this he has been by no means alone among African rulers) and, perhaps more importantly and significantly, has taken pains to ally his country with the economic and political groupings most favourable to its development, irrespective of their stance on black/white relations. With Britain he has maintained consistent friendship, as befits a country whose recurrent budget is expected to depend upon British subventions until at least 1975. In August 1967 the Portuguese foreign minister, Dr Alberto Franco Nogueira, visited Malawi; in March the same year a trade agreement conferring MFN status on imports had been signed with South Africa; in May 1970 Dr Vorster visited Malawi; and in August 1971 Banda's return visit to South Africa met with considerable acclaim from white, as well as black, South Africans. Diplomatic representation between the two countries had been arranged, and considerable numbers of South Africans were to be found as advisers in government, industry, technology and agriculture; most significantly, the director of information in Malawi was an Afrikaner. South African financial support for the construction of a new capital city at Lilongwe was forthcoming when other western nations were averse to contributing.

For all this, notwithstanding the very real benefits it may have conferred upon his country and people, Banda had to pay a very real price. He largely forfeited friendly relationships with those more militant black countries on his borders, Zambia and Tanzania – with the latter of whom developed a wrangle centred on

59

the demarcation of the boundary in relation to Lake Malawi, greatly fomented by the presence at Dar-es-Salaam of Banda's opposition-in-exile. His difficulties with his domestic opposition continued, and the macabre series of axe killings in 1969 and 1970 near Blantyre (discussed in the chapter on law, pp.91–2), held considerable political overtones. In dealing with these difficulties Banda seems to have adopted two main courses of action. Firstly, he consolidated his personal position to the point where it was difficult to claim that either his ministers or parliament contributed to the business of ruling the country; in 1970 Banda put through legislation to make himself life president of Malawi, and the general election held in 1971 was an entirely MCP affair; but one candidate, and he a member of the MCP, was permitted to stand for each constituency. Although these individuals were selected by local committees, Banda himself exercised the final choice (although there is no evidence that he ran flagrantly counter to local opinion). Secondly, Banda either from deliberate trade policy or by way of bowing to mass opinion actively discouraged the business operations of the non-Malawian, non-black communities. It should be mentioned here that the Asian community in particular experienced difficulties in obtaining trading licences, particularly in rural areas where Africans could reasonably assume trading responsibilities themselves, and that although Banda sounded forth against the principle of widespread nationalization of foreign enterprise he did, nevertheless, embark on a measure of state participation in certain trades and industries. This trend is one that will almost certainly be continued. Banda rides high, but he rides alone; and his personal belief in contact and dialogue with the whites of his own and surrounding countries leaves him exposed.

Zambia

Zambia became an independent republic on 24 October 1964 under the presidency of Dr Kenneth Kaunda, leader of UNIP, with a lively opposition centred on the ANC led by another of the architects of the independence struggle, Harry Nkumbula. Most of the outstanding difficulties appeared, at the time of independence, to have been resolved; thus, Barotseland, which formed a large semi-autonomous enclave in the country somewhat similar to Buganda within Uganda, became a more or less integral part of Zambia, while the re-allocation of the assets held in joint ownership with Rhodesia proceeded amicably and, in addition, a *modus vivendi* was reached with the great copper companies which dominated the economy of the country.

Nevertheless, serious problems remained. On the economic front there was and continues to be a profound imbalance between those employed on the Copper Belt with its high wage rates, and those eking out a living at bare subsistence level in the rural areas, or attempting to exist in conditions of dire urban poverty in the towns. The presence of white miners on the Copper Belt has provided flashpoints of difficulty, but this was a self-liquidating problem as between 1964 and 1968 the ratio of white to black mine employees dropped from 1:7 to 1:14. Indeed, with the number of white miners reduced to 4,000, the problem has been not to get rid of them but to induce them to stay and continue to make available their essential skills. The importance of copper to Zambia can hardly be overestimated; with 93 per cent of her export receipts normally derived from this source, it is clear that any interruption in supply, difficulty in marketing, or sudden drop in price would greatly harm development prospects for the whole country. Kaunda was spared this catastrophe until 1970–1.

Meanwhile, the inevitable play of politics became concentrated upon tribal divisions. Government at the time of independence seems to have been inherently unstable, both because the leaders were jockeying among themselves for power and also because, as in so many other African states, there were too few jobs to go around for ambitious men – and little or no prospect of sharing them among others outside the charmed governing circle. Kaunda himself managed to remain above or beyond a tribal label, no doubt partly because of his personal qualities, but also because he was by birth a Nyasa (although brought up in the country of the Bemba, the dominant tribe in Zambia whose power base is on the Copper Belt). This was not, however, true of Simon Kapwepwe, the close personal friend of Kaunda's who was for some years his vice-president, who was born a Bemba, whose friends and political affiliates were Bemba, and who has constantly played politics on tribal lines. Matters came to a head

61

at the 1967 conference of UNIP, when disputes over office-holders in the party organization resulted in the election of Kapwepwe to vice-president, but polarized opposition to the Bemba hegemony to an alliance between the Lozi tribe of Barotseland and the Angoni.

In December 1968 the first post-independence elections were held. The UP, created as a breakaway party from UNIP, was banned, and the election resulted in UNIP winning 81 of the 105 seats contested with the ANC taking 23. Considerable political tension and unrest followed, which Kaunda attempted to assuage by a greater degree of decentralization of government powers. Cabinet ministers were moved to head the administrations of the eight provinces into which the country was divided, while at the same time the concept of cabinet government was dissipated by the growing practice of holding cabinet meetings only once or twice a month. In what appears to have been another move to coordinate political and administrative matters it was also decreed that top civil servants should be UNIP supporters.

The year 1969 saw the growth of further difficulties for Kaunda. Anti-white feeling increased, caused by poor relations with white miners on the Copper Belt and also by the continuing intransigence of Rhodesia following UDI; there was also very considerable general insecurity, and dissatisfaction engendered by the inequitable distribution of wealth in the country. The 1966–70 Development Plan had failed to deal with one of its objectives, that of social justice; for although it attained a gross national economic growth rate of 11 per cent, this was very unevenly distributed. From 1964 to 1968 peasant farmers' earnings had increased by 3 per cent, those of men employed outside the mines by 52 per cent, and those of the miners by 35 per cent. Real *per capita* incomes had risen by some 66 per cent, a huge increase but one that was totally erratic in its distribution. All this was at odds with the personal philosophy of Kaunda, as it had been expressed prior to mid-1969 and as was to emerge later. Kaunda believed in a humanist state, one in which African socialism and the function of the cooperative should help to spread riches from town to rural areas; he held out strongly against graft and the exploitation of man by man, and in 1971 he was to publish a declaration curiously akin to that of Nyerere's Arusha declaration, in that it outlined a proper code of behaviour for top civil servants, politicians and UNIP leaders and attempted to restrain the rise of persons or classes who promoted their own interests at the expense of the nation. It is these personal beliefs of Kaunda that explain the content, just as it is the political imbalances of his country that indicate the timing, of the series of economic measures that were promulgated at the same time as many of his political measures to restore political order.

In April 1968 the Mulungushi declaration had reserved certain classes of business for Zambian citizens, controls on local borrowings were imposed on local firms, the remission of dividends outside Zambia was limited, and twenty-four large industrial undertakings were instructed to offer 51 per cent of their equity to Zambian state interests. Kaunda's difficulties in 1969, already mentioned, were compounded by a resounding dispute with his country's judiciary that had the mobs in the streets sacking the High Court and putting justices in fear of their lives; at the same time the ebullient Kapwepwe was further damaging the prospects of inter-tribal amity. On 17 June 1969 Kaunda achieved a flexibility of action by holding a referendum that authorized him to change the constitution on a two-thirds majority vote in the National Assembly, rather than by recourse each time to a referendum (as laid down in the constitution).

In August 1969 came the UNIP conference at Matero, where Kaunda's announcement that the state would assume a 51 per cent ownership of the great copper companies did much to distract attention from the inter-tribal rivalry that was bubbling to the top of the cauldron. He dissolved the UNIP central committee and suspended its constitution, setting up a commission of enquiry under Attorney-General Chuula to work out a new constitution, and himself assumed much of the personal power to run the government until the Chuula commission should report. Kapwepwe resigned, for reasons that are obscure but are probably connected with his belief (now disproved) that he could count on support from non-Bemba sources, and thus enhance his own political prospects; two days later he withdrew his resignation. In October Kaunda put through certain constitutional changes, among them that no one might stand as a parliamentary candidate and also for the office of president at the same time, that Barotseland was to lose some of its special privileges (a blow to the Lozi tribe, this), that the government should take powers to redistribute land left by absentee landlords; and, most important, that the president was to have extended rights to detain people for up to one year without a judicial review of their case, and in declaring a national emergency to be able to suspend fundamental rights.

If these measures were designed as a holding operation they met with little success. There were renewed difficulties over labour relations throughout 1970, unrest among the urban poor and dissension between members of UNIP and the ANC. Kaunda's attempts to placate all shades of the political spectrum led him to make reshuffles of cabinet and government posts on 8 January, in March, May, October and November (this, on grounds of individual misappropriation of funds). On 7 December, Sardanis, the permanent secretary of state participation, the architect of economic reforms, left; and on 16 December eleven permanent secretaries also departed. The report of the Chuula commission, which came to hand, was roundly criticized for its proposals to confer more powers on the UNIP central committee. It seemed that radical changes in all departments of government were needed.

Kaunda was at this time still opposed to the formation of a formal one-party state, or to the banning of the opposition – on the grounds, he stated, that as they had so little to offer the electorate they scarcely presented a threat to orderly and effective government. In August 1970 local government elections had led Nkumbula, leader of the opposition ANC, to claim ballot rigging in favour of the UNIP (which gained 609 seats that were unopposed). The ANC took some 80 seats, and independents held 15, out of 968 seats that were at stake. When the UNIP conference was held in December 1970 Kaunda was no longer embarrassed by Kapwepwe as vice-president, for his term of office had expired. When the party met again at Mulungushi in May 1971 this probably made it easier for him to achieve the changes that were essential if more individuals, and all segments of opinion, were to have some form of participation in government. Kaunda made it clear that from now on, the president was to be free to choose his vice-president in the party hierarchy and that neither this appointment, nor other party appointments, need bear any relevance to cabinet or other government positions. In this way he was widening the pool of jobs for which individuals could compete, and he was cutting himself loose from the necessity of following-up the appointment of a person to party office with the appointment of that same person to government service. It is probable that he was realizing that the old guard of those who had fought for independence for so long were not necessarily those who were best fitted for running the country in later years, under different conditions; it is certain that he realized the urgent necessity of admitting elements of all seventy-three of Zambia's tribes to the work, and the rewards, of government.

In other spheres, also, the 1970–1 government reforms were far-reaching. In economic affairs the numerous changes made in INDECO, FINDECO and MINDECO as organs of state intervention in trade and industry indicated that machinery of this degree of sophistication could function efficiently only with difficulty, and the businesses transacted under the aegis of these organs were accordingly transferred back to be controlled by those government departments to whose tasks they bore most relevance. This action appears again to be pursuant to Kaunda's desire to associate more individuals with the working of business. As regards party organization, the UNIP conference began with a meeting of the 350-strong National Council to ratify the new party constitution before it was put to the 600 delegates from each province, the twenty other members of the central committee and the five special members nominated by the secretary-general. Kaunda was unanimously voted secretary-general, and his nominees for the central committee were all returned unopposed. The central committee was in future to be elected on a national, instead of a tribal, basis – and membership of the committee was no longer to be an automatic passport to a government post.

In thus establishing two possible power bases, one in government, the other in the UNIP hierarchy, Kaunda was hoping to rid his country of the in-fighting by the party hacks that had impeded its political progress; he was, too, trying to divest himself of the legacy bequeathed him by the independence struggle, in the form of the fighters for independence whose talents did not lie in politics, nor in nation-building. Kaunda was not wholly successful, as the 1972 declaration of the intention to create a formal one-party state indicated. Kaunda was experiencing real difficulty in bridging tribal animosities, which were resulting in party divisions along purely tribal lines.

Rhodesia

The Central African Federation had meant many things, frequently self-contradictory, to many people. To Rhodesians it suggested, variously, that white rule would be perpetuated in Central Africa; or that the interests of Southern Rhodesia would prevail over those of her two partners; or that the power and prospects of the whole would be immensely enhanced by political unity; or that federation was the final stage, and one from which there could be no retrogression, towards complete independence. We have already seen that since 1923 Rhodesia had enjoyed an anomalous position, that of a self-governing colony in whose affairs the British government, although constitutionally competent, did not in practice interfere.[1] When, therefore, the Central African Federation broke up in 1963–4 and the other territories were clearly progressing to complete self-rule, the Rhodesians assumed that for them, too, independence on 1923 terms would be resumed and that in a short while thereafter the residual powers of the British government would be abolished by the UK Act of Parliament conferring the complete independence which most of the rest of Africa was attaining.

The story of Rhodesia from the break-up of Federation to the present day, therefore, is the story of the attempt by the 250,000 or so whites who enjoyed political and economic power to gain independence from Britain and the control of some $4\frac{1}{2}$ million of their black fellow-countrymen. It is the timing that is crucial here. While the latter years of the Federation saw the horrors of the Congo anarchy and grave doubts as to the shape of things to come in Kenya (all of which confirmed the whites of Rhodesia in their refusal to countenance black rule or anything likely to lead to it), they also bore witness to the worst of the evils of *apartheid* in the Sharpeville shootings in South Africa and to the then apparent successes of self-rule in Ghana and Nigeria, and to the hopes for the rest of the emerging countries of Africa (which encouraged British governments in the rightness of their decolonization policy, especially from the comfortable distance of London). At the same time it seems that the British government still cherished the concept of a Commonwealth that included the independent African countries; it was prepared to lend an ear to the vocalities of the United Nations Committee on Colonialism; government ministers are known to have concluded that the Rhodesians had had their chance to create a multi-racial state and, having failed to bring it about, that they were unlikely to do so in the future; and, probably, that a possible link-up of a white-controlled Rhodesian state with a South Africa apparently irrevocably and eternally ruled by an Afrikaner nationalist government would increase, not decrease, tensions in Africa itself and lend ammunition to the Asian and American critics of the British colonial record. Had it all happened ten years later, most of these arguments would have been exposed as the myths they now appear to be; and it may well be, one felt, that with the change in the British role in the last decade from that of a would-be world power to that of a European satellite, capitulation, in 1972, seemed not far off.

However that may be, the British government was not prepared to give independence to Rhodesia when the Federation broke up. For the time being she continued to be ruled under her 1961 constitution, which provided for a legislative assembly of sixty-five members and a governor representing the Queen. The franchise produced thirteen African, one Asian and fifty-one white MPS, functioning through two separate voters' rolls, the qualifications for which depended on varying circumstances of age, property and income, and educational attainment. A very few whites, some Asians, a few coloureds and perhaps $1\frac{1}{2}$ million Africans were thus unable to vote; in 1964 it was estimated that about 100,000 Africans and approximately the same number of Europeans were actually eligible to vote. Another element that has loomed large in Rhodesian politics has been the place of the chiefs and their role in sustaining tribal unity. It is true that elsewhere in Africa the breakdown of tribal society has wrecked the fabric of family life and produced a stratum of poverty-stricken, ill-educated and rootless men and women. It is equally true that in Rhodesia an essentially self-ruling system, accepted by rural people and conferring delineated and respected powers upon local chiefs, is an essential ingredient of stability. Chiefs receive salaries from government; they are consulted by government; and on the whole, in the last decade or so, their powers and responsibilities have increased. It must also be pointed out, in view of the claims of Rhodesian governments, that to consult the chiefs is to arrive at a consensus of native opinion, that chiefs represent the traditional element of society, that they experience the same criticisms of their rulings and *mores* as does the Establishment in Britain, and that they have the same vested interest in preserving the *status quo* in Rhodesian African society as did the property-owners of Britain before the Reform Bills – or as did the Fulani in Northern Nigeria, the chiefs in Ashanti or the kabaka's government in Buganda.

These, then, were some of the elements present during the demise of the Federation. Rhodesians were to claim that Britain wrote in limitations to Rhodesian sovereignty after agreement had been reached with Sir Edgar Whitehead's government; however that may be, it is true that Britain retained powers in three important spheres of legislation. She reiterated British control over African affairs; a Bill of Rights to prevent discriminatory legislation enabled individuals to appeal to the High Court, and ultimately to the Privy Council in London; and a constitutional council was set up to examine every bill presented to the legislative assembly and to report to the governor if it contravened the Bill of Rights. To these limitations on Rhodesian sovereignty the political reactions were swift, and varied. Whitehead's United Federal Party (UFP) was opposed by the DP led by Winston Field, who headed it in the federal parliament until the break-up of the Federation. The African chiefs signified agreement to the 1961 constitution, but the African nationalists, led by Joshua Nkomo and Ndabaningi Sithole in the National Democratic Party, embarked on a campaign of active dissent and intimidation which led to the party being banned in December 1961. Within one week it had been re-formed, under Nkomo, as the Zimbabwe African Peoples' Union (ZAPU); it survived until September, when Whitehead again banned it.

In December 1962 came the general election in which Whitehead's government was defeated by the right-wing Rhodesia Front (formed from the old DP in March 1962) under Winston Field; the RF took thirty-five seats and the UFP twenty-nine, of which fourteen were held by Africans. The extremists among the African nationalists boycotted the elections, but those on the right of the country's white electorate did not and these elections, therefore, saw a significant swing in sentiment – brought on to some extent by Whitehead's attempt to work the constitution as agreed with Britain, but also by his alleged soft treatment of African terrorist activity. Field's deputy prime minister was Ian Smith, responsible also for the Treasury, and who had earlier left the UFP because he claimed that it had misled people over the nature of the 1961 constitution.

The end of the Federation witnessed, therefore, a new right-wing government in power in Rhodesia, composed of men resentful of what they termed British double-dealing over the constitution, and determined to get full independence from Britain. Field's first attempt to gain independence came when he refused to attend the federal dissolution conference unless Rhodesia were promised her independence; nevertheless, he was persuaded by R. A. Butler, the British Central African secretary, to attend the London conference on independence, and was finally manoeuvred into going to the Victoria Falls Conference at which the Federation was split up. It was apparent that the Rhodesians were out on a limb of their own and that the British, thrust forward by their own political pressures both domestic and foreign, would not agree to Rhodesian independence without the considerable safeguards for the future of the African people and against constitutional amendment that Field could not agree to make. In the meanwhile, African nationalist agitation in Rhodesia was again erupting, and despite the split in ZAPU which resulted in Sithole's formation of a rival nationalist party, the Zimbabwe African National Union (ZANU), serious unrest was in the making.

The formal ending of the Federation came on 31 December 1963, and by this time the political strains among the Rhodesians were beginning to tell. Winston Field was commonly believed to have thrown away his best bargaining counter for the independence of his country by his attendance at the federal break-up conference; there was dissension within as well as outside his cabinet on how best to handle the politics of the situation. Further negotiations on Rhodesian independence took place in England in October/November 1963 between Field's deputy, Ian Smith, and the British Commonwealth secretary, Duncan Sandys, but these proved abortive and by now Field was being pressed by his close advisers to take a stronger line. Field undertook a visit to England which, though nominally private, was an attempt to renew negotiations which again came to nothing. On his return to Salisbury he resisted domestic pressures for an immediate unilateral declaration of independence; then, in April 1964, Field was prevailed upon to resign by his colleagues. He was succeeded by Ian Smith.

Smith, the first Rhodesian-born prime minister of Rhodesia, did not inherit a strong power base; when Field resigned, J. H. Howman, minister of the interior, went with him to the back benches and Smith's party in legislative assembly had a majority of only five. Almost immediately he resumed the negotiations for independence, but he received little change from British governing or official circles and his failure to receive an invitation to the Commonwealth Prime Ministers' Conference in London in July (Rhodesia had always, by custom, attended these gatherings) indicated the lack of support from white, as well as black and brown, Commonwealth members. In September 1964 he travelled to London for talks with government leaders; these proved no more successful than those held after October with members of the new British Labour government. A referendum held in Rhodesia on 5 November 1964 indicated that a smallish majority, with a considerable number of abstentions, thought that Rhodesia should obtain its independence on the basis of the 1961 constitution; meanwhile, the British government was countering threats of a unilateral declaration of independence (UDI) by declining, at this juncture, to implement certain of the financial details worked out at the Victoria Falls Conference. During 1965 negotiations proved no more successful. The visit of the Commonwealth secretary, Arthur Bottomley, to Rhodesia in February merely widened the gap; at the same time, support for Rhodesia was indicated by South Africa, which offered a low-interest loan, and by Portugal. A Rhodesia government white paper, published in April on the economic aspects of a possible UDI, was by no means pessimistic as to the possible outcome.

On 7 May 1965 Ian Smith's government went to the polls in a general election, and the result was a landslide victory for the Rhodesian Front which got all the fifty A-roll seats. The Rhodesia Party, comprising what was left of the UFP, won ten of the B-roll seats while independents won the remaining five B-roll seats. The Rhodesia Party then announced that it could no longer function as a multi-racial party in parliament, and the mantle of the opposition passed to the ten Africans who had won the B-roll seats for the Rhodesia Party, and who now christened themselves the United Peoples' Party. Smith had his overwhelming support for his politics; for the next few months correspondence, negotiations and visits between London and Salisbury continued, but to no avail. UDI was declared on 11 November 1965.

Since then, virtual stalemate has continued. It is worth here recapitulating the British government's five (later to become six) principles upon which it has said it has been willing to confer *de jure* independence upon Rhodesia :

(i) unimpeded progress to majority rule
(ii) guarantees against retrogressive amendments to the constitution
(iii) immediate improvement in the political status of Africans
(iv) progress towards ending racial discrimination
(v) the British government to be satisfied that proposals for Rhodesian independence are acceptable to the Rhodesian people as a whole
(vi) regardless of race, no oppression of the majority by the minority – or of the minority by the majority.

The door has never quite been shut on discussions. In December 1966 came the talks aboard HMS *Tiger*; in October 1968 those on HMS *Fearless*. In February 1967 the Rhodesians appointed the Whaley Constitutional Commission, whose report, published in April 1968, rejected both partition and some form of a federation in favour of a unitary system of government, and which also rejected the concept of eventual African majority rule in favour of race parity in representative institutions. This parity concept was unacceptable to the RF, which formulated its own proposals and narrowly secured their passage in party caucus that met in September 1968. Among the most important of its recommendations were the establishment of a republican form of government, the setting up of a twenty-three member senate and an interim government of sixty-eight, or sixty-four members, to give way later to a national parliament and three provincial councils, of which one should be European and two African. It was probably this shift towards republicanism, coupled with

Smith's dropping of two of the most hard-line members of his cabinet, that enabled the *Fearless* talks to take place at all.

In June 1969 the mainly European electorate in Rhodesia endorsed by referendum a series of proposals to set up republican government and to reform the constitution; this was the constitution that was brought into effect on 2 March 1970. It provided for a House of Assembly of fifty Europeans and sixteen Africans, for a senate of ten Europeans, ten African chiefs and three to be appointed by the president (of whom one was to be coloured), and for a president to be appointed by the cabinet for a term not in excess of five years. The country was to be divided into fifty European constituencies and eight African, and the franchise exercised through two electoral rolls, one European and the other African.

In June 1970 the new Conservative government in Britain initiated further talks with the government in Rhodesia, as a result of which proposals for a settlement of the independence issue were agreed upon subject to their approval by the people of Rhodesia as a whole. To test this agreement, a British commission under the chairmanship of Lord Pearce was despatched to Rhodesia at the end of 1971 and it reported to the British government in March 1972. Its views, if widely regretted, were unambiguous; the whites of Rhodesia might be in favour of the proposed settlement, so might the chiefs so far as their views could be ascertained, but for the ordinary people, the mass of reasonably politically conscious Africans and for the handful of fervent nationalists both in and out of gaol whom the commission had been able to canvass, the answer was a clear 'No'. As with Africans elsewhere on the continent of Africa, they wanted independence, majority rule and one-man-one-vote with no possibility of the reneging on entrenched clauses that has been so widespread elsewhere.

Botswana: Lesotho: Swaziland

These three countries which in pre-independence days were collectively designated the 'High Commission Territories', denoting their special protectorate status *vis-à-vis* Great Britain, are still commonly confused with each other. As a recent and very helpful study[2] of the three countries brings out clearly, however, the mechanics of their governments stemming as they do from their individual societies differ greatly from each other. The following brief accounts of their political evolution since independence attempt to give a practical impression of the main political issues with which they have been confronted and which may become more important in the future.

BOTSWANA: The pre-independence elections held in March 1965 brought twenty-eight of the seats in the National Assembly to the Bechuanaland Democratic Party (BDP) led by Sir Seretse Khama, paramount chief of the Bechuana tribe; three seats only fell to the opposition Bechuana Peoples' Party (BPP). At independence on 30 September 1966 Sir Seretse became president, being elected by the National Assembly sitting as an electoral college. His powers included the ability to summon or dissolve the assembly at any time, legislation was to be initiated with his approval, but he could not withhold his approval if the assembly passed legislation for the second time.

Politics in Botswana does not have the turbulence, say, of Lesotho, for the ruling party of Botswana seems to be an alliance of traditional elements with the small opposition party consisting of a very few of the more modern chiefs, and some of the younger elements among the townspeople. A measure of coexistence with South Africa is inevitable, indeed welcomed by the Botswana government, but South African influence is nowhere nearly so marked as it is in Lesotho.

On 18 October 1969 the first post-independence general elections were held; four parties contested for power and 76,543 votes were cast (a poll of only 54 per cent of the registered 156,0000 voters). There were 52,341 votes for Khama's BDP, which took twenty-four of the assembly seats; 10,362 went to the Botswana National Front (BNF) which thus newly won three seats; 9,234 votes and three seats went to the BPP, and 4,601 votes and one seat went to the Botswana Independence Party (BIP). The rise of the BNF, a hitherto untried party and one which consisted of a coalition between some of the most radical and some of the most traditional elements in the country, together with the fact that the BDP's share of votes cast was 11.8 per cent down from its 1965 total, may indicate a significant shift of opinion away from Sir Seretse Khama's party, particularly in a year which saw a boom in mineral diamond discovery in Botswana by Banangwato Concessions and de Beers' diamond interests. 1970, however, saw a continuation of the calm progress of the past, perhaps the most significant event being the construction of a new road against the wishes of the South Africans, who feared its use as a guerilla highway; and the passage of the Tribal Land Act which reduced some of the powers held by the chiefs and served to split conservatives and radicals in the BNF, thus lessening its influence as the major opposition party. The main possible sources of political acrimony appeared to be the somewhat slow rate at which the localization of jobs was being carried on.

LESOTHO : Independence on 4 October 1966 was marred by the difficult relationship existing between the king, Moshoeshoe II, and his prime minister, Chief Leabua Jonathan who headed the Basotho National Party (BNP) which had an effective majority of six in the sixty seat lower chamber. The opposing Basutoland Congress Party (BCP) had twenty-five seats, which it had obtained in the pre-independence elections of May 1965. Its demands for a further pre-independence election (which might have given them the power) were turned down by the British but supported by the king. The king was strongly placed politically, for although he was nominally a constitutional monarch his following was considerable and he was constitutionally enabled to nominate eleven of the thirty-three strong members of the senate. In December 1966, shortly after independence, the king was placed under house arrest and was only released (in the following January) when he had pledged the government and the college of chiefs that he would function in future as a constitutional monarch.

In March 1967 however the college of chiefs rescinded the king's pledge and Chief Jonathan, himself a member of the royal family, gave warning of possible stern action. The main point at issue was the government's policy of cooperation with South Africa, and in August 1968 the prime minister stated that he could no longer tolerate criticism of his actions by the opposition, which was, indeed, aggravated by the activities of political refugees from South and South-West Africa. 1969 saw a repetition of the tensions between the protagonists of a more active role for the king, those of the government who wished to keep the king in check and seek whatever support was necessary from South Africa, and those radical nationalists who wished to discredit both the parties and follow an extreme anti-*apartheid* line.

Considerable unrest led up to the general elections held on 30 January 1970. The two main contestants were the BNP of Chief Jonathan, and the opposition BCP. Conflicting claims of the seats won were made, and half an hour after the opposition leader, Ntsu Mokhehle, claimed victory with thirty-two of the sixty seats, he was arrested. Chief Jonathan announced that conditions of bribery and intimidation had falsified the election results, and on 3 February the sittings of the High Court were suspended so as to prevent the hearing of electoral appeals. On 16 February it was announced that the constitution had been suspended and the election invalidated, and that Chief Jonathan had assumed emergency powers. Soon afterwards, a rapprochement between government and opposition parties took place, but in March the king, whose predilection for the opposition was well-known, was sent into exile despite a four to one majority on his side in the House of Chiefs.

There is no doubt that the power behind Chief Jonathan's ability to stage and sustain this coup was South Africa. South African officials were to be found in the civil service, the police (Lesotho has no army), in the intelligence services, and as organizers of the elections. There is no doubt, either, that the South African government was gravely embarrassed at the disorders occurring in this, its client, state. British aid to Lesotho was halted at the time of the coup, and the rest of 1970 saw Chief Jonathan attempting to placate opposing elements and restore order to his country. In December the king was fetched back from his place of exile in the Netherlands, on his undertaking to perform his proper duties as a constitutional monarch. Whether, this time, he would be successful did not seem at all certain.

SWAZILAND : Swaziland became independent on 6 September 1968 as a constitutional monarchy whose king enjoyed some very real powers, among them the right to nominate six of the twelve senators and six members of the thirty-member House of Assembly, and powers to control the use of land. The king is Sobhuza II (the Ngwanyama – the lion) and it was his party, the

Imbokodvo National Movement (INM) that took all thirty of the seats in the assembly, the opposition party, the nationalist Ngwane National Liberatory Congress (NNLC) being too weak and divided to win any.

The INM has become a coalition of the traditional rulers' party with modern nationalists, and after independence had four main problems with which to contend – the question of the ownership of land (much of which was alienated to foreigners, South Africans in particular); the dispute over the ownership of mineral rights; the country's economic dependence on South Africa; and a boundary dispute also with South Africa. The ownership of minerals was settled by vesting them in the king, not in his persona as constitutional monarch subject to the government of the day, but in his capacity as the Ngwanyama, or trustee for the people in general. In 1969 a land commission was appointed to deal with the land question; it appeared to be proceeding amicably if lengthily.

So far as Swaziland's general relationship with South Africa is concerned, however, it was and probably always must remain close; although it has resisted setting up a diplomatic mission there, and has refrained from showing cordiality towards Banda of Malawi who had been foremost in initiating a dialogue with South Africa. In the same way, Swaziland maintains close diplomatic links with the more militant African countries such as Zambia and Tanzania. She has also expressed the as yet unconsummated desire to be associated with the East African Common Market, probably because of her fears of total dependence on South Africa and the Southern African Customs Agreement area. Localization of the civil service has proceeded as fast as reasonably possible, and in November 1969 three Swazis were appointed to senior posts hitherto held by expatriates; by 1970, 85 per cent of the public service had been localized.

South Africa

The overwhelming power south of the Limpopo, and indeed the equally overwhelming influence extending far to the north of that river, is that of South Africa. The Union Act of 1910 found a formula for sticking together some of the disparate groups, ideals, and interests that had come to be associated together under the

British flag after the subjugation of a proud and independent people with nowhere else to go; the next fifty years were to see these relationships transmuted beyond recognition. It is unfortunate that *apartheid* evokes such responses from those who care most about it, either one way or the other, as to obliterate almost entirely consideration or knowledge of what else has been happening in South Africa during the last half-century, or even a reasoned appreciation of what has led to the imposition of the philosophy. The near-total polarization of opinion on *apartheid* means that to fail to praise it brands one, in certain circles, as a fellow-traveller (if not worse); to fail to condemn it brings accusations, in other circles, of fascism (at best). A welcome exception to the quality of most of the literature on the subject is the recently-published *Oxford History of South Africa*.[3]

In fifty years South Africa has raised herself from the level of a defeated nation struggling to develop a farming industry and an infant industrial empire, attempted to accommodate numerous different races of men with totally alien credos and customs, and has established an identity for herself in a shrinking, collectivist world. She has had to contend with internal tensions that have led her close to civil war, with external threats to her territorial integrity, and with a kind of tortured doubting of her own cultural and religious destiny that few countries, save perhaps the early USA, have experienced. That being said, we should note that in fifty years she has erected a system of power and control of those who do not subscribe to her political ethos whose success, at the moment of writing, must be the envy of all other totalitarian states seeking to marry law and order with material prosperity, to the total disregard of the liberty and stature of the individual. Yet we must also say that most of these challenges that faced South Africa in 1910 and many of the answers she has evolved to overcome them are curiously similar to those that today face the countries to the north of her who are among the most vocal of her critics.

In 1910 the first Union cabinet was headed by Botha with Smuts as his close lieutenant, and it included Hertzog – the embodiment of Afrikaner separatism, the advocate of the separate development in the same country of the two major races, the Dutch and the British. This government was a coalition of representatives of the South African Party of the Cape Province, and

77

the Orangia Unie and the Het Volk parties which in 1911 came together to form the South African Party on a truly national basis. In opposition were the Unionist Party, largely English-speaking, as well as the Labour Party; Botha claimed to be mid-way between Hertzog with his separatist views, and the Unionists. It was Hertzog who early alarmed the English-speakers with his active advocacy of strict equality between the Dutch and the English languages in education, and he took the lead, also, in opposing unthinking South African support for contributions to the British navy, although this was supposed to be the Empire's navy for the protection of all those far-flung areas painted red on the map. After 1912 Hertzog had been excluded from the government for his advocacy of his views, and in January 1914 he established the National Party, an anti-imperialist and pro-Dutch political party which cared little for the fusing of the Dutch and English strains so dear to men of Smuts' political leanings. Later in 1914 came the great controversy as to whether South Africa should be involved in war on Great Britain's side; and although Hertzog was not one of the actual rebels, this episode marks the moment after which total South African support for the British Empire and all that it stood for could never be taken for granted.

In the general election of 1915 the National Party secured twenty-seven seats and 78,000 votes, compared with the 92,000 who supported the majority SA Party led by Smuts; and in 1920 the NP emerged as the strongest single party, with forty-four seats to the SA Party's forty-one, the Unionists' twenty-five, and Labour's twenty-one. The 1924 election, held under the shadow of grave industrial unrest and loss of life on the Rand, produced a winning coalition party of the National Party under Hertzog and the Labour Party led by F. Creswell, which gave them power with an overall majority of eighteen; but the years intervening until the next election, held in 1929, showed that many Afrikaners still identified themselves with the Smuts brand of unity with the English speakers of South Africa. Nevertheless, in 1929 the NP won an outright majority of seats on its own, seventy-eight to the seventy of the opposition combined; but this did not yet give Hertzog enough support fully to implement his language policy and to put through some of the racial/colour legislation that he favoured.

The next four years saw the slump and the depression, coupled with a fundamental difference of opinion within the NP between Hertzog and the adherents of Malan, which in turn produced a coalition between Hertzog and his old colleague Smuts; in 1934 the parties of these two merged, to form the United South African National Party. Malan's section of the NP, that at the Cape, opposed the coalition on the grounds that it was essential to preserve South Africa's right of secession from the British Empire; his views gained currency throughout all four of the South African provinces during the 1930s and gave birth to the ideals and separatist principles of the Afrikaner Bond.

In 1938 the NP increased its total of parliamentary seats from twenty to twenty-seven, winning 247,000 votes, but the coalition of Hertzog with Smuts retained power. The following year saw the fall of Hertzog, whose wish to keep his country neutral in the war in Europe was countered by Smuts' advocacy of declaration of war and by the eighty to sixty-seven vote in parliament in favour of war on the British side. Hertzog demanded a parliamentary dissolution, which would have involved the country in a general election on the issue of war versus neutrality, but Governor-General Duncan refused him a dissolution on the grounds, then held constitutionally correct, that another MP was capable of forming a government with the requisite parliamentary support. This was Smuts, who thus led South Africa as premier throughout the Second World War. Hertzog and Malan formed a somewhat uneasy alliance in opposition, particularly in view of Malan's advocacy of republicanism; but by the end of the war Hertzog, through advancing age, was no longer in politics.

At the end of the war Smuts and his policies were no longer in favour. At the 1948 general election the National Party and the Afrikaner Party united, the result thanks to the weighting in favour of rural constituencies giving the National grouping seventy-nine of the parliamentary seats to the seventy-one mustered by the combined opposition – despite the fact that the NP polled 100,000 fewer votes. Smuts, the veteran of three major wars, the constant advocate of Anglo-Boer unity and Empire solidarity, died in 1950. The 1948 election that for the first time put the Afrikaner elements in power by themselves was but the precursor of elections in 1953, 1958, 1961 and 1966 all of which

79

confirmed them in power and reinforced the claims made for the validity of their policies.

It is a conventional belief that the National Party's victory in 1948 paved the way for the introduction of the policies and executive actions that make up what we know as *apartheid*. This, from the evidence we have, seems to be far from the truth. The laws and conventions that prevented the majority of the men and women living in South Africa from exercising the vote, living where they pleased, following the occupations of their choice and disposing of the fruits of their labour in their own pleasure, long predated 1948. Milner the architect of Union was far more preoccupied by the question of race, conceived in Anglo-Dutch terms, than ever he was by colour; and successive British governments, while they still retained practical power as well as legal rights to influence South African affairs, did nothing to secure for black, brown, yellow or coloureds the civil rights that were cherished by their own people. Nor did international opinion intervene, for a very long time; the deliberations at Versailles in 1919 spared few thoughts for the majority of people living in one of the countries to whom was granted a mandate to rule an ex-German territory.

Nor does much of what we now term *apartheid* legislation itself date from post-1948; its seeds were sown in the social and economic conditions at the time of the First World War, and in many cases they seem to have little to do with colour, much to do with the common wish of those who exercised the vote first to secure, then to aggrandize their own personal situations. The regulation of land, for instance, furnishes an early example; the 1913 Native Land Act and the 1936 Native Land and Trust Act enforced land segregation in rural areas. In 1937 came an amendment to the Natives (Urban Areas) Act that curbed native rights in urban areas; in 1946 the Asiatic Land Tenure and Indian Representation Act divided Natal and the Transvaal into areas where no Indian might own fixed property, save with the permission of the minister of the interior. By 1913 the problem of the poor whites was already exercising the government of South Africa.

In the mines, the 1911 Mines and Works Act, the 1926 Mines and Works Act and the 1922 Apprenticeship Act effectively reduced the numbers of Africans able to enter skilled occupations by denying them opportunities for training. Attempts to segregate Africans in industry began in 1920 with the Native Affairs Act, which was followed in 1923 by the Natives (Urban Areas) Act, and in 1927 by the Natives Administration Act which sought to separate African workers from European. This was not successful, for the census of 1936 indicated that over half a million more Africans lived outside the native areas than inside them.

The political disenfranchisement of Africans began at the time of Union, when the South Africa Act retained the disenfranchisement of Africans in three out of the four provinces of the new dominion, and in addition enabled the Cape franchise to be abolished. The tendency was for African franchise rights to be whittled away both by legislation, and by failure to enact legislation touching the newly acquired rights of whites so that it applied also to non-whites. In 1936 the Representation of Natives Act removed the African voters in the Cape from the common roll.

Industrial control began soon after Union. In 1913 there was a general strike among white workers; in the same year, the man who was later called 'Mahatma' Gandhi organized a general strike of Indian workers in Natal, which was conducted by means of passive resistance. The war with its other preoccupations intervened, but in 1920 an all-African trade union was formed and during agitations African workers were fired upon by an all-white force. In 1922 came a major disruption to industrial harmony, caused by Britain's return to the Gold Standard and the consequent damage this did to the economy of the South African gold workings. To reduce costs the Chamber of Mines tried to increase the ratio of black miners to white; the (workers') industrial federation demanded a 1 : 3.5 ratio, the Chamber offered 1 : 10.5 and the resulting fracas had to be put down by the army and led as related previously to the first accession to power of the nationalists, in coalition with the Labour Party, in 1924. This led in turn to positive action to protect the interests of displaced white persons by the encouragement of secondary industry, and also to the protection of skilled (white) workers by measures that had their origins in early Transvaal ordinances to protect whites against the challenge posed by the importation of Chinese labour in the days of Milner. The Industrial Conciliation Act of 1924, the Wages Act of 1925, and the Mines and Works Act Amendment Act of 1926 set up consultative machinery, regulated wages and established the principle of a colour bar in certain mining jobs.

All this is not, of course, to say that the Nationalist governments that have remained in power since 1948 have not greatly reinforced discriminatory legislation; patently, they have, and the list of their legislation makes long and perplexing reading. The Group Areas Act of 1950, the Promotion of Bantu Self-Government Act of 1951, the Natives Resettlement Act of 1954, the Group Areas Development Act of 1955, the Urban Bantu Councils Act of 1961 are all examples of a wealth of legislation designed to regulate every aspect of people's lives. The enforcement of the pass laws, of educational and religious segregation, of household and family disruption and of the apparatus of police control that enforces it has been told elsewhere. What has been achieved since 1948 is the spreading of a rationale of segregation, in the arguments for the merits of separate development based on the view that differences in skin colour demand differences in background that are incapable, it would be argued, of being bridged. It this had not been proved false north of the Zambesi, the dedication and sincerity with which spokesmen for the white South African regime argue the case for *apartheid* might earn them credence.

5 What of the Safeguards?

It will be clear from the foregoing chapters not only that the African constitutions have suffered far-reaching changes (and not necessarily for the worse, either), but that these have taken place in spite of, and perhaps because of, the very precautions that were supposed to prevent them ever taking place. Event has piled on event. Despite this, a general pattern has emerged.

As early as 1961, one of the foremost authorities on the attempted transformation of Westminster model to African reality could write:[1]

'Among the characteristic features of modern Commonwealth constitutions are the limitation of parliamentary sovereignty, guarantees of fundamental rights, judicial review of the constitutionality of legislation, the transfer of the responsibility for terminating a superior judge's tenure of office from a legislative to a judicial forum, and the vesting of full control over the public service and the conduct of elections in the hands of independent commissions. The aim of many of these provisions is to capture the spirit and practice of British institutions; the methods of approach involve the rejection of British devices and the imposition of un-British fetters on legislative and executive discretion.'

This was one analysis which has proved totally correct, and largely accounts for the extent and direction of African constitutional change. Twelve years or so later we can perhaps take the argument a little further. British institutions, if they are to succeed, require British devices; if they do not get them, we may expect to see the demise of British institutions. And what then – anarchy, perhaps, or the constitution of the USA, or the thoughts of Chairman Mao; or perhaps a return to the autochthonous or home-grown constitutional school of thought? That is for the future. For the present what we should be asking ourselves, as we try to typify the changes that have taken place, is: are these countries in fact moving closer to, or further from, a

83

form of British-style democratic government – albeit one which has highly individualistic features about it?

It is clear that one of the prime causes of change has been the urgent necessity for African governments to become truly sovereign. Nkrumah's dealings with his Ashantiland chiefs and Kenya's abolition of the provincial Houses of Assembly were both manifestations of the desperate need for the central governments to be able actually to govern, free of the shackles imposed by institutions that held a delaying or refusal power. So too, in another sense, have been the fates meted out to the traditional rulers like the kabaka of Buganda and King Moshoeshoe II of Lesotho who were unable to bring themselves to function as constitutional monarchs. In the British abdication crisis of 1937 Winston Churchill said of Edward VIII, 'our cock won't fight'. The Africans did, and have, and as a result have had to be flown away. This represents, also, the war of the generations; the African chiefdoms have little relevance to, or authority over, the young men of their tribes who cannot stay to work on the land because there is too little to go around and, also, because the modicum of education that they have received brings with it contempt for work on the land. The reason why the chiefs in Rhodesia and the heads of the South African Bantustans do not truly represent the feelings of their people is because the young are no longer constrained by the ties of society into belief in, and conformity with, the decisions of their elders; the occasions when the young join with their elders in a genuine alliance against outsiders are confined to the crises that threaten not just a segment of the tribe, but its whole existence. So it was when Sir Andrew Cohen banished the Kabaka of Buganda in 1953.

The true sovereignty of African governments has had to be achieved externally as well as internally. Each country's expression of itself as a republic is not so much a form of rebellion against so slender a tie with the British monarchy, but rather a demonstration that a limitation on action that is no longer even effective, should be seen to disappear. It is also, frequently, an act of convenience; for it enables crafty and subtle play with titles and status to take place. Kenya, for instance, at this time of writing has a president (of a certain age) but no prime minister; all men are mortal, and when the president passes from the scene it is possible that it will be easier to accommodate conflicting claims to power if there are two top jobs to be filled, not just one; although most probably this in itself will provide a source of strain on future political stability. The Commonwealth tie has long been one of convenience and trade alone; South Africa no longer belongs, and this fact coupled with the knowledge that at any time they may opt out probably keeps the African countries inside this particular cobweb of relationships.

Sovereignty, too, is expressed in the ability of African governments to change their own constitutions. The original clauses written into the constitutions in the interests of all those minorities (and majorities) have easily been circumvented, and in circumstances of strict legality. South Africa saw the inflation of numbers in her senate, Ghana resorted to the simple expedient of using the CPP majority in the central House of Assembly to amend the constitutional requirement that changes in the regional houses required a two-thirds majority in the regional houses themselves. This lesson was a long time in the learning by the British constitution-makers (or perhaps they did not really care what happened to the constitutions after independence); but why in that case, one wonders, has it only been in relation to Rhodesia's UDI that serious attempts have been made to frustrate subsequent alterations to the constitution. Either a government is sovereign, or it is not; and if it is sovereign, it must be able to change its own constitution.

Governments have become more fragile as they have become sovereign and centralized. One has only to look at the ease with which some of the military coups have taken place to realize that underlying stability is conspicuously absent. In part, of course, this is a self-stimulating mechanism, and as such it bodes ill for the future. But it is also caused by solid accountable factors. Some of these are inherent in a situation where national cohesion is rudimentary, where the inequalities of wealth and opportunity are glaring and where the processes of change and development are lauded but the direction they are to take is unclear. Governments have come to expect disaster; individuals within them have the lifelines out to friendly territories and the bank accounts in Switzerland. It is difficult to decide whether the incessant emphasis on one-man, strong-man government is a cause or an effect of this fragility, or even whether, on the contrary, it prevents it from being even worse than it is; but normally one would expect a government to derive strength from the full utilization of talent, and a sense of moral security from the knowledge that substitutes for the First XI exist. One cannot stigmatize these African governments as dictatorships in the European/South American sense of the word, but they are nevertheless widely regarded as the product or preserve of one man; one thinks of Nyerere's Tanzania, Nkrumah's (still) Ghana, most definitely of Banda's Malawi and Kaunda's Zambia. In part this is because they are young countries, but in part it is because of the deliberate attempt to create personal charisma. Too rarely do the critics declare it mere headline-hogging.

One-party government, too, poses its own problems. It is a gross oversimplification to assume that because a country has adopted a one-party system, that this is necessarily either undemocratic or restrictive of the ordinary person's ability to cast his vote. In Nkrumah's Ghana, probably, it was of this kind. But we have plenty of evidence from the widespread changes in parliamentary and ministerial personnel that have followed elections held in one-party states like Tanzania, to show that in fact ordinary people exercise a very effective choice in the composition of their governments and hence in their policies to a certain level.

It is generally true that the influence of parliaments themselves has greatly declined; usually the quality of debate is abyssmal and the cut-and-thrust of contention absent (an exception to this is the Kenya House of Assembly, where dissension still has quite the colonial air about it). The speed with which legislation is put through can be truly breathtaking (all three readings of one bill in one day, for example, in Tanzania), and frequently the number of days that parliament actually sits in the year is minimal. This reflects not so much a decline in the only available national forum of discussion – as it would, say, in England – but rather the recognition of the inadequacies of one forum only in countries where education and communication are so circumscribed. In Tanzania discussion takes place at local levels and disseminates upwards very satisfactorily, so far as one can detect, so that local interests and opinions are heeded to an extent to be envied in many of the Western democracies. What, in fact, is going on is that a single forum for discussion (parliament) is being replaced, often very effectively, by other fora of discussion and decision far better suited to ascertain the will of the people at this stage of their development.

Yet, for all of this, there is little genuine evidence of innovation, of true root-and-branch consideration of the whole problem of government by and with the consent of the people. Again, perhaps Tanzania with her particular brand of African socialism is an exception; so too is South Africa's *apartheid* policy. Most of the other countries with which we are concerned can turn up, if pressed, some form of coherent statement concerned with its governing will and philosophy. But few of their methods are innovatory at all – the Tanzanian ombudsman commission, perhaps, despite its European derivation, could in certain aspects be an exception.[2] In a sense this lack of innovation does not matter, because innovation for the sake of innovation is like the snake swallowing his own tail – remarkable, but counter-productive – but where previous methods have so clearly failed to produce required results, one would expect more attempts to discover truly new methods and institutions of government. There are of course powerful arguments against this happening; lack of financial and intellectual resources coupled with genuine admiration for the orderly functioning of events as perceived in the West, perhaps, may account for it. Or perhaps, when one can instance two very different systems of government such as those of Britain and the United States (both of which *work*, however imperfectly, and are reasonably stable), it does not matter which system with whose details in what admixture the African countries choose, or evolve; the only thing that matters is that they should be confined to their own arena and left to choose and evolve, not just in the light of theory but according to their own practice. It is all very well to frame a theoretical federal constitution with the aim of governing peaceably and equitably a large and disparate area; it may or it may not work. But once the horrors of civil war have been experienced by the people intimately involved, then they indeed have that first-hand knowledge of the price of failure that is essential to success. What is needed in Africa is not autochthony of institutions or methods or theories, but the thrust of personal experience.

These, then, are some of the broad trends behind the individual events in Africa today. The general impression is one of considerable instability, interspersed with the influences that still exist and constitute the normal safeguards of a stable state. One of these major influences, the army and the incidence of military takeover, is discussed on its own at length in the following chapter, because to date the armies have played a spectacularly large part in effecting change despite their more normal role as a conservative force in society. The other major influences making for an ordered society with safeguards for the individual – the rule of law, an impartial and efficient civil service, and the press, radio and television – are now to be discussed. So, too, in brief, are those enemies of the individual, society, and the state alike – bribery, graft and corruption.

The law

Trade may have followed the flag, or *vice versa*, but almost before either of them arrived in the Englishmen's knapsacks the law of England had taken root. The importance attached to the rule of law is mirrored today in the attention paid to the independent countries' legal systems.

In pre-colonial times there already existed two major sources of law in Africa : Islamic law, found mainly in North and East Africa, and the unwritten customary law obtaining elsewhere. This latter varied considerably according to the tribal society in which it operated; a greater element of self-help law was to be found where central tribal institutions were sparse, but in the well-defined tribal states of West Africa, for instance, customary law tended to be more susceptible of central administration. The importation of English common law, the British felt, was one of the indispensable attributes of sovereignty over an area; but they acknowledged at the same time that an individual was entitled to retain at least a modicum of the law under which he had been born. Thus, the colonial era saw in effect a dual or triple system of law come into operation; both customary and Islamic law were permitted to continue, although their scope and status were closely defined and in some cases demoted, and on top (and in many cases interlarded between) was to be found the operation of English common law. Nor was this all; for in pursuit of their belief that the individual was entitled to the benefits of his own as well as English law, the British allowed Roman–Dutch law to spread northwards from South Africa to embrace also

Lesotho, Swaziland, Botswana, Rhodesia and South-West Africa.

The retention of a measure of traditional law and institutions aided British colonial rule with its principles of indirect rule operating through such chiefs as could be discerned, and it was not, therefore, swamped by English common law; considerable coexistence persisted, but on the whole English ideas prevailed in criminal law and also in ideas as to what constituted the law of evidence. Customary law operated in particular in spheres relating to marriage and the family, property, and land usage. In East Africa a certain codification of English common law took place through the importation from India of the Indian Penal Code of 1861, and the Indian Code of Criminal Procedure and the Indian Evidence Act, both of 1872 – the latter the work of Sir James Fitzjames Stephen, and reproduced almost in its entirety in East Africa.

It will be obvious, therefore, from this very brief summary of a complicated subject that while the legal systems of British Africa may have worked, they offered enormous scope for amendment when independence came. Certain basic principles, however, have always endured. Almost all Commonwealth lawyers learned their law in the English Inns of Court, to return to practise in a fused profession (that is, in one where the British distinction of solicitor from barrister in regard to function did not exist); this fact has often seemed to reinforce the strength with which British principles of the rule of law are held, but it has occasionally meant that advocacy has triumphed at the expense of the more solid virtues normally associated with an English solicitor's work. There has indeed been a new interest expressed in African customary law in its relevance to African culture and personality; efforts have been made to fuse African law courts with those formerly operating English law, but it has been more difficult to unify western law codes with those of Africa despite the growth of local law schools and centres for advanced legal study.

At independence every effort was made to preserve the three main principles underlying the practice of English law: judicial independence, the common law insistence on the rights of the individual, and the integrity of the legal profession. We have already seen that the appointment and termination of the tenure of the judiciary, the operations of the courts themselves, and the choice and conduct of such officers as the attornies-general and directors of public prosecution were removed as far as possible from the political arena. In addition, the British wrote a Bill of Rights into all the independence constitutions save that of Ghana (which was drafted too early to incorporate it). This helped to allay the fears of the racial minorities at independence, but as with the limitations on politicians' powers over the judiciary, the Bills of Rights were frequently abolished or their scope confined as the independence constitutions suffered the changes consequent upon the attainment of republican status.

This was, of course, one aspect of the government's bid for sovereignty; the ability to create or wreck one's own judiciary, to control the rights of one's own citizens is essential to a sovereign government, just as the ability to refrain from doing so is the mark of a mature, self-confident one. The most clear attack upon the independence of the judiciary came in Nkrumah's Ghana, when tension between the judiciary and the regime came to a head in December 1963 when Nkrumah dismissed the chief justice, Sir Arku Korsah – as, indeed, he was by then constitutionally entitled to do, even if in terms of custom and precedent he should not have done so. The case had concerned the trial of two former cabinet ministers, Adjei and Adamafio, on charges of attempting to take the life of President Nkrumah; they were acquitted, and Nkrumah thereupon dismissed the chief justice. This case led on to the holding of a referendum in 1964, by which Nkrumah was empowered, as he had not previously been, to dismiss justices of the Supreme and High Courts. The same year saw the greatly increased use by Nkrumah of that other commonly-utilized form of repression, the Preventive Detention Act.

A prime example of the difficulties encountered in ensuring the responsiveness of the law to local conditions took place in Zambia in July-August 1969. Justice Ifor Evans quashed a magistrate's sentence of two years in prison for two Portuguese soldiers who had strayed over the border, and incurred the wrath of local (Bemba) nationalists who insisted on exemplary punishment. Kaunda, who had been out of the country when the matter first came to public attention, returned to find a public uproar which seems to have compelled him to take a strong line with the chief justice, James Skinner. Notwithstanding this, Skinner issued a statement in support of his colleague Ifor Evans; mobs composed of members of the Zambia Youth Service went into action and sacked the High Court, the chief justice went into hiding and later resigned, and so did two other senior judges. It is worth noting that at this time all the judges were white, although all except two of them were Zambian citizens (as was Skinner), and that Kaunda was hard-pressed, as so often, by his nationalist wing.

There are three interesting postscripts to this saga. The chief justice who succeeded Skinner was another white, Brian Doyle. The first black Zambian judge sworn in on 3 November 1969 was Godfrey Muwo, who had been the magistrate before whom Nkumbula (Kaunda's rival) had appeared in 1968 on charges of insulting the president; Muwo had ruled that he had no case to answer. And James Skinner, a personal friend of Kaunda and a longstanding UNIP supporter, kept his head well down after the affray, and his profile low, and attracted little attention when at the end of 1970 he became chief justice of neighbouring Malawi.

It is Malawi that exemplifies the extent to which English common law is not competent to deal with all types of African cases. Malawi's chief justice, Sir Peter Watkin-Williams, had resigned his post, together with Malawi's three other high court judges, in February 1970 following the passage of the Local Courts Amendment Act. This allowed African traditional courts to impose the death penalty, and the need had come about following the bizarre series of axe murders that had wracked Blantyre during 1969 and early 1970. About thirty people had been hacked to death and mutilated in what seemed a spate of senseless murders; rumours swept the country that a minister of the government was involved, that blood and/or some of the organs of the dead were to be sent to South Africa for, doubtless, nefarious purposes, that elements of the exiled opposition or the Tanzanian or Zambian governments were involved. The story illustrates very well the extreme difficulty that African governments have in bringing many of their people within the mental framework of the twentieth century; and Banda was in consequence deeply anxious to end the murders before rumour should get entirely out of hand. Five men accused of the murders appeared before Justice Bolt of the High Court, who acquitted them for lack of evidence. It was Banda's contention that although the rules of English evidence might not allow a conviction, nevertheless these men were guilty and were known to be so locally, and that means should exist to secure conviction.

The law and its operation in Africa has been a matter for contention, but on the whole it seems to have survived with its principles relatively unimpaired. In Nigeria, it is the opinion of one of the foremost authorities on the country's government[3] that

'even during the tense crisis of late 1964, all parties were careful to observe the law and the advice of the chief justices of the federation and Eastern Nigeria and of the federal attorney-general was of great importance in deciding the outcome'

even if he has to add that 'the notion that power must be used or held on to, and that there is no merit in observing any limitation, is widespread'. In 1961 a federal government attempt to establish a commission of enquiry into the affairs of a bank was nullified by a Supreme Court decision. There was, however, real strain over the Action Group crisis in the western region in 1962, when an action of the governor was ruled invalid by the Supreme Court, whose decision in turn was reversed by the judicial committee of the Privy Council, in London, in May 1963; this revived fears about the reality of the sovereignty of the parliament and the courts of Nigeria; an All-Party Constitutional Conference was convened in Lagos, and this led to the abolition of appeals to the Privy Council in September 1963.

Another intense drama took place over the case of Chief Enahoro, charged in England under the Fugitive Offenders' Act of 1881 (an anachronism if ever there was one) as a by-product of the treason trial that arose out of the same western region affray of 1962. This had the satisfactory result of drawing international attention to the absurdities of the application of English law and to the necessity for doing something about it, but not before Chief Enahoro, having suffered the rigours of the English appeals system and Brixton gaol during an icy winter, was summarily returned to Nigeria to be tried and convicted there:[4]

'How ironic that I should have been arrested in London, the centre of the Commonwealth; that I should appear, or be represented, in the courts ten times, and that my arrest and subsequent extradition under an out-of-date Act should have brought about political crises in the British parliament which almost led to the downfall of the Conservative Government of the time, while in employing that Act to bring about my extradition, the Nigerian Government seemed almost to deny their own hard-won independence.'

If the application of English law has had its absurdities, that of international law has been almost totally ineffectual as the story of South-West Africa indicates. This is an area of some 300,000 square miles which supports about half a million people; its land is barely cultivatable and over 10 per cent of it is uninhabitable; it is valuable for its diamonds and the base metals mined there, but, save to those who live there, significant for little else. It has, however, to a certain extent come to embody the conscience of the world, perhaps because the world likes hopeless causes, perhaps because it cannot speak for itself, and most of all, perhaps, because it offers one of the few ways by which to challenge the *apartheid* apparatus of South Africa.

The territory passed to South Africa under mandate in 1919, and battle was joined early over the rights of the original inhabitants as against those of the latecomers – the Germans who remained there, and the South Africans who now sought farms there.

'Throughout the history of its control over South West Africa, the South African government has always found enough land—and the best land—for white farmers, and never enough land for the African tribes. [The 1920s and 1930s] were lean and hungry years for the tribes. The state of South West Africa today is the legacy of those years.'

Thus has written an avowed enemy of *apartheid*,[5] and the quotation is included here not to give one side of an argument but to illustrate the intense feeling the subject has engendered.

The supervisory powers of the old League had been nothing if not sleepily exercised, and despite the hopes of interested parties the UN after the Second World War achieved little more. South Africa's policy was then (as it had been for years) to bring about the integration of South-West Africa into her territory, and when this was denied her by the UN she refused to conclude a trusteeship agreement and, furthermore, declined to deliver annual reports on her administration to the UN. Between the end of the Second World War and 1960, the UN General Assembly and other committees of that body passed over sixty resolutions in condemnation of South African policy. Meanwhile, three opinions handed down from the International Court at the Hague stated that the demise of the League had not altered South Africa's responsibility and accountability for South-West Africa.

South Africa's view has always been that the matter is one that is internal to her, and that to broach it in an international forum is a breach of her sovereignty. In 1960 a further effort to amend the situation was made by Ethiopia and Liberia, acting on behalf of all independent African states, to bring the matter before the International Court to secure not an advisory opinion but a compulsory judgment on whether South Africa was fulfilling her international duties in her administration of the territory, and whether her *apartheid* policy as applied in South-West Africa was consistent with the terms on which the original mandate had been granted. While this case was being prepared and heard, numerous debates and votes in the UN Assembly and in the Committee on South-West Africa called for action against South Africa. In July 1966 the outcome of the Liberian and Ethiopian action was reached; the International Court's verdict was that it was not able to give judgment on the merits of the dispute because neither of the two countries bringing the suit had a legal interest in, or right deriving from, the matter under complaint.[6]

Despite a ruling from the International Court that South Africa might not act unilaterally in altering the status of South-West Africa, South Africa now intensified her policy of integrating South-West Africa within her borders. Windhoek's legislative assembly was reduced in status, and Pretoria took over responsibility for internal security and related issues, and also handled the revenues which had hitherto been under the control of Windhoek. The Bantustan policy was extended to South-West Africa, and in implementation of *apartheid* measures the Herero people were removed from Windhoek to a new township. New legislation in 1969 further incorporated the area into South Africa and made her status close to that of a mere fifth province in the Republic, with ten proposed Bantustans and one central area for the whites.

UN condemnation of South Africa has continued since 1966, but to little or no avail; protest votes have had no visible effect, and attempts to send UN official observers to the area were thwarted. In 1970, however, the Security Council resolved to request an advisory opinion from the International Court as to the legality of South Africa's continued presence in South-West Africa. When hearings began early in 1971 South Africa offered to hold a referendum among all the peoples of South-West Africa as to whether they wished to stay under South African rule. When the Court produced its judgment in June 1971, its advisory opinion was that South Africa should withdraw from South-West Africa immediately; South Africa herself could take refuge in the fact that the judgment, although recognized as authoritative, was not binding in international terms.

It is clear that litigation of this kind produces no practical effect, because it cannot be enforced, and that it benefits only the lawyers engaged on the cases. Nevertheless it is sure to continue, because it is not without its side effects; it focusses world attention on the South African policy of *apartheid*, it enables the independent African nations to form a common front which in other areas it is difficult for them to achieve, and it is even useful to South Africa herself, if her official publications are to be believed, because it enables her to spread understanding of her *apartheid* policy and hence win converts to her cause. Above all, of course, it is about the *only* course open to those who wish to bring about the fall of *apartheid* – unless an uncharacteristic lapse should occur in South Africa's security affairs.

Otherwise, the state of the law in the African countries today seems remarkably healthy. It is not without its lapses, some of which we have noted, and from time to time it is clear that events force unwelcome decisions from beleaguered rulers. The undoubted acceleration in the careers of some African judges has not significantly altered the quality or the unbiased nature of the opinions handed down. Changes have already occurred, and we may expect many more, and no doubt they will be misunderstood by those whose wish is to see the nature and content of the law preserved at the expense of the people whom it is supposed to serve. The best epitaph[7] seems to be that of a British ex-solicitor-general of England, and a man well noted for his championing of African causes:

'With one outstanding exception, it is broadly true to say that the judges throughout the Commonwealth have jealously preserved their traditional independence. The exception was in Southern Rhodesia where, after prolonged indecision, Sir Hugh Beadle and the majority of his colleagues accepted the illegal regime. The breaking point was reached in 1968 when they refused to give effect to the Queen's reprieve of men who had been sentenced to death. These judges stand alone in the Commonwealth. They were false to the oaths of allegiance which they had taken on assuming judicial office. Even so there were two honourable exceptions of Rhodesian judges who refused to follow their example and resigned.'

The civil service

Close behind the law comes the civil service as a defender of the *status quo* in government and a bastion of the ruling system rather than a possible agent of its downfall. The civil service in the African countries, consisting as it originally did of expatriate Englishmen, was geared primarily for pacification and for imperial rule; hence, a more positive role involving development policies and the active participation, as opposed merely to the cooperation, of Africans themselves, took a long time to evolve. During the colonial era the service was divided into senior posts, in the main occupied entirely by Europeans, and the junior posts which fell to the local inhabitants. Complications arose in East and Central Africa, where the presence of Asian immigrants and of a settled European population which had come to stay interposed a middle layer between the senior and the most junior posts, and was to prove a most effective barrier to the translation of Africans from the bottom to the top of the pyramid of jobs.

At independence, then, the adequate functioning of the civil service and its ability to serve its new masters was clearly difficult to achieve. Before the Second World War the amount of localization that had taken place in colonial services was marginal indeed, and even as late as 1947 development policies to encourage the rise of Africans were passive only. In this area, the civil service was far outstripped by developments in the political sector which it was supposed to serve. Not only was there a lack of trained and experienced Africans who would be able to take over; the presence in civil services of Europeans who had had to receive special inducements reflected in salary payments for their services, and of Europeans and Asians in East and Central Africa whom it was felt necessary to remunerate on scales in excess of those laid down for Africans, meant job confusion. In later years this was to lead to the considerable disenchantment of the Africans appointed to many formerly European or Asian held posts, who expected (not unnaturally) to draw all the pay and emoluments, and to be entitled to the leave privileges, that their predecessors had had. Nor should it be forgotten just how sensitive the whole question of the civil service was to prove, for upon the efficiency of the service has depended the efficiency with which legislation has been handled, administrative details attended to and policy decisions assessed.

As in other spheres, independence caught the civil services of the countries concerned at very varied stages of preparedness.[8] Ghana's approach, for instance, had been fairly gradual; in 1954 there were four African heads of departments and ten assistant secretaries; by 1958 Africans occupied 69 per cent of posts in superscale and the next two grades; but in 1959 half the permanent secretaries were still expatriates.

In Nigeria the question of standards raised its extremely awkward head. Existing standards had to be abandoned in 1957, because, with independence clearly only just over the horizon, the 55 per cent of the whole country's population that was contained in the north contributed only 1 per cent of the federal civil service. By June 1960 about 60 per cent of the federal senior posts had been Nigerianized, but the process was always a much faster one in the west and the east than in the north. In Sierra Leone another problem had to be met; between 1953 and 1959 the number of Africans in senior posts increased from 166 to 381, but the number of expatriates employed, far from falling, also increased; this was of course due partly to the absolute expansion of the civil service that was a feature of the times in Africa, but it also reflected the need to retain the services of professionals with the qualifications, such as engineering, that local Africans lacked (and still lack), and were to need so greatly.

In East Africa Africanization came late, partly because of the speed with which independence arrived and also because of the late development of western-style education for local people; and it has never been clear to what extent the new rulers meant 'localization' when they spoke of jobs for locally born people. There had always been less economic pressures on the colonial governments to train Africans for civil service jobs, simply because there were always Asians ready to take the jobs that required certain skills and knowhow that the Africans did not yet possess, and for practising which the Europeans demanded higher salaries. East Africa held two options for every would-be civil servant; he could seek to join the High Commission (later the Common Services Organization) which served as a rudimentary federal civil service, or he could choose to join the civil service of his own territory. Most opted for their own national services, as nobody could be sure if the Common Services would continue after independence. The Udoji report of 1962 on Africanization in EACSO showed that, of the 567 top posts in the administrative grades, 88 per cent were held by Europeans, 4 per cent by Asians and 8 per cent by Africans. Of the 3,624 executive and technical posts, 42 per cent were held by Europeans, 46 per cent by Asians and 12 per cent by Africans. Africanization was urgent, for political and also for financial reasons; and also because over a thousand expatriate officers, having secured good financial terms and scenting trouble to come, had either retired or handed in their notice.

In Tanzania there were few signs of Africanization at senior levels just before independence, but Nyerere's multiracial approach to the problem had to be abandoned in favour of Africanization in 1962 because of the severe nationalist pressures to which he was subjected. That year saw the exodus of many British from high levels, and also that of their wives who had formed the top secretarial cadre; the following year saw the departure of many Asians from government service.

Uganda had always been furthest ahead in progress of all the East African states, for as early as 1929 it had been policy to advance Africans in government service. Even so, by 1952 there were only five of them in top posts; but by 1961 there were 130. In Kenya in 1960 only five Africans held senior posts, but the next year several African assistant secretaries were appointed and with independence there was a complete replacement of the British permanent secretaries by Africans, all of whom were university graduates. Kenya has seen many moves to oust Asians from government service, but, nominally at any rate, the policy there has always been to localize rather than merely to Africanize the public service.

The degree to which the public services in ex-British Africa had been Africanized/localized, and the speed with which it had taken place, clearly varied very greatly. Symonds draws attention to a most interesting feature of the process; Ghana and Uganda, which were relatively speaking always the most advanced countries, kept British permanent secretaries for longer than the other countries – because, he feels, an Africanization policy had been seen by the public to be in operation for so long they could believe in it, and they did not therefore need to exert the pressures experienced elsewhere to Africanize speedily at the expense of efficiency.

Having been established, how then was this localized civil service to fulfil its functions? A greatly distinguished member[9] of the Ghanaian civil service, later to serve in East Africa and elsewhere, gives an account of the new nature of the tasks now required of civil servants, who now had to be concerned with the intricacies of ten-year economic development plans and so forth; social services had to be integrated with the needs of a new state, and politicians and civil servants alike had to be trained to use each other as well as their own resources. One of the few works on how the new civil services have performed[10] fills in a few of the available details. Omorogbe Nwanwene tells us that in spite of all the guarantees of civil service independence, all Nigerian governments have taken a hand in directing the public service commissions; so far from the civil service being non-political, when the new mid-western state was created in 1963 over 3,400 employees of the western public service who came from the Mid-West were dismissed. Ladipo Adamolekum says the usual practice is to appoint administrative heads to the technical ministries, because of the shortage of Nigerian technical specialists all of whom are needed on the job; he notes a high turnover of personnel, especially at the permanent secretary level, and draws attention to the strained relationships that exist between politicians and their civil servants at the highest level. As for the public corporations, dealt with in the section dealing with graft and corruption in high places, Owodunni Teriba says that a great problem is that of striking the correct balance between autonomy and public control, and that government control is established through ministers' powers of direction and supervision, and staffing.

Presumably most of the African civil servants remain, for the most part, within their own beehives just as do their English counterparts, and for that reason – and also because of the long-standing English tradition of civil service silence – we know comparatively little about them, aside from what we can glean from the occasional personal anecdote. It is clear that they have a very grave basic problem in the relationship with their ministers; on the one hand there is the professional training that urges them to be non-political, non-partisan and pragmatic in approach, on the other hand there are the efforts of government to mobilize all resources for the support of the state. The same needs that produce the one-party states and that fuse administrative and political procedures and personnel give rise also to demands that civil servants abandon aloof attitudes and, *ipso facto*, embrace the party faith; because to do so means in so many cases also to embrace the cause of the country. In Zambia civil service reshuffling has often been used to aid government reshuffles, of which there have been excessive numbers. Permanent secretaries of ministries have been affected by the parcelling-out of the assets and functions of the former ministry of state participation, finding themselves appointed the chairmen of great holding companies. When this expedient proved not too effective the civil servants were made full-time managing directors of their organizations, relinquishing their former permanent secretary posts.

In Uganda, General Amin's nominally military government contained no less than six career civil servants, subjected (one understands) to military discipline to maintain order. In Tanzania, Nyerere's policy of total popular involvement has served to blur the edges of the functions assumed by party, politicians generally, the state, the people and the civil service, but he has nevertheless not been without his quota of problems in bringing change to rural Tanzania. The Christmas Day 1971 murder of Dr Klerruu, Regional Commissioner of Iringa, indicates intense local resistance to Nyerere's policy of *ujamaa*, or cooperative farming. In Ghana, Dr Busia's 1970 expulsion of 568 civil servants from their jobs on grounds that they had served Nkrumah was widely felt to be unfair and led to a conflict with the judiciary, which held the dismissals to be invalid. To be a successful civil servant in Africa today requires dexterity and the capacity for change; not necessarily attributes inherited from Whitehall, but towards which Whitehall might reasonably set its sights.

The press, radio, television

At independence the news media no less than the other organs of protection of the civil community seemed poised to play their part in society, to afflict the comfortable and comfort the afflicted – as some have it. On the whole it was a well-developed press, particularly when compared with the literacy rates for the countries concerned which, as the table on p. 148 shows, varies from about 10 per cent to 40 per cent of the adult populations. The larger countries of West Africa, for instance, Ghana and Nigeria, had vigorous and competing morning, evening, weekly and monthly publications, of colourful and vigorous mien and reflecting to quite a large extent the national characteristics of the countries they served. The smaller countries, in particular Gambia, were poorly served. Over in East, Central and South Africa in the countries most influenced by British settlerdom, the press had early taken on a more sober tone, and at independence were tending to regret not always having supported the nationalist cause. Nevertheless, problems there were. Those of purely newspaper technology such as the quality of print, distribution and the like will not detain us here because, although they are of course essential to the well-being of the papers concerned, we are more interested in the purely political problems posed by the mass media and the ways in which they have been overcome. At independence these problems were of two main types : one stemming from the undoubted foreign elements in the mass media; and the other relating to the role that it was envisaged should be played by the media in national development.

An important element in the press has been the extent of foreign ownership.[11] The British Daily Mirror Group took over the *Daily Times* of Lagos in 1947, founded the *Daily Graphic* in Ghana in 1950 and also ventured into Sierra Leone. The Thomson Group founded the Nigerian *Daily Express* in 1960, owns the Malawi *Times*, was a cofounder with the Aga Khan of the *Daily Nation* in Kenya, and, until it was banned by the government in 1964, controlled the *Daily News* in Rhodesia.

David Astor of the London *Observer* attempted the rescue of the *Central African Examiner*. The conglomerate company Lonrho took interests in the *East African Standard* of Kenya, the Zambian *Northern News*, and in Tanzania. The Argus chain of South Africa is prominent today in Rhodesia.

The tendency is to see these foreign ownerships as part of a (concerted?) plan to control and subvert the African continent from without; but, although one at least of current writers on African press affairs is very alert to these dangers,[12] the evidence does not seem to bear this contention out at all. The Mirror and Thomson groups entered the fray partly, it seems, because the British tax structure at the time favoured investment in overseas businesses, and they scented the making of good profits there; although the groups themselves stress the benefits their intervention has brought to African countries, in particular the journalistic expertise, modern printing methods and advertising systems that have been undoubted legacies. The Aga Khan's interest in the East African press was stimulated at least as much by his wish to promote the logical development of his industrial and packaging interests there, as by his desire to benefit the followers of his Ismaili sect. Lonrho's reasons for participation are as obscure as many of the other motives and commitments of this little-publicized group, but it picked up a rare pocketful of assorted assets in its efforts to found a latterday industrial empire – for which it has been rewarded by the 'risk' status attaching to its share rating. On the whole, the foreign owners went into it for the profits and associated *kudos* they thought would be forthcoming; and when they failed to get their profits (for instance, Thomson's in Nigeria) they ceased publication, and when their ownership became incompatible with nationalist ideals and they lost local *kudos* (for instance, the Mirror group in Ghana and the Argus chain in Zambia) they sold out. Apart from this it has, as we shall see later, proved perfectly easy for local governments to ensure that locally produced papers and other media respond to national aspirations.

Quite apart from ownership, it is clear that a measure of foreign control of, and influence on, the African press, TV and radio still survives. Technologically speaking, this was inevitable at independence simply because of the need to ensure that the presses kept running; as time passes far fewer white faces are seen over the presses, at the reporters' desks and in editorial chairs, and this is because the means of substitution is available quite as much as the financial pressures for it to take place are great. Thomson interests are frequently found behind the establishment of TV networks, but as these are manipulated by local people little foreign influence seeps through. More serious is the almost total foreign ownership and control of the agencies serving Africa with news and pictures; Reuter's, UPI, AP, Agence France Presse, Tass are but a few of these, and the seriousness lies not so much in the fact that they may, or can, constantly push a non-African political influence, as in the overwhelming extent to which the news that floods along the wires is non-African. Just as the railways ran up-country from the ports to the hinterland and the shipping lines connected local with metropolitan ports, so today the African countries experience the same difficulty in learning about each other. This was especially true in the Congo crisis of the early 1960s and it remains true today, because the conditions that would remedy it, namely the availability of large sums of money and local inter-African cooperation and initiative, are still lacking.

Since independence there has, naturally, been a far greater penetration of Africa by the news media of the eastern bloc than could take place in the colonial period. Nevertheless the seeds were sown in pre-independence days. By the end of 1956 a daily English news service had been started by Radio Peking for African editors. Early in 1958 the New China News Agency opened its first office on African soil in Cairo, and this was followed by branch offices elsewhere as fast as Chinese diplomats could get themselves accredited; branches such as these, of course, offer a two-way service (just as do those of the Western bloc) in that they report back to China as well as disseminating Chinese news, and Chinese comment on and interpretation of, news from elsewhere. In September 1959 Radio Peking began to transmit a one-hour English programme twice daily, and since then its transmissions have increased and French, Portuguese and Swahili programmes have been added. It is thought that Chinese broadcasting hours number as many as those put out by the Russians; and it is clear that the internal tensions of the communist world, those between the Soviet Union and her satellites as well as those between the Soviet and Maoist interpreters of the communist line, are played out over the radio bands of Africa as well as elsewhere in the world. It is easy to wax paranoid over the growing influence of the eastern bloc and to urge more concentrated efforts by western interests, and there is no lack of people who do so, but on the whole their concern is not justified. In the first place, Africans are no more foolish than anyone else in giving propaganda its due assessment; and secondly, as the general din of noise and propaganda levels increase, it seems very probable that nothing is closely read or listened to any longer. The ingredients added to the cooking pot do not stop it boiling; all they do is enrich the flavour.

Apart from these considerations related to foreign elements, one must also consider the relationship between domestic political events and the press. What is it the African governments actually want from their media? – because nothing is more certain than that the press, like other organs of society such as universities, rural cooperatives and urban developments, has a place assigned to it in national planning. The role of the press is, in many ways, similar to that of the press in the West; it exists to inform, to warn, to prod and pester and occasionally to be immensely unfair – as well as to be astoundingly right on occasion. Its role as entertainer is probably less, and as educator greater, in Africa than in the West.

In the way in which it is regarded domestically we should note an interesting hangover from colonial days; great importance is attached to it as a possible vehicle for rebellion. The nationalists' struggle for a voice in colonial days leads governments to invest the press with a significance which it does not hold in the West. Because the medium is still in its infancy it is suspect, and this leads African politicians to exhibit a lack of confidence in it. To an extent this is because of the insecurity and fragility of the regimes. The dissemination of the press is hindered by the low literacy rate, by the multiplicity of languages and lack of English save among a very small élite, and by the fragmentation of society; the press therefore enjoys the overwhelmingly major portion of its distribution in a few congested urban areas, so that the nightmare of the newspaper cartoon, the irreverent caption or the single illicit broadsheet sparking off revolution is not so far from possible realization.

African governments tend to over react; there are many

examples of offence taken at laughable incidents, such as the joke White Man's Burden Party in Kampala in 1964 which resulted in several deportations. Partly this arises because it does not matter so much what happens, as what is seen to happen; there is a large element of face-saving in press restrictions rather than an honest attempt at regime-saving. On the other hand, it is also true that governments face press opposition that is very genuine and very political in content, in circumstances that hold local overtones of Dunkirk or Pearl Harbour. The nationalist parties that were so united at independence often split soon afterwards, and the tradition of using the press as a political tool continued. Then, too, there is always the difficulty of the crusading journalist, whose battle is never won even if the skirmish of the moment is ended.

It is probably inevitable, then, that the press should be a scourge as well as a salvation. Means of controlling it in Africa vary widely. In most black African countries there is a strongly developed editorial sense of what will get by. This can rarely afford to be wrong. Formal censorship is not much used, save in moments of real crisis – such as the East African army mutinies of 1964, or during the Biafra War in Nigeria. Countries such as Tanzania, Zambia, and Ghana during the Nkrumah regime end up with an official government press (occasionally in competition with a non-official press), but this is not always as successful an experiment as one might imagine because it gets so boring to the local readership, and hence is used only for packaging.

A bad offender as regards censorship has been Rhodesia since UDI. The *Central African Examiner* had been founded in 1957 by Rhodesian (later Roan) Selection Trust (one of the mining houses) and by the *Economist* of London. In May 1960 it was taken over by a group that included David Astor of the London *Observer* and Theodore Bull, an Englishman gone to Rhodesia whose family had had long connections with the diamond interests. According to Bull, they 'tried to hold to a steady line of common sense realism based on simple principles of justice and human rights' in the *Examiner*, but the issue of December 1965 was their last; the censor cut about half the issue, and after an unsuccessful court case to challenge the validity of censorship the paper ceased publication.[13] Another case occurred in October 1969, when the financial editor of the *Rhodesia Herald* and the

Salisbury correspondent of the London *Financial Times* were sentenced to eighteen months' gaol for passing economic information to an agent of an enemy country (widely believed to be the us consul in Salisbury). Rhodesian journalists were forbidden under the Emergency Regulations to disclose the names of people or details of this case; or those of Trevor Gallaher, the Salisbury lawyer, who was sentenced to four years for espionage. South Africa does not operate a formal censorship as such, but press freedom is gravely compromised by such government measures as the 1950 Suppression of Communism Act, the Criminal Law Amendment Act, Prisons and Riotous Assemblies Acts, and the Police Act. The 1964 General Laws Amendment Act allowed political suspects to be held incommunicado for ninety-day periods without appearing in court, and the 1965 amendment to the Political Secrets Act prevents the publication even of the names of persons arrested for political offences. The 1971 Publications and Entertainments Act established police powers to enter private houses and seize publications on suspicion. The 1971 clash between Prime Minister Vorster and the press over allegations that South African police had crossed the Zambian border in pursuit of guerillas took place with Vorster not denying the facts, but infuriated that they were reported. Over this matter he mainly criticized the English-language press, which has certainly been less subservient to the government than has the Afrikaans-language press, which has, of course, often been under the ownership and direct management control of members of the government.

In closing this section it must be remarked that, in reciting some of the apparatus by which censorship is achieved under the Rhodesian and South African governments, the intention is not to gloss over the censorship and undue influence that persists in black Africa today. The intention is, however, to draw attention to the fact that censorship and control are so marked in the two areas under white Anglo-Saxon political control, and are actively subscribed to by the numbers of white people who rest their claims to exercise power over the majority of their countries' citizens on their supposed adherence to western, civilizing values which include the rule of law and freedom of speech.

Graft, bribery and corruption

One cannot honestly disregard the existence of graft, bribery and corruption in Africa today, both because the evidence that they exist is so overwhelming and because the problem is so grave in its implications. But if it is widespread, it is also widely condemned by government ministers and officials and it is therefore the duty of a work of this nature to aid them by throwing a little light on the subject; we must remember, too, that the reason we can quote instances is because they have become the subject of government enquiries whose work deserves recognition.

Corruption, then, is widespread, and it occurs in many different sections of society, over a wide assortment of activity. A general warning of its all-pervasive character was given by Nkrumah of Ghana, in his famous dawn broadcast in April 1961, to little avail it would seem in the light of subsequent enquiries undertaken when his regime had toppled. Of corruption in public corporations, the Coker Commission of enquiry into the affairs of certain statutory commissions in western Nigeria in 1962 found that the political party in control of the region had obtained some £6 million of public money through its control of the economic life of the region and the functioning of statutory boards.

When a government falls, the signal is frequently given for an enquiry into the affairs of its predecessor; and Uganda under Amin has been no exception to this general rule, for he set in train enquiries into the functioning of the General Service Unit (a para-military unit) under Obote; into corruption in ministries and public bodies; and into the affairs of the Coffee Marketing Board and the National Trading Corporation. Heads of state have been foremost in trying to root out corruption. In Zambia at the end of 1970 President Kaunda suspended some officials, including two of his cabinet ministers, on charges of misappropriation of public funds relating to the unlawful lending of money from agricultural funds. In March 1971 both cabinet ministers were found guilty of scandalous conduct and were fined and given suspended prison sentences.

Perhaps one of the most significant enquiries of all took place in Sierra Leone, with the publication of the Dove-Edwin Report in December 1967 on the conduct of the general election of March the same year. Among its conclusions was:

'The whole of the Government's arrangements for the 1967 election was rigged and corrupt . . . they were determined to use all means fair or foul to win and remain in office and if all failed to get Brigadier Lansana to take over.'

The methods used included a sudden increase in the amount of money required from candidates as deposits, an increase in the cost of electoral petitions, the withdrawal of the right to appeal in cases concerned with the election, and the increase of the votes needed to save a candidate's deposit from forfeiture, from one tenth to one quarter of votes cast.

Ghana, Nigeria, Uganda, Zambia, Sierra Leone : this list is nowhere near exhaustive and could be extended throughout all the countries of Africa, not excluding the white south; a very well-known and respected legal authority could write in 1967 :[14]

'When some years ago I met a body of South African public accountants the main question they asked was what their duty was when they found items in the accounts which undoubtedly represented bribes to public servants. It was, they said, a constant worry.'

These are some of the facts. Comment on them has always been short, for obvious reasons. One of the most recent writers on the subject, who may be too severe, says :[15]

'Everybody who has lived in any of the African states knows that venality is a common practice there . . . the conspiracy of silence on the part of the great majority of European intellectuals, due to inverted racialism, prevents the dissemination of knowledge about the phenomenon.'

He goes on to cite instances of corruption among police and petty clerks, and the origin of the phrase *ten-per-center* among Nigerian businessmen; the foreign companies, he says, do not hesitate to use their financial power to gain advantage and says they have 'entire teams whose job it is to operate vast networks of corruption . . . the official names for these activities is public relations'. As a former practitioner of public relations in Nigeria, this writer is in a position to refute this last claim; yet the point is valid in its general application, that those who offer bribes are as culpable as those who receive them.

Two earlier writers[16] offer a more balanced appreciation of the problem. They analyse two approaches: one, that the problem exists but does not matter (an opinion held, they claim, by Christian ministers, among others); and the second (put forward by the anthropologists) that it exists but is not corrupt because it is really something else,

'essential parts of the culture patterns of people who differ from ourselves, and the offering of a gift in return for a service has the honourable sanction of custom and is part of the cement that binds society together.'

Little that happens in Africa today could possibly be worse, they say, than what went on in eighteenth and nineteenth-century Britain; an interesting antithesis of one of Andreski's assertions, that there is more corruption now in the USA than in Britain, and more in Britain today (or in 1968, when his book appeared) than ten years before that.

Wraith and Simpkins score in their assessment of how best to overcome it. Salvation, they say, will not be found in statutory legislation; it may possibly come through the sanctions of religion, law, and the family; it will be aided by law enforcement, and by the generalized application of standards of efficiency in, for instance, building and construction, and public accountancy. The development of the professions and business associations will help, as will the gradual alteration in the present concentration of power, wealth and status in a few hands instead of in many, as in western societies. Above all, they say, the growth of a strong, well-rooted, wide-branching democracy deserving and retaining the respect of its members will go far to remove the phenomenon.

6 The Military

To include a chapter on the military as a force in politics would be unthinkable in a work dealing with the major western democracies; to omit the subject from a book on African countries would be to gloss over one of the major factors determining African politics since independence. Or so it might be thought. But is this quite true; and are the African countries now quite so far from the mainstream of the western traditions in which they were steeped before independence, as this statement (if true) would imply?

The intervention of the military into politics is, if unusual, by no means unknown in western states. The near-treason of elements of the British army over events in Ireland in 1912–14, the circumstances of General MacArthur's recall from Korea, the outright mutiny of part of the French army in Algeria in 1962 – all these are examples of military reactions to political situations whose solution appeared at the time to be impossible by constitutional-political means. There is, therefore, respectable precedent for military incursions into politics in African countries, particularly in view of the extreme shallowness of political roots there. If one is to cavil at the coups one can only do so on the grounds that they appear to be addictive, not because they have occurred at all; one may regret them, or alternatively welcome them as affording the only means of relief from an outmoded and unpopular system of government impossible to change by means of the ballot-box, but they must be seen in the general political context rather than as phenomena in their own right.[1] Military governments come to power, not because of the original sin or the superior firepower of the military, but because the civilian political order has proved unsatisfactory, particularly in its capacity to undergo peaceful change.

The politicization of the military

It may be that the idea of military incursions into politics never dawned on the constitution-makers and the politicians, for while the constitutions contain safeguards concerning the control of, and appointments to, the public service, judiciary and sometimes the police, little is said about the military beyond providing for the commanders-in-chief to be appointed by heads of state on the advice of premiers. On the other hand, as early as 1958 there was disquiet among northern Nigerians at the preponderance of Ibo from the eastern region in the officer corps, so that in Nigeria, at least, the pressures to achieve tribal balance in the federal army were apparent well before independence. If the constitution-makers gambled consciously that the apolitical traditions of the British army coupled with hasty changes in the territorial balance of the officers would suffice to soothe growing tribal consciousness, then the gamble did not pay off. It is ironic that it was the very steps taken to redress tribal imbalances that served to reinforce the latent suspicions that the military service, far from being a professional one whose members were recruited and held commissions by virtue of their fitness to do so, was staffed according to political/tribal, not military, dictates. And these tribal strains, so apparent in Nigeria, have been repeated in Sierra Leone, Kenya, Uganda and Zambia.

Even in retrospect, however, it is difficult to see what else could have been done to deal with them. Political pressures on the newly independent governments sought to Africanize the officer corps, i.e. to phase out white (mainly British) commanders-in-chief and officers (see *table 3*, p. 112, *Army Africanization*) and to replace them with local nationals, and to achieve a tribal balance in officer and non-commissioned ranks that adequately reflected the national make-up. Many of the governments concerned were content to postpone the full Africanization of officer strength, either because they feared the loss of efficiency, or because they believed that an army led by British officers would remain subservient to government control, or, perhaps, because they feared the international political implications of an accelerated dismissal of representatives of a major western power. Nyerere of Tanganyika, who thought as late as 1961 that Africanization could not be completed until 1971, attempted until the army mutiny of January 1964 to preserve a non-racial approach as well as efficiency by refusing to accelerate the departure of his British officers. Although the mutiny in Tangan-

Table 3

Army Africanization

| | Date of independence | Approx. size of army at independence | Commissioned officers | | |
			European or Asian	African	% African
Ghana	1957	7,000	184	27	12.8
Nigeria	1960	8,000	320	57	15.1
Sierra Leone	1961	1,000	50	9	15.2
Tanganyika	1961	2,000	58	6	9.4
Uganda	1962	1,000	50	14	21.9
Kenya	1963	2,500	85	80	48.5
Malawi	1964	750	40	9	8.4
Zambia	1964	2,200	134	1	0.7

Source: J. M. Lee, *African Armies and Civil Order*, Chatto & Windus, London, 1969.

yika is thought to have been motivated as much by army displeasure with pay and promotion prospects as by other considerations, the presence of the British officers exacerbated grievances and from that time onwards they were rapidly phased out of the army. In Uganda the pressures to get rid of British officers began immediately after independence, and while they may have been increased by the poor personal relationships between some of the individuals concerned, the real causes appear to have been centred on the need to expand the Uganda army to deal with problems on the frontiers with the Congo, the Sudan, and north-western Kenya; Uganda nationalism and tribal rivalry within the army, both of which inflamed emotions and harmed the cause of national unity; the rapid training and subsequent difficulties in fitting into the army of young Ugandan officers; and, probably the immediate cause of the mutiny, very real grievances over pay and promotion which could only be redressed if British officers, the block to promotion, were ousted.

In contrast to these cases where the presence of British officers undoubtedly inflamed feeling and thus *ipso facto* involved elements of the army in political dissent, Nigeria in 1964 provided an example where the presence of a British commander-in-chief, Major-General Welby-Everard, kept the army from assuming a role in the reconstruction of the federal government after the elections (even though the explosion averted by Welby-Everard was merely postponed, not aborted). The problems of a British commander-in-chief of an African army after independence have been vividly recounted by the last British head of the Ghanaian army, who[2] relates his conflict of professional and patriotic loyalties when instructed to despatch young Ghanaians for training in eastern bloc countries. An army whose basic drill, equipment and supplies originated from diverse sources would be hopelessly inefficient, and the response of a British national instructed to cooperate with a scheme to replace western influence by that of Soviet Russia could never be wholehearted. In these circumstances it would be impossible for British officers to preserve professional reticence; and their very presence could trigger off the troubles they were supposed to prevent. The insurance policy had become a liability.

It would be wrong, however, to assume that the removal of the British eliminated all sources of strain among the officers in the newly independent armies. Replacement and expansion could be achieved only by accelerated training. This in turn meant that numbers of young men of lower intellectual attainment and levels of professional competence were commissioned, frequently to serve under older men whose rise sometimes from the ranks, had been considerably slower and whose grounding in military competence, in consequence, was better founded; and so a battle of the generations would be joined. This was especially true in Uganda, where the arrival from Sandhurst of a number of young Ugandan officers greatly exacerbated relations with British officers before and during the mutiny of January 1964. In Nigeria the preponderance of Ibo officers at independence – 75 per cent of all African officers – meant that in succeeding years special effort was expended on seeking out non-Ibo, mostly northern, candidates to redress the balance of regional representation. In 1962 a quota system which gave 50 per cent of commissions to northerners was instituted, and because educational levels in the east were generally higher than in the north, selection had to be consciously biased in favour of northern candidates. In Kenya and Tanganyika at the time of independence numbers of senior other ranks were commissioned, but their lack of formal schooling caused them and their wives to feel aloof from other members of an élite service, with resulting tension among the whole. In Ghana the leader of the unsuccessful 'lieutenants' coup' of April 1967, Lieutenant Arthur, had but recently failed a promotion examination which barred him from the further advancement that he felt was his due. We are informed that he held his superiors in contempt, and that he had hoped to be the first lieutenant ever to carry out a coup.

In Sierra Leone a split began among army officers very shortly after the British force commander was replaced in January 1965, and the rationale of subsequent confused events is made even harder to establish because tribal cohesion was not absolute. The officer appointed to head the army, Brigadier David Lansana, became closely associated with the prime minister, Sir Albert Margai – both men being Mende from the south, and united in opposing the northern Temne – and following the elections of March 1967 in which the former opposition party headed by Siaka Stevens was returned to power, Lansana placed the governor-general and the new premier under house arrest, seemingly in the wish to retain Margai as prime minister. Lansana was in turn dislodged three days later by other Mende officers, who apparently feared the combination of Margai and Lansana, and Lieutenant-Colonel Juxon-Smith, a Temne, was installed as chairman of the National Liberation Council which ruled the country. Juxon-Smith was himself overthrown in April 1968 in a coup organized by army other ranks, in protest (so they said) against the failure of their officers to surrender power to civilians.

While one has no means of knowing what the effect of the continued presence of British personnel would have been, whether it would have papered over the cracks in army cohesion and discipline or whether it would merely have attracted other expressions of dissidence, it seems safe to conclude that the most it would have done would be to postpone them. At some stage of national development some form of trial of strength was inevitable among members of the armed services, most of whom were insecure in the positions they held and of necessity closely associated with the politicians in a small arena. It is important to realize for the purposes of foretelling the future that while the coups may be over, the emotions and conditions that produced them are not. The play for power continues, albeit with a changing cast and, perhaps, upon another stage.

New sources

After the British, who?

As we saw earlier in this chapter, political pressures from within as well as outside African countries resulted soon after independence in the speedy and almost complete replacement of British personnel in the armed forces, except for some still serving in non-executive, strictly advisory capacities. Other pressures have operated to replace the training methods and supplies formerly obtained from British sources by those of non-British origins.

Some of these pressures stem from expediency. Among the problems experienced in training African soldiers in Britain have been the difficulty in finding men with the requisite purely educational qualifications to enter, for instance, Sandhurst; and the questionable relevance of a Sandhurst, or for that matter a West Point, military training to conditions encountered in Africa. It is at any rate arguable that what is wanted is not a highly professionalized army on British or American standards, but rather a militia that can be mobilized to meet local needs – such as riot containment or famine relief – by the use of local resources in manpower, organization and supply. Although preliminary courses can be devised to precede Sandhurst, it has become clear that the prolonged isolation of the military in foreign training institutions causes major difficulties when they return to their own countries. There is evidence for this from one of the architects of the 1966 military coup in Ghana,[3] Major A. A. Afrifa, who (rightly or wrongly, as it may be) became sorely disillusioned with his country's ruler when he was on his second visit to England after having served with his national contingent in the United Nations force in the Congo. Allied with the élitist isolation of the military in barracks so that communication and the creation of a sense of identity with the people in general are effectively barred, radical criticism of the conduct of the country's government can only be vented by unilateral military action to usurp civilian government. This is what happened in Ghana in 1966 and 1972, in Sierra Leone in 1967 and again in 1968, and in Uganda in 1971.

The remedy, even though it may be only a partial one, is to train on the spot. On the whole, the old pre-independence notions of joint organizations to accommodate men from different countries within broad geographical areas, such as the Royal West African Frontier Force (created by Lugard in 1897) and the King's African Rifles (covering Kenya, Uganda and Tanganyika) did not survive independence; even the East African Land Forces Organization, formed in 1957 to maintain a federal structure for the armies of the three East African territories, withered away. One of the reasons for this has undoubtedly been interterritorial jealousy; who is to have the *kudos* of the military training establishment in their country? This factor loomed large over negotiations in Nigeria concerning the siting of an air force base and training centre;[4] if this can operate to such a pitch of intensity within a country, it will clearly exert even more influence on the relationships as between different countries – and as nationalisms grow, so it will increase. Another reason concerns the very different rates of political progress and the different political philosophies at work in the various countries. For instance, both Zambia and Malawi at one stage sent cadets for officer training to East Africa, but found themselves unable to fall in with the programmes for speedy Africanization current there and therefore preferred to resume training in England itself, as the lesser of various evils. Again, governments fear the infection of their own armies by neighbours' military coups, or other troubles; the mutinies of the East African armies in January 1964 were very swiftly followed by action in Zambia and Malawi to improve pay and conditions of service. And governments lose their freedom to choose their own sources of help if they share long-term training arrangements with their neighbours which require standardization of selection, procedures and equipment.

As well as these reasons of expediency, political reasons also lie behind decisions to train forces locally and decisions as to from whom to accept training missions, arms, and equipment. Politics is also at the root of most of the decisions of foreign countries to become involved with the forces of African countries.

It is very clear that the great-power rivalry that gave rise in the nineteenth century to the scramble for Africa has been revived, undeterred by manifest pitfalls, in this latter half of the twentieth century. Those who do not actually seek power and influence in Africa nevertheless continue to dabble, in hopes of denying the spoils to their rivals. The Israelis are nearly ubiquitous in their search for friends in the face of a hostile Arab world, although early 1972 saw a grave setback to their hopes in Uganda; the Chinese dispute the leadership of the communist bloc with the Russians, seeking converts to their cause in the same way as did the rival churches in Europe during the Reformation; the Czechoslovaks temper the economic difficulties of membership of the Comecon organization by selling arms; Canadian training teams pursue their own interpretation of Commonwealth leadership; in Zambia the Italians have added to their commercial successes by sending a mission to train the Zambian air force; the Bulgarians, Albanians, Egyptians and Algerians offer their own brands of training to the freedom fighters; – and if France and the United States are conspicuously absent from this list, it is only because they have their hands full, and their essential interests preserved, respectively, with *la francophonie* and Ethiopia. It is, similarly, politics as much as economics or morals that lies behind the actions of those willing to sell arms to southern Africa. It is, however, far too simplistic to see the modern scramble for Africa in terms of an extension of the cold war, mainly because the stakes are such small change and, in total, so low value (to foreigners, if not to local inhabitants). It is nearer to the truth to recognize the immense fragmentation of motive and opportunity, and to conclude that each country indulging in this scramble does so on the basis of its own self-interest, however local, limited and self-contradictory that may be, according to the needs of the moment – exactly in the way in which the scramble a hundred years ago took place.

The recipient African countries' motives in choosing the sources of their foreign military assistance are as idiosyncratic as those of the donor countries. Independence brought an immediate demand, in almost all cases, for the withdrawal of forces and the evacuation of British bases, but it seems that this was more an expression of the need to demonstrate true independence of the former colonial power than a serious evaluation of the usefulness or effectiveness of British, as opposed to other foreign, arms and training.

Independence brought, also, pressures against the formation of defence agreements with Britain, mainly because of the new nations' wishes to represent their policies as non-aligned in world affairs. A major exception to this general rule, and one which was later to prove its validity, was Nigeria, which at independence in 1960 expressed the wish to sign a defence agreement with Britain.[5] One of the original motives may have been the Nigerians' wish to steal some of the thunder in African affairs from the Ghanaians, with whom an intense nationalistic rivalry had sprung up concerning pan-African leadership, but the agreement fell victim to the actions of the Nigerian opposition party led by Chief Awolowo in the federal parliament which ran the issue as a convenient stick with which to beat the government. It generated immense heat in domestic politics and proved in the end too much for the government, which had to bow to the weight of national disapproval and abandon the defence agreement with Britain. It is interesting to note that Awolowo was in fact in favour of such an agreement both before, and for a short while after, independence, and that his opposition to it began only when he fathomed its possibilities as an embarrassment to the government; on such factors do many policy decisions depend in Africa, as, of course, in Britain, the USA and most other parts of the free world.

It is, however, rare for opposition parties to seize such an opportunity in Africa, and most of the decisions as to sources of military aid are taken by governments which lack an effective opposition. One of the major determinants of their actions is the extent to which they are prepared to be non-aligned. All the African countries claim to be non-aligned with the big power blocs, and thus claim an aloofness in attitude that prevents them being labelled neo-colonialist. Nevertheless, some countries are more non-aligned than others; it is generally justified to indicate Nigeria as an example of a country that tends towards a more western point of view, and Tanzania as an example that justifies its leftist course by arguing that a genuine non-aligned stance requires withdrawal from many of the western ties with which she attained independence. Accordingly, Nigeria's military links tend towards the British model (although the course of events during the Biafra war turned government attention to the Soviet bloc in looking for armaments), while Tanzania has accepted aid from the Chinese and East Germans as well as from the Canadians (and, also, temporarily, while reorganizing from the mutiny of 1964, from a Nigerian contingent). Ghana under Nkrumah turned to Russia and China; latterly she has swung more to the western orbit.

Another element in the decision-making process is the wish to divide-and-rule. African governments function uneasily, fearing as they now do the incursions of the military into politics, and one defence for them is to fragment the army by splitting its training, and hence possibly its allegiance, between two or more benefactors. Thus Obote called upon Israeli and Chinese instruction for the Uganda army, and installed the Russians in the air force base at Gulu – as it happened, to no avail. A subsidiary and potentially very great danger of this policy, of course, is its tendency to draw two or more powers into any country where a coup has taken place, particularly where the legality of action taken or the legitimacy of rival regimes is in question.

A further factor is the difficulty in arranging payment for arms or instruction. Not only are balance of payments problems chronically bad; without exception, the countries where African governments have come to power are desperately poor, and what wealth they have is in the form of mineral or primary agricultural produce which is at the mercy of international demand and pricing mechanisms. There has been a tendency for barter deals to be concluded with the eastern bloc, under which arms can be paid for by cocoa, say, from Ghana, or cloves from Zanzibar. On the whole this has not resulted in a net expansion of trade, because of the limits of world absorption of a commodity like cloves; but it has served to distort the apparent direction of trade from Africa, for the cocoa which formerly was marketed through London (some of which went on to the Soviet Union and points eastward) now goes direct to its destination behind the Iron Curtain. Barter deals such as these are extremely welcome to the Iron Curtain countries, which also suffer from balance of payments problems (being generally overloaded with roubles to the detriment of dollar and sterling balances) and are able to build up cherished foreign reserves by this kind of deal. They also generally lack manufacturing capability for consumer goods, so that the export of arms or industrial machinery may be their only means for paying for imports of produce from Africa. There are thus extremely sound commercial reasons on both sides for trade between Africa and the eastern bloc, and the existence of such trade and its increase should not be taken necessarily as evidence of an ideological commitment.

The element of patronage in decision-making should not be overlooked. Although many of its niceties in Africa remain obscure to us, being less well charted, say, than are those of Texas, the obligations of African politicians to their kinsfolk, constituents or tribes are both far-reaching and firmly held. The disposal of supplies or the bestowal of the means of getting a training are facilities of great value to many individuals, and they play a sizable part in determining the direction of military policy.

Finally, there is the factor of ideology, of which Tanzania is probably the best exemplar with her system of compulsory national service (unique in ex-British Africa) and her close links with China. Of all the African countries Tanzania's brand of African socialism is the most original and the firmest rooted in the ordinary people, and she has gone further than any of the others in evolving a specifically African answer to many of the social and economic problems with which she is faced, particularly that of mobilizing the people. She has shown herself ready to draw on the experience of many different countries, of which China is only one among many, and whose 'everyone a soldier' movement[6], launched in August 1958 at the beginning of the Great Leap Forward, offers one means of transforming a predominantly agricultural population into a permanent mass movement for defence. In China the movement met with many setbacks and suffered considerable change in the course of five or six years, but its all-inclusive nature, coupled with its close political commitment to the whole of society, may well have posed an alluring vision to Nyerere, faced as he was with the need to transform and motivate his poverty-stricken country. This is not to claim that Nyerere is necessarily a Maoist; merely that he may have seized his chance to capitalize on a useful idea.

The role of the military

Only four of the ex-British countries – Gambia, Botswana,

Lesotho and Swaziland – have refrained from raising an army. Embedded as Gambia is in Senegal, Botswana, Lesotho and Swaziland in South Africa, they rely on their police forces for internal security and upon the goodwill of their neighbours for survival.

Table 4

Strengths of Armed Forces (Excluding Gendarmerie and Police) at April 1970

	Regular armed forces	Size of force at independence	Date of independence
Ghana	15,000	7,000	1957
Nigeria	163,500	8,000	1960
Sierra Leone	1,600	1,000	1961
Tanzania	7,900	2,000	1961
Uganda	6,700	1,000	1962
Kenya	5,400	2,500	1963
Malawi	1,150	750	1964
Zambia	4,400	2,200	1964
Rhodesia	4,600		
South Africa	43,800		

Source: Richard Booth, *The Armed Forces of African States, 1970,* Adelphi Paper 67, May 1970, Institute for Strategic Studies, London, 1970.

Elsewhere, armies have not only been maintained but increased in size. *Table 4* shows their strengths (for convenience of comparison, some of the figures in *table 3* are repeated). Some of these figures need explanation. Since 1966 Ghana's forces have been reduced, with the disbandment of Nkrumah's POGR (President's Own Guard Regiment). The immense increase in the Nigerian military force is accounted for by the Biafran War. Uganda has had to face threats to external security from the Sudan, Somalia and the Congo, as well as internal difficulties; Kenya has had to fight a considerable war against the Somali *shifta* in the north. Nevertheless it is clear that there has been a general increase in the size of military forces which is not reasonably accounted for by any threats posed, and that there is no general tendency to abolish or reduce forces.

What, then, are these quite considerable forces used for? It has been said, rather unkindly perhaps, that apart from staging coups African armies have nothing to do, and it is of course quite true that the army that is busy fighting an external army has no time for internal domestic meddling. There is nevertheless more to matters than this. A chronological list of the main military actions to date, which have hit the headlines of the world but which have confused rather than cleared public awareness of the issues involved, may suggest guidelines for an analysis of military function to help the all-important assessment of whether the African 'military disease', as it has been called, is epidemic or merely episodic in African politics.

Table 5

A Decade of Military Action

Jul. 1960 start of the CONGO crisis
Dec. 1963 beginning of action against Somali shift, KENYA
Jan. 1964 mutinies in KENYA, UGANDA and TANGANYIKA
Jan. 1966 federal government replaced by Gen. Ironsi, NIGERIA
Feb. 1966 Gen. Ankrah replaced Nkrumah, GHANA
May 1966 kabaka overthrown, UGANDA
Jul. 1966 Ironsi replaced by Gen. Gowon, NIGERIA
Mar. 1967 Sir A. Margai replaced by Brig. Juxon-Smith, SIERRA
            LEONE
Apr. 1967 Lt Arthur's abortive plot, GHANA
Oct. 1967 attempted secession of Biafra, NIGERIA
Apr. 1968 rankers' coup replaced Juxon-Smith by Stevens, SIERRA
            LEONE
Jan. 1971 Obote overthrown by Gen. Amin, UGANDA
Jan. 1972 Dr Busia overthrown by army, GHANA

The list indicates that the African military action about which so much has been heard can be divided into roughly six categories. *(1) Mutiny*, as in the East African countries in 1964: *(2) Internal Peacekeeping*, riot control etc. in support of normal police activity, extending perhaps into major actions such as took place in Nigeria to prevent the secession of Biafra: *(3) the Military Coup* proper: *(4) External Peacekeeping*, as with

United Nations forces in the Congo: *(5) War*, openly conducted though possibly formally undeclared: and *(6) Freedom Fighting*, as on the borders with white-dominated southern Africa. These categories are not wholly satisfactory. Overlapping can occur – as for instance when grousing soldiers attempt to elevate the incoherence of their actions and win public support for a coup by claiming to support true democracy – and the boundaries between them are not always clear. Nevertheless they provide a reasonable enough framework.

MUTINY: Mutiny is, or it should be, the easiest factor to control. All the East African countries, as well as Zambia which also at the time felt itself vulnerable, took immediate severe action against mutineers in 1964 while at the same time increasing pay, improving conditions of service and ridding themselves of some of the barriers to promotion imposed by the presence of British members of the army. Yet there have been reports that steps taken were not as drastic as might be advocated by thoroughgoing reformists; and it does appear to be the case in Nigeria that failure to punish adequately the plotters of the January 1966 mutiny contributed greatly to the sense of strain that culminated with the July 1966 murder of General Ironsi and other officers. The steps taken appear to have been successful in East Africa in preventing further action founded purely on discontent with service conditions; but it is worth noting the danger that such mutinous action may be put to use by discontented politicians in their turn (as happened in Tanganyika and also in Uganda), who do not necessarily provoke mutiny but use it to better their own political fortunes.

INTERNAL PEACEKEEPING: There is no doubt that using the army for internal peacekeeping runs severe risks of arousing political discontent in African countries, and this discontent makes itself known not just outside the army, say among those whom the army is being used to control or the population at large, but also within the army as well. This of course is because the army very swiftly becomes identified with one or other, if not both or several, of the civilian factions that have caused the employment of the army on duties outside its normal purview. This is not a problem that is confined to African countries – one has seen this factor at work in British Ulster in 1970, 1971 and 1972 – but it does seem to give rise to a greater degree of political polarization in African armies than takes place elsewhere; and this polarization in turn increases the difficulty of the army in living with itself and with those members of the general public with whom its individual members may not be in political agreement. The deterioration of the situation in Nigeria throughout 1966 and 1967, and the ill-fated attempt to retrieve matters by organizing officers and men to serve in areas of their own origins, are evidence enough of this.[7] On the other hand, the more successful action undertaken to subdue the Tiv in eastern Nigeria in 1962 may indicate that, while internal army action of itself may not create doubts as to the army's political impartiality, the use of the army in support of political/tribal decisions will afterwards give rise to suspicion as to the motives lying behind the use of the army.

MILITARY COUP : The military coup proper, the replacement of an established government by forcible means employed by an army, has taken place nine times in Africa in the last twelve years or so – twice in Nigeria, three times (once unsuccessfully) in Ghana, twice in Uganda and twice in Sierra Leone. It does not always place an army government in power – the coup of the rankers in Sierra Leone which restored civilian government in April 1968 was itself a protest against the undue prolongation of military rule; and governments such as those of General Amin in Uganda have been composed mainly of civil servants rather than military personnel (although it has been reported that these same civil servants have subsequently been obliged to undergo some degree of military training and subjection to military discipline since the coup took place). In all cases so far, the military have professed an eagerness to return to civilian rule; and in the case of Ghana this actually happened, with the election to the premiership of Dr Busia in 1969, although his replacement in 1972 would argue the case against the disappearance of the army from the political scene in Ghana.

Not all coups overthrow the central element of government; that in Uganda in 1966 which effectively overthrew the kabaka of Buganda, the head of state, was staged by the prime minister, Milton Obote, who had seized his opportunity to remove a very considerable threat to his own power. And not all coups are successful; that of Lieutenant Arthur in Ghana in April 1967 failed, although he came very near to destroying the government, and perhaps the most remarkable thing about it (as is made clear in one of the latest works on the subject),[8] is that nobody wanted to know about it while it was going on. A tiny force, a handful of men, seized Flagstaff House and the Castle, shot General Kotoka and narrowly missed killing or capturing the head of state General Ankrah. No counter-attack from government forces was mounted, no alert sounded and the army totally failed to react; indeed, members in command are said to have shut themselves away, out of trouble and away from the necessity of taking sides. The trouble is that coups debase the currency that is government so that legitimacy of a regime depends not upon the vote of the people but upon the success or otherwise of the coup mounted to establish it. Lieutenant Arthur was to argue, at the military tribunal that sentenced him to death, that the only difference between his attempted coup and the February 1966 one was that his failed. One can only conclude that coups breed later coups; and the fact that the nine (at the moment of writing) that have taken place in Africa have been distributed among only four countries bears this contention out.

EXTERNAL PEACEKEEPING : It is the external peacekeeping function, however, that has done most of all to expose the new African countries to the push and pull of conflicting policies. The tragic history of the first years of the Congo has been exhaustively chronicled.[9] The Congo episode was vitally important to the rest of Africa. For the first time the armies of the newly independent countries took the stage, and those of both Ghana and Nigeria were to win richly-deserved praise for their conduct. Yet the Congo operation sowed many seeds of dissension and disaster. It produced the first great open rift between the African nations, between the moderates of the Brazzaville (later Monrovia) group and the radicals of the Casablanca group who favoured the cause of Lumumba. It fostered enmity and competition between Ghana and Nigeria, both of which aspired to leadership of the continent. It cast ridicule upon the politicians who had exposed the troops to arduous and unpleasant service, in particular upon the Ghanaians Andrew Djin (ambassador to the Congo) and

Nathaniel Welbeck whose conduct appeared by turns absurd and cowardly to the military who witnessed it. Disenchantment with the United Nations, for its policies and its personnel and for its secretary-general, Hammarskjöld, as well as contempt for those who attempted to manipulate it became rife; and disillusionment set in over the conduct of all the great powers, the US, Russia, Great Britain and Belgium. Reading the record, no one escapes unscathed and the memories of follies, cowardice and treachery were to accompany the soldiers and the camp-followers back to their homes when the fighting ceased, to fester and later to flare into discontent. This was the time when the Africans first found they had the tiger by the tail, when fears of 'another Congo' prompted the nightmares not just of the western and eastern blocs but of the Africans as well; fears of the total breakdown of civil order that had resulted in the second time round of western intervention in Africa. For a long time to come the Congo will serve as an argument in favour of the self-containment of strife, lest intrusion by one force open the door to a host of interfering agencies from outside, as well as inside, Africa, and lead eventually to the recolonization of the continent.

WAR: Fighting on the African continent there may have been, but so far Africa has had little experience of the conduct of war in the sense of action against a declared and identified national enemy. To date there has been little tendency to question the validity of colonial boundaries, curious perhaps when it is remembered how irrelevant to conditions on the spot most of them are; not so curious, however, when one realizes that to question one places all in jeopardy. Live and let live is the rule, lest in robbing your neighbour your other neighbour seek to rob you, with as much or as little right on his side. There have of course been some boundary altercations, that between Tanzania and Malawi being perhaps an example where the existence of antipathetic political philosophies seek an outlet for expression; and at various times the free flow of local peoples across national frontiers has been impeded so as to prevent smuggling, or preserve employment, or as an instrument of blockade (as with the Cameroons border in the Biafran fighting).

One of the few available examples of outright war has been seen on the border between Somalia and Kenya, where a largely unsung mini-war flourished from Kenya independence in November 1963 until the latter part of 1967. The cause of this lay in the path of Kenya's north-east boundary with Somalia, which cut haphazardly through the middle of groups of mainly Muslim nomadic tribesmen who felt themselves to have little in common with the predominantly Bantu peoples of Kenya, and who wished to secede together with the territory over which they and their herds wandered, to join Somalia. The issue was one of even more than ordinary import to Kenya, not only because the area claimed by the Somalis amounted to a large portion of Kenya (though economically it was nearly worthless, being mostly desert), but also because Somali secession would furnish a precedent to other restive tribes in Kenya, such as the Masai, who also wished to opt out of a country dominated by the rival Kikuyu and Luo tribes. It was also a matter of concern to Ethiopia, whose borders march with Kenya and Somalia and whose territorial integrity was also threatened by the Somali nationalists' claims to the Ogaden area.

When the British withdrew from Kenya in November 1963 the attacks from the Somali shifta (bandits) intensified, to ebb and flow for the next four years despite all efforts at settlement. The OAU conference at Addis Ababa in November 1964 failed, despite general exhortations, to bring peace; nor were the efforts of President Nyerere of Tanzania to mediate in December 1965 any more successful. Through 1966 and the early part of 1967 matters worsened, bringing disrepute upon the OAU for its inability to achieve settlement and threatening to involve the great powers in the dispute, for Russia, Egypt and China were reported to be supplying Somalia's military needs, the US was heavily committed to the defence of Ethiopia (which had ratified a mutual defence pact with Kenya in 1964), and Great Britain was committed to the cause of Kenya. Matters did not improve until after a new Somali government took office in June 1967; then in September 1967 a summit meeting of the OAU at Kinshasa achieved out-of-session talks between Somalia and Kenya, and the way was thus paved for the successful mediation of President Kaunda of Zambia in October. In January 1968 Kenya and Somalia resumed diplomatic relations. Little credit has been given to the OAU and to Kaunda himself for this successful mediation, but there is no doubt that this four-year war might, if unchecked, have proved as costly and disastrous to Africa and the rest of the world as the Congo episode.

FREEDOM FIGHTING : We come finally to freedom fighting, the reaction of the African countries to the outrage (to them) of white domination in southern Africa, to *apartheid* and protestations of separate-but-equal. For obvious reasons little is known of these activities, and of the little that is known, much is of suspect veracity because reliable eye-witness accounts are few and rumour, in consequence, is rife. The organizational centre is at Dar-es-Salaam in Tanzania, where the secretariat of the OAU committee for freedom is located. It is known that camps for training fighters are maintained in southern Tanzania and in Zambia, from where fighters are infiltrated into Portuguese Mozambique and Rhodesia; freedom fighters are also training in Algeria, Morocco and Albania. Little success in freedom fighting activity has so far been established, due mainly, one understands, to the erratic nature of the financial support it receives and also to the fact that the long arm of retaliation is feared by those African countries nearest to the scene of operations. The chief protagonists of an active policy have tended to be those countries at a safe remove from punitive action, such as Uganda; those nearest to it, like Malawi, have tended to explore the advantages of coexistence. It is important to realize that, so far from freedom fighting against southern Africa proving a uniting force in African international relations, it is in fact a divisive one; not only are the independent African countries bitterly divided as to the stance to be adopted towards the freedom fighters, but there is a tendency for the shreds and remnants of opposition parties to attach themselves to the insurgent groups, in the hopes of soliciting support for their cause and in the certainty that arms, ammunition and disaffected men are available. Thus one finds Presidents Kaunda of Zambia and Banda of Malawi concerned to protect their own political position from certain segments of the freedom fighters. It seems almost certain that freedom fighting activity will intensify in the future; *apartheid* grows no less obnoxious, while training effectiveness will improve and African governments themselves remain worthwhile targets for an armed opposition. It also seems probable that it will inspire the whites' backlash of counter-action, which will probably be vented upon those countries nearest at hand to the borders of South Africa, Rhodesia and Mozambique. If one seeks a future source of extreme political tension, as between black and white Africa and also between differing elements of black Africa, the issue of freedom fighting would seem to be the prime candidate.

7 Politics and the Man on the Shamba, or Land, Labour and Learning

The man and his family who eke out their livelihood from their shamba[1] constitute the norm of African populations, and although the twin pressures of landlessness and the lure of the towns are drawing people away from their traditional occupations we will use this term to denote what elsewhere might be called the man in the street. Almost all of these are vitally affected, in ways and to a degree not experienced in the western world, by land policies, by labour – its existence, organization and rewards – and by the spread, or lack of it, of education at all levels. These are the most important factors to affect the mass of the population; and the extent to which their needs are met sympathetically and efficiently by governments is a guide to the general happiness and prosperity of ordinary people, and hence to political stability.

The land question

This is, perhaps, the most critical of all those that haunt African governments. This is not because overpopulation in relation to the land area available is yet so great that famine and starvation stalk the land as they do, say, in India or Indonesia (see *table 6* opposite); but rather because immense social and economic pressures connected with the use and ownership of land do exist, and it seems probable that they will continue to be felt for many years – if not for ever.

African countries have been exposed to political strains on two main counts. In the mainly 'black' countries of West Africa, and to a certain extent in those of East and Central Africa that lacked large white settler communities, the problem has been

Table 6

Population, Population Growth and Density of Population

Country	Population (millions)	Growth rate % p.a.	Persons per sq. mile
Botswana	0.6	3.0	3
Gambia	0.4	2.0	82
Ghana	8.6	2.8	93
Kenya	10.8	2.9	48
Lesotho	0.9	2.9	80
Malawi	4.4	2.5	96
Nigeria	52.8	2.7	148
Rhodesia	5.1	3.2	34
Sierra Leone	2.5	1.5	91
South Africa	19.6	2.4	42
South-West Africa	0.6	1.8	2
Swaziland	0.4	2.5	60
Tanzania	12.9	2.5	36
Uganda	8.3	2.5	91
Zambia	4.2	3.1	14

Source: AID *Economic Data Book*, Africa, USAID,
Washington DC, Feb. 1970.

comparatively simple to define; in the main it is one of development, of sustaining and organizing the movement of peoples from an agricultural way of life to an increasingly urban, commercial and industrial existence. Two or three centuries of western experience have had to be compressed into ten years, rather as though the Enclosure Acts, the industrial revolution, the frontier moving westward and the cattle versus crops controversies of the USA had all happened, at once, in the same place. But in the white settler countries such as Kenya, Rhodesia and the Republic of South Africa, another problem has been experienced; that of the white settler community, those who came with their families to farm and ranch, to rear their children and in many cases to grow up as white Africans. They brought with them high standards, intricate skills and organizational techniques that the economic imperatives of the twentieth century demand; but their presence, dominating great areas of country and imposing sophisticated mechanisms upon infant states, has constituted an affront to landless Africans intent upon scratching a bare livelihood from the land. In a sense, the problems of 'black' and 'white' Africa merge into the one urgent necessity to maximize agricultural surpluses so as to provide the wherewithal for industrial expansion. In the meanwhile, however, African governments are faced with the need to accommodate the poor, feed the hungry and educate the juveniles; an efficient, profitable agricultural sector of the economy is incompatible with full bellies for the mass of the people. Herein lies the political threat of the land question.

The statistics of the proportions of the population dependent on land and agriculture for their livelihood are misleading, because they take no account of the ability of the land to support people – which is very varied throughout Africa, the continent of droughts and floods, deserts and fertile pockets, jungles and savannah. But it is safe to assume that all those who live outside the larger towns are dependent for their livelihoods upon farming or cattle herding. It is also the case that many, possibly the majority, of those who are town dwellers are also socially and economically dependent upon the land, either because their tribal roots are there and in times of difficulty they retrace their footsteps to kith, kin and a square meal; or because their wives and children remain behind within the structure of tribal life; or because the stream of relatives seeking their fortunes in the towns serve as a constant reminder of the family, the tribe and the ancestral origins on the land.

This merging of the pastoral with the urban life gives rise to many problems. For instance, 20 per cent of adult male Botswana are at any given time absent on work in South Africa, and the mines of South and Central Africa have always exercised a powerful pull over men from a great distance away, seeking money to pay for the bicycle, the transistor or the brideprice. Whether individual and national monetary gains make up for the terrible personal and social strains inherent in the break-up of families is a fertile ground for argument; and it is clear that a great many hostages to fortune are thus created.

But the migration of peoples even within national boundaries is no less a cause for concern. In Kenya, for example, in colonial days it was used as an excuse for the construction of wage rates upon racial lines, the argument being that as an African could rely on maintaining his wife and children on the shamba back home, he therefore needed less pay to maintain himself in the town. There was just enough truth in this theory to ensure its carry-over well into independence days. And both public and private housing was planned upon the same premise, namely that as the families remained at home on the shamba the living space and facilities provided in towns could be kept to the minimum needed for *de facto* bachelors. Whatever economic merits such schemes may once have had were more than cancelled out by the tremendous social demerits that flowed from them, in terms of split loyalties, deserted families, rootless urban dwellers and prostitution – rife in the towns of West Africa, as in Nairobi and the other towns of East, South and Central Africa, today.

To what extent the land problem can be expressed also as an urban problem, or as a social problem in that it was either a cause or an effect of the break-up of tribal life, or as a purely economic problem depends very much upon the standpoint taken as to relative priorities and organizational necessities. It can, indeed, also be expressed as a legal and property-owning difficulty, for tribal occupation of land areas meant that the important thing to be noted about the relationship of human beings to land was occupation, not ownership; instead of legal title to ownership of land being vested in one person, a notion of land occupation had arisen whereby what counted was that those who had always worked an area were entitled to assume that they and their descendants could always continue to do so. Neither individuals, nor chiefs purporting to act on behalf of the tribe, were entitled to alienate land. But neither, in later days, could land thus collectively held be deemed adequate security for bank loans for improvements, or for the purchase of machinery; and so the relative security of tribally-occupied land has become a twentieth-century liability, and the source of complaints that western banking systems have operated contrary to the needs of small African farmers needing credit.

African land that was alienated to Europeans, however, was always a different proposition. Generally speaking, the 'black' countries of West Africa and Uganda, where tropical climatic conditions and vigorous local communities discouraged Europeans from settling, experienced no large-scale alienation of agricultural land to foreigners; even the commercial interests who sought to establish plantations were prevented from doing so by Colonial Office policy, which was anxious to protect Africans from the consequences of untramelled commercial exploitation. Matters were different, however, in places like Kenya, where the climate was attractive to European settlement, where large areas of land appeared, at the moment of colonial expansion, to be unoccupied, and where the profitability of the Uganda Railway (built to bolster the military presence) depended on the development of some kind of lucrative traffic along the five hundred odd miles of track that separated the port of Mombasa from its hinterland.

KENYA: From 1902 provision was made for the government of Kenya to lease, sell, or issue temporary occupation certificates to individuals (necessarily, at this time, Europeans) conferring rights over land in Kenya. From the beginning the white settlers contested with the Colonial Office the terms on which they might hold land, and more particularly the possibility that members of the Asian community might occupy land in the highland areas thought most suitable for European settlement. From 1908 it became the custom not to grant land in the highlands to Asians, and in 1915 this custom was superseded by a degree of legal restriction written in to the land ordinance of that year. In 1923 the Europeans' privileged position in the highlands was reinforced *vis-à-vis* both the Asians and the Africans, seemingly as a *quid pro quo* for the announcement of the paramountcy of African interests over those of the other races in Kenya, wherever they should clash. By contrast, African rights to land were slow of establishment and, particularly in the case of the Masai tribe, subject to alterations which, whatever their legality or the high-minded intentions of those who made them, caused much resentment and insecurity among the indigenous dwellers in the country. By the time legislation had been passed in 1938–9 to confirm and reinforce Africans' and Europeans' rights to land ownership and occupancy, mutual distrust and resentment had grown and the barriers between the races had become only too clearly etched in the delineations of the White Highlands.

To what extent land policy contributed to the Mau Mau movement, that African rebellion of the 1950s which centred on the Kikuyu tribe (which was the tribe most affected by the White Highlands policy), cannot be known exactly; but it is probable that frustrations over landholding, land shortage, and restrictions as to land use by Africans, as well as suspicions of white settlers' aims played a major part. The Royal Commission on Kenya that published its report in 1955 recommended the ending of racial barriers in the colony and, in particular, called for the White Highlands to be opened for settlement by all races. No attempt was made to implement this section of the report until 1959, when some form of radical constitutional change was clearly imminent; from then until independence in 1963 it was a major concern of the outgoing colonial regime to order the land question so as to avoid, on the one hand, a white settlers' rebellion caused by too direct a repudiation of their interests, and on the other hand the complete collapse of the agricultural sector of the economy through premature African acquisition of their lands.

In this it was largely successful, and its gradualist approach seems to have been followed by the successor, African, government. All racial barriers to the holding of land were removed, and all parties understood that Africans' land hunger would have to be assuaged by settling numbers of them on land formerly occupied by Europeans; because the Africans would not be able to pay for the land thus taken over at anything like the Europeans' valuation of it, upwards of £15 million was made available by grant from the British government to buy out the settlers. Outgoing whites received special consideration from the Kenya government in that they were absolved from exchange control measures that governed the movement of capital from Kenya; incoming African farmers received assistance with grants, loans and advice to aid their movement into the former European areas.

Whilst it cannot be said that the level of agricultural production was maintained, the political results of this policy have been quite outstanding. A large enough number of Africans have been resettled to assuage the most extreme demands of the landless; a reasonable level of agricultural production has been reached in a country whose prime industry, until the advent of tourism, had always been agriculture. Above all, action has been seen to be taken; numbers of European farmers have been seen to leave, without question many African families have moved in to replace them, most certainly the African government has redeemed some of its pledges to its people who voted it into power. The general trend of land legislation and regulation has been to favour African interests above those of the Europeans and Asians who remain, particularly in regard to productive land up-country that can support numbers of people, and land at the coast whose developmental value is greatest. It is not to be expected, of course, that events in Kenya will commend themselves to the embattled white settlers of Rhodesia. But those who heard the gloomy relish with which the Kenya settlers prophesied murder, mutilation and mass expulsions will acknowledge that the worst has not occurred. Most importantly, perhaps, time has been won with which to mend race relations, construct a new economy and instil greater confidence in an untried government.

Hard on the heels of this diminished white settler problem, the government of Kenya has been beset by another aspect of the land question which bears an altogether closer resemblance to the normal play of national politics. As a very enlightening book[2] makes clear, the resettlement of Africans in the former White Highlands immediately gave rise to controversy among politicians as to the terms upon which the newly won lands should be held. Roughly the debate polarized around two extremes: on the one side the government view that individual ownership of land should prevail, on the other the opinions held by political radicals such as Bildad Kaggia who maintained that individual ownership was in breach of custom and also of equity. The debate reached its height in 1965. Government supporters emphasized the success, in both economic and human terms, of the agricultural policies followed by the colonial government in its latter days under the Swynnerton Plan, under which smallholder agriculture had been encouraged together with determined – and successful – efforts to foster the growth of cash crops and to register individual title to land holdings. A considerable body of African smallholders now existed, each with a title to his land and the prospects for making a reasonable living for himself and his family; men like these did not support the standpoint of Kaggia's followers, who based their opposition to land holding by individuals on two main points. First they disputed the validity of restricting access to land to those individuals who had been granted title to it; and secondly they disputed the social injustices inherent, they claimed, in the selection of those to whom the land eventually found its way. They could thus rely on support from those who yearned for the retention of the old customs of landholding, and also from the landless, the disaffected, and the poverty-stricken who had not succeeded in obtaining land.

The debate was in the end resolved in favour of the transfer of land to individual ownership, but not before the controversy touched upon many points of dissension. It was, of course, a good stance from which an opposition could attack government policy generally. As the row developed its protagonists retreated to more extreme positions until the opposition's standpoint embraced a whole critique of capitalism, private enterprise and the existence of private property. One should guard against the too simple deduction that this land issue was merely one element in an inevitable polarization of political theory along lines more familiar to political scientists of the western and eastern blocs; while, undoubtedly, Kaggia's allies tended to look towards the east for inspiration and support, the land controversy was a very genuine one in terms of individual need and echoes of it will certainly recur in the future. One can expect the controversy to be revived at moments of stress, as when population pressures grow too great to be contained within present bounds, or when land allocation grows too partial, or when famine or flood – still, as always, liable to occur in this predominantly agricultural country – come again.

SOUTH AFRICA : Further south, however, where the white man's influence is still supreme, the outcome of problems and conflicts similar to those found in Kenya has been very different. Here the trend of older legislation has continued, in reinforcement of racial barriers – whatever the original intentions of those who framed the legislation. In Rhodesia the Land Apportionment Act of 1931, originally brought in to regularize land tenure so as to preserve at least a portion of the land to the indigenous inhabitants, has been frequently amended. At present, 44 million acres (including 4 million available for individual purchase) is set aside for Africans; 36 million acres for Europeans; and 6 million is open for purchase by anyone. About 11 million acres have been retained as national property, for wildlife parks and nature reserves. The constitution prevents whites from occupying African areas, and the Land Apportionment Act prevents Africans from occupying white areas; exceptions are made for lodging government officials such as agricultural advisers and the police, and about one million Africans are working, for wages, on white farms. Of the 16.8 per cent of Rhodesian land designated as of high fertility soil, slightly over half is found in African areas. In Rhodesia 37 per cent of the land has a rainfall of over 28 inches a year, and about half the African area is located within this limit. All urban areas are designated as European and Africans are not allowed to buy property in them (except in the townships); but all Africans who work under labour agreements are exempt from this regulation, and the Natives (Urban Areas) Accommodation and Registration Act of 1946, consolidated in 1951, compels white employers to supply free accommodation to their African employees and wives. Other exceptions allow Africans to occupy town premises for educational, religious or other reasons benefiting Africans; all public places are open to Africans; hotels may apply to be multi-racial.

The conclusions to be drawn from this style of legislation are bitterly contested, as are the motives behind it; there is little profit in pursuing the subject here, except to remark the obvious that, while much trafficking between the different races takes place, the mere existence of legislation such as this strengthens the apartness of the races. It does not yet, as it does in South Africa, belong to a whole apparatus of legislation and philosophy that teaches that *apartheid* is the only means of ensuring the separate development of each race and colour group, and that such separate development is not only beneficial to all but inevitable, given the religious and natural order of things. The roots of *apartheid* are, indeed, traced back to the Afrikaners' occupation of the *platteland* rural areas in South Africa, 'the cradle of Afrikaner life and nationalism'.[3] As the Afrikaners' frontiers spread northward so their contacts with the races they displaced increased and became embittered; the Zulu wars and finally the Boer War saw them spread widely, and still precariously, through the Union. Early land problems, and indeed economic problems generally, were legion. They included labour shortage as well as unemployment, the fragmentation of land holdings, under-cropping or total lack of cultivation in some areas and land shortages elsewhere, the presence of Africans among whites as fellow farmers as well as employees, and the presence of Indians and Chinese as yet another exotic infusion among the differing, disputing races. Many of these problems were, or appear to be today, mutually contradictory, and for an explanation of them Francis Wilson's account already referred to is admirable; attempts to resolve them concern us more closely, for upon them the edifice of *apartheid* has been constructed.

It is the South African Land Act of 1913 that is generally taken as the fundamental measure from which derives much of the further legislation to regulate black/white relationships, although its purpose at the time appears now to have been more closely directed at economic distresses. It attempted to solve the labour shortage felt by many of the white farmers, while preventing blacks from taking over, or indeed continuing to work on an independent basis, land that it was thought should more properly be worked by whites. The practice of farming-on-the-half, by which Africans could formerly work white-owned land so long as they handed over half the produce to the owner was forbidden; this, it was thought, would release numbers of independent Africans to be absorbed by those farmers who needed black labour. It was also made illegal for a white to sell land to a black. The results of this Act were far-reaching indeed. Many thousands of Africans with their families were rendered homeless, and an embryo lower-middle-class of successful African contractors and entrepreneurs was destroyed. More tellingly, perhaps, the land set aside for African use and the arguments deployed in favour of the Act succeeded in uniting several disparate strands of South African opinion, which might otherwise never have united to make possible the future structure of racial exclusiveness; both economic interests, of farmers as well as of industrialists on the Rand, and religious/charitable interests could find points of agreement in certain aspects of the Act.

The modern Bantustan areas are a direct and logical development from this early land legislation. Much of its ideological basis rests upon the arguments deployed by Prime Minister Verwoerd in the early 1960s to make separate development assume a more intellectually respectable guise. The first Bantustan was set up in the Transkei in the eastern Cape, as the homeland for 1½ million Xhosa people. Seven other national units have been envisaged, for other peoples. The defects of this system as an exercise in practical self-government are obvious; the areas are too small to accommodate all those for whom they are supposed to be designed, they are fragmented so that national or racial unity can only be illusory, and although control over day-to-day domestic affairs is granted to Africans living in Bantustans, control over security, foreign policy, trade, currency and the like are reserved to Pretoria. This continuing white control over African affairs in the Bantustans is not matched, nor is it ever designed to be, by any sort of exercise of African influence within the 87 per cent of South African territory that is designed for exclusively white existence.

Labour – the unions

It is not possible in a book of this size and nature to do justice to all the aspects of labour that influence the play of local politics. Mention is made elsewhere of some of these aspects, in particular the difficulties caused by low employment levels and the lack of job opportunities for younger, educated people anxious to share some of the rewards of independence. Here we must confine discussion to some of the aspects of the development of trade unions, for one of the most striking, and disturbing, things about African political life is the almost complete absence of organized labour as a force to be reckoned with. We should ask ourselves why this is so, and, in particular, how long this state of affairs is likely to last.

The growth of unionism started late, and it has been slow. In the ex-British territories its start was prompted by Colonial Office concern in the late 1930s for the conditions and wages of workers. The Office also feared the growth of labour organizations hostile to government and to the accepted colonial order. The first permanent labour adviser to the colonial secretary was appointed in 1938, and the English Colonial Development and Welfare Act of 1940 maintained that none of the territories under Colonial Office control might receive aid unless it possessed legislation protecting trade unions' rights, embodied a fair wages clause for work in which aid was to be used, and forbade the employment of persons aged less than fourteen. This was followed up in 1942 by the establishment of a Colonial Labour Advisory Committee, to function at the Colonial Office in London, which included British TUC members, representatives of employers' organizations, academics and civil servants.

An authority[4] on the development of trade unions in Africa points out some of the inherent difficulties. While the British Labour party and the TUC wanted to see the unions grow as model democratic institutions rooted in African society, civil servants and the colonial governments themselves merely wished them to function along lines tolerable to the administration; hence they were never viewed as organs of social or economic change and betterment, but as a possible means of ensuring the maintenance of the *status quo*. They did not grow, as had the British unions, out of a sense of intolerable grievance at industrial conditions; nor were they in any way rooted in African custom, save as occasional extensions, perhaps, of family/tribal affiliations. Indeed, by their inevitable emphasis on unity by occupation or industry, they contributed much to the breaking down of old forms of cohesion – although at the same time offering a means of forging new groupings.

The unions were slow to grow, as the example of Nigeria shows.[5] Although a few unions, such as the Nigeria Union of Teachers, the Civil Servants' Association and the Railway Workers' Union, existed prior to the Second World War, the country had no trade union legislation and their position was legally obscure until 1938, when the first trade union ordinance gave some protection to trade unions and also provided for the appointment of a registrar of unions. Registration of all unions was made compulsory. In 1939 a small labour inspectorate was formed. In 1942, however, a separate department of labour was formed, with specialist branches dealing with factory inspection, workmen's compensation and employment exchanges, trade testing, minimum wage legislation and the whole gamut of industrial relations. Meanwhile unions themselves grew but slowly. In 1940, five employees' unions were registered, with 3,500 members, and by 1942 sixty-two unions had been registered with 21,000 members. In December 1947, eighty unions had been registered, of which twenty to thirty had lapsed, and a total of 75,000 workers were members. In 1956, nearly 200 unions remained registered, of the 332 which had registered during the past seventeen years; a total membership of 170,000 had been reached. These unions were of very small average size, and their numbers were overstated as well as inaccurate.

Reasons for this kind of disappointing record are not far to seek. Unions themselves had difficulties in communication, organization and in internal administration. A large contributing factor lay in the low levels of wage labour in the territories generally; in Nigeria in 1959 it was said to be a mere 2 per cent of the total population.[6] Where the majority of occupation is on a self-employed basis and where the wage earner is a rarity, unionism is slow to start. Again, much of labour in Africa was then, as it is now, migratory in character; both as within countries, for instance within Nigeria with Ibos from the east moving westward and, in particular, northward, and also from country to country. West African coal and iron ore deposits, and above all the great mines of southern and Central Africa, drew people from hundreds of miles away to work on contract and at the end of their time to return whence they came. It is estimated that in 1959, only one third of mineworkers in South Africa were South African born. These conditions of limited work periods interspersed with periods spent at home and of contractual work, militated against the formation of unions whose purpose in most of the western world was to enforce job security and raise wage levels and conditions of work.

During colonial days, trade unions were encouraged by the administrations but they were considerably circumscribed as to the activities they could actually pursue. They had to register with labour departments, and such registration could be withdrawn and the union thereby rendered illegal. They were obliged to submit accounts for examination, a wise precaution; but political activity was prevented so far as was possible, and rights to strike whittled away by designation of 'essential services', such as water, electricity, transport and the like, the supply of which it was illegal to disrupt. This control of union activity, and the idea that it could and should be exercised by governments, has been yet another carry-over of British practice into colonial days.

In South Africa the growth of unionism has always been affected by the racial situation. So far as Africans were concerned, right from the time of Union, laws and regulations were concerned to discriminate as between whites and other races in matters of wages, conditions, job opportunity and recognition. The Mines and Works Act of 1911 and Mines and Works Amendment Act of 1926, as well as the Apprenticeship Act of 1922, resulted in Africans being excluded from skilled work. The operation of the Pass Laws and other legislation controlling residence and passage of Africans greatly influenced their possibilities for employment. The whole of the inter-war years and what has been called the Civilized Labour Policy begun by the Nationalist/Labour government that came to power in 1924 acted to hoist employment opportunities, rewards and skills for whites (in many cases displaced, like many blacks, from the land) far above those obtainable by blacks, coloureds or Indians. This is not to say that the treatment meted out to white unionists was, or has been, ideal, as witness Smuts' treatment of the miners on the Rand in 1922, when eighty-one were killed and 315 wounded during police action on his instructions. It would seem to indicate that intolerant treatment of other races does nothing to secure proper treatment for all sections of the ruling race; and the reasons why this should be borne are psychologically puzzling. It may well be that government control of white unions in South Africa is tolerable for the whites only because they know that the blacks, further down the pile, are having an even worse time. (This kind of reasoning may also be held to account for white Rhodesians' present acceptance of the outrage, in a so-called democracy, of persistent press censorship.)

The story of the rise and fall of Clements Kadalie's Industrial and Commercial Workers' Union of Africa (ICU)[7] is an interesting and instructive one. Kadalie and his ICU rose on the boom-and-bust conditions after the First World War; by 1925 the discrimination practised against Africans had led him to become actively hostile to whites as such – 'The ICU appeared to be transforming itself from an organization attempting to win wage increases and minor patronage from electoral participation to a movement which was set on challenging the structure of society'.[8] In 1926 came an unsuccessful effort by the ICU to exchange delegates with the white-dominated South African Trade Union Council (SATUC); in 1927 Kadalie was suggesting the whites join the ICU as a single trade union body to bring conditions in South Africa before the world. By 1930 Kadalie personally and his efforts at union solidarity were shattered by internal union quarrels as much as by action from outside; although he still continued in 1936 to fight for the cause of Africans in his attempt to prevent the disfranchisement of Cape Africans.

South African labour conditions continued after the Second World War in the same mould as before. The 1956 Industrial Conciliation Act did not recognize Africans as employees. African wages and conditions were dealt with as part of the agreements reached between employers and white unions at Industrial Councils, where a member of the Bantu Labour Board, i.e. a white government official, would be present to take decisions as to African interests. Two centres of trade union activity were registered under the Act – one, the all-white South African Confederation of Labour, the other the Trade Union Council of South Africa (TUCSA). Until February 1969 the latter took under its mantle the affairs of some of the non-registered African trade unions that were affiliated to it; after that date, however, as a result of decisions taken by a white voting majority, it has not functioned on behalf of African unions. It now has forty-nine predominantly white affiliates and a membership of 166,398, and continues to represent the interests also of a minority of affiliated coloured and Indian unions. All skilled and semi-skilled jobs are prohibited to Africans, and the Ministry of Labour controls the replacement of workers of one race by another to operate an effective total colour bar. In addition to legislation designed specifically for labour matters, African workers are greatly affected by legislation designed for other spheres; an example of this is found in the Suppression of Communism Act 1950, which has been used to dismantle African trade unions.

Much the same kind of effect was created on the Rhodesian Copper Belt, where before independence white miners enjoyed skills, conditions and rates of pay far above those of the other races; since independence it has been a major part of the Zambian government's policy to achieve some semblance of parity. It should be remembered that Zambia among the 'black' African states represents an anomaly, in that a high level of employment and a very major part of her domestic product is derived not from agriculture and allied occupations, but from mining; and the government has experienced extreme difficulty in pursuing its political, together with its industrial, interests in the matter. It has been an undoubted fact that Africans on the Copper Belt are not yet technically capable of conducting all mine operations themselves – although there is of course no reason why they should not in time do so. The Zambian government has had to juggle political pressures for the removal of whites with its economic needs to retain whites' services, and also contend with whites' wishes to leave a delicate and sometimes dangerous area (the midst of Bemba country, on whom the political agitation in the country has centred) in numbers and at times when it has been necessary to retain their services.

Throughout Africa the post-independence conduct of trade unions has had two aspects: one, their external relationships with world bodies and in particular their standing *vis-à-vis* the western and communist blocs, and the other their role and standing inside their own countries. The 20 per cent of African workers that were unionized in the 1950s were split between membership of the International Confederation of Free Trade Unions (ICFTU), a non-communist body, and the World Federation of Trade Unions (WFTU), a communist-inspired organization. Soviet policy in the matter inclined to support the formation of independent African trade unions, and to create a bloc of them together with the WFTU. This purpose was aided by Nkrumah's policy, in the furthering of pan-Africanism and, in particular, Ghana's role in it, of subjugating his trade unions domestically but in encouraging them to play a pan-continental part. Thus, in May 1961 the All-African Trade Union Federation (AATUF) was formed under Ghanaian leadership, and throughout Africa battle was joined among trade unionists as to which grouping should be supported. On the whole, the ban by the ICFTU on dual affiliations meant that unions that wished to support the AATUF adhered also to the WFTU; but the very militancy of these organizations also proved their undoing, because governments feared their influence over national unions – and in any case, those countries that took a less militant line than Ghana in the early 1960s or resented her leadership in African affairs also rebuffed attempts by the AATUF to win adherents.

Internally, these jealousies had considerable effect. The Nigerian trade union movement, for instance,[9] split into two organizations – the Trade Union Congress (Nigeria) (TUC(N)) and the Nigerian Trade Union Congress (NTUC), of which the former adhered to the western-oriented ICFTU and the latter to the AATUF. Personalities and policies in these two organizations were bitterly opposed and made for erratic labour relations in the early 1960s when each was bidding for adherents. In 1964, however, they came together in an organization called the United Labour Congress of Nigeria and achieved a general strike that did much to shake further the already-tottering foundations of the Nigerian federal government.

All the African countries have needed to control their unions, in the absence of meaningful political activity for them; as with the nationalist movements, the achievement of independence left many in the unions with little constructive work to be done and in seeking a role they undermined governmental authority. Tanzania offers possibly the best example of post-independence union control, for before independence the union movement played a major part in politics and in the agitation for independence itself, more so than in most of the other African countries.[10] The National Union of Tanganyika Workers (Establishment) Act of 1964 altered the whole structure of unions in Tanganyika (as it then was) and brought them under government control. The Tanganyika Federation of Labour and its eleven member unions was dissolved, and one central union with several industrial sections was set up in its place. The general secretary and his deputy were to be appointed by the president of the republic, and the union itself was to be affiliated to TANU as one of the party's organs; its structure is very similar to that of TANU itself. Its defects, according to an academic observer, were considerable. It suffered from top-heavy structure and insufficient coordination; its office-holders lacked experience; and centralization at Dar-es-Salaam led to weakness at the branches and in regional organization. Despite later attempts to remedy them, accounting procedures and financial control are still weak.

Similar efforts to those of Tanzania were made elsewhere to achieve higher standards within the union organization and to impart some sense of national destiny in which the unions had a role to play. The quality of union leadership is glimpsed from a book written by one of the Kenya leaders,[11] whose intense feeling for the future of union activity is paralleled by a certain incoherence of story. An account of union activity in Uganda[12] stresses the lack of union cohesion there, brought about partly by the fact that the unions there were never closely identified with the nationalist struggle for independence, and also partly by the fact that so many of the union's leaders, and indeed the inspiration of the whole Ugandan movement (the Kenya politician Tom Mboya, who moved in with Fabian and ICFTU backing in the late 1950s), originated from outside the country – from Kenya. A telling assessment of the quality of union leadership was made in a study of the Nigerian Coal Miners' Union.[18] 'Contrary to expectations, power within the NCMU was more highly centralized than in the majority of European and African unions ... a group of persons coming from a tradition of direct, participatory democracy had structured and were operating the union in a highly centralized and autocratic manner. Models offered both by Ibo tradition and by Western trade unions had been rejected and new power forms created'. The author went on to cite the gap between the leaders and the rank-and-file of the movement, difficulties of communication and the imposition of centralized control, and the lack of democratically reached decisions as contributing largely to the union's lack of cohesion. He also noted the tendency of the leaders to copy the politicians in their efforts to hang on to power, to manipulate for their own ends the divisions among the rank-and-file and to do all that was possible to ensure the continuance of power in the hands of the then leaders.

Learning – education

Education is a politically explosive subject in Africa, and it is likely to become even more so in years to come. There is pressure on governments from the most basic grass-roots levels all the way to the top of the social pyramid, urging the expansion of educational opportunities. This pressure conflicts with, even if it sometimes complements, national development plans which call for money and skills to be used elsewhere. In a very real sense, a hundred pounds spent on education has to be wrested from general development funds already, maybe, earmarked for infrastructural or industrial spending, and a system of priorities worked out – which it is then essential to try to communicate to the ordinary people.

Meanwhile, pressures mount at the other end of the educational process, from those who have painfully and with luck on

their side made their way through the educational system, survived the enormous amount of weeding-out that takes place en
route and emerged with a coveted certificate or, in some cases, a
diploma or degree at the end of it all. The accompanying table
on literacy rates indicates the extent of the work that remains to
be done, simply to furnish some of the basic tools needed by a
society – the ability to read and write. On top of that are more
sophisticated needs, for doctors and engineers and the like as well
as for lawyers and teachers, which can only be met by the expenditure of money and forethought on future national needs.

Table 7

Literacy Rates

Country	Literacy rate %
Botswana	20
Gambia	10
Ghana	25
Kenya	20–25
Lesotho	40
Malawi	15
Nigeria	25
Rhodesia	25–30
Sierra Leone	10
South Africa	35
South-West Africa	27
Swaziland	36
Tanzania	15–20
Uganda	20
Zambia	15–20

Source: AID *Economic Data Book, Africa,* USAID,
Washington DC, Feb. 1970.

It is at this stage that governments meet another crucial challenge; how to ensure that national needs are met by higher educational plans, and how to ensure that those who emerge from
the educational process can actually use what they have learned
in their future careers. There is nothing that makes for more

discomfort in governing circles than the knowledge that a swelling tide of newly-literate youngsters is coming on to the employment market which is already suffering from a surfeit of them. Government is faced with a 'heads you win, tails I lose' situation where educational expansion can be as dangerous to national stability as educational stagnation.

Table 8

Schooling: Attendance Figures

Country	Primary students as % of 5–14 age group	Secondary students as % of 15–19 age group	Primary+secondary students as % of 5–19 age groups
Botswana	42	3	33
Gambia	17	12	16
Ghana	70	27	57
Kenya	52	7	39
Lesotho	83	5	61
Malawi	36	3	26
Nigeria	30	6	23
Rhodesia	58	3	42
Sierra Leone	19	6	15
South Africa	n.a.	n.a.	57
South-West Africa	n.a.	n.a.	40
Swaziland	46	9	37
Tanzania	27	2	20
Uganda	29	10	23
Zambia	44	6	33

n.a. = not available

Source: AID *Economic Data Book,* Africa, USAID, Washington DC, Feb. 1970.

So far, governments have held the view that educational expansion is the least of the evils with which they are confronted. The accompanying figures of recent school enrolments show not just the low levels (by western standards) of school enrolments at various levels, but the extent to which each stage of the educational system functions as a bottleneck rather than as a point of entry to the next stage. These are pessimistic figures, but they should be interpreted carefully. In the first place they take no account of regional variations within countries; in the Muslim north of Nigeria, for instance, a far lower proportion than the national average attends school (in particular, girls receive very little schooling) while the east of the country has always boasted considerably higher figures for school attendance. Again, the figures give no indication of the considerable amount of part-schooling that takes place. A better way of gauging national progress is to examine national plans for education, both because they indicate weaknesses in the system which African governments are concerned to rectify and because they suggest the pressures to which governments are subject.[14]

Thus one finds that Zambia, for instance, aims to have 75 per cent of children in eligible age-groups in rural areas, and all children in urban areas, complete a seven-year primary course; and secondary education, teacher training and technical educational facilities are to be expanded to keep pace. In Uganda in 1966 it was estimated that 65 per cent of children aged six to twelve years were attending school and by 1971 it was hoped numbers would have been raised to 75 per cent. Kenya aims at seven years' primary education for all children, and a rise from the 60 per cent enrolment rate of 1968 to 75 per cent in 1974; development plans stress the importance of teaching science, mathematics and engineering, and the need to produce people to meet the requirements of the expansion of the economy. Tanzania is aiming to increase primary school enrolment by 300,000 in 1973/4, but this will result in an increase of the primary school enrolment ratio only from 46 per cent to 52 per cent; in fact, secondary school education, teacher training and university work are to attract the lion's share of educational expenditure in the country.

Turning to West Africa, Gambia's long-term educational plan envisaged a rise in primary school enrolments from 11,504 in 1964/5 to 30,000 by 1975, and in secondary school figures from 2,992 to 4,340 in the same period. In Nigeria the objective is to increase primary school enrolment to 50 per cent of the relevant age group by the mid-1970s, and secondary enrolment to 25 per cent. Sierra Leone has been attempting to increase primary enrolment from 139,413 in 1968/9 to 269,000 in

1971/2. Ghana's two-year plan to 1970 called for a development expenditure of some £2¼ million on education generally.

Educational statistics in South Africa and Rhodesia follow the same expansionist trend, but are complicated by factors of race and are made harder to compare by racially-compiled statistics. There is no doubt that educational facilities for all races are being improved and expanded. In South Africa, enrolment in African schools at primary level has increased from 1,770,613 in 1964 to 2,298,482 in 1968, at secondary level from 59,790 to 98,670. Coloured enrolment at primary and secondary levels together rose from 386,574 in 1963 to 455,562 in 1968. In Rhodesia, total educational enrolment rose between 1964 and 1968, in respect of Africans from 634,518 to 713,170 and in respect of category 'other' (i.e. whites and mixed races) from 58,769 to 63,376. In 1965, 90 per cent to 95 per cent of African children were receiving five years of lower primary education and 50 per cent received upper primary education. The 1970/3 Public Sector Investment Programme envisaged a seven-year primary course for all African children who could reach a school, 12½ per cent of whom could go on to four years of secondary education and 37½ per cent of whom could continue with a two-year vocational education course.

In promulgating these programmes, it is interesting to note that Rhodesia and South Africa have been faced with precisely those problems which today confront the rest of black Africa; what to do with the great mass of the under-educated. In the case of South Africa, educational politics have been framed to reinforce *apartheid*; the black population should not undergo too bookish an education, but should concentrate upon the practical. The first sources of education for Africans had been the churches and missionary societies, which had been partially supported by funds from government sources. To consider the whole question of education for Africans, the nationalist government established the Eiselen Commission in 1949 and its subsequent report embodied most of the principles upon which educational policy has since rested – in particular, the need for a separate African social framework. It recommended that responsibility for education should be transferred from the churches to the government, that there should be extensive revision of the curricula, and that extensive development plans should be undertaken. This report's principles and recommendations were enshrined in the Bantu Education Act of 1953, which brought far-reaching changes. The most important of the measures were twofold. African community schools were established, run by Africans guided by government officials; and the Native Education Finance Act of 1945 was repealed. This had effectively made the whole of the South African community responsible for financing African education, because schools for Africans were partly or wholly financed from general revenue sources; now, however, a special account for financing African education was to be set up, into which £6.5 million of general revenue, plus four fifths of the 'Bantu' tax paid annually, was to be paid. In this way, education for Africans would come to depend upon revenue from wholly African sources. An additional provision in the Act which would have far-reaching social consequences lay in the ruling that African languages were to be used as the medium of instruction in schools; clearly this would have the effect of increasing the Africans' isolation from the other races, and from other African tribes.

In higher education, too, the nationalist government has framed its policy in accordance with wider political designs. Until 1959, what higher education there was for Africans took place mainly in the English-language universities, albeit under restricted conditions so as to minimize social mixing; it was in that year that the two main pillars of *apartheid* in higher education, the Extension of University Education Bill and the University College of Fort Hare Transfer Bill, were enacted. By these measures all non-Europeans not registered by January 1959 were banned from entering any white institutions of education, except for the medical school at Natal and the correspondence courses of the University of South Africa. The government was also empowered to take over Fort Hare and to establish new institutions for non-white attendance only. The first 'Bantu' College was opened in March 1960, with close control being exercised by its Rector over students and by the deputy minister for Bantu Affairs over faculty appointments; this pattern was followed in the setting up of Fort Hare for the primary use of the Xhosa tribe, the University College of Zululand at Ngoya for the Zulus, the University College of the North (at Turfloop) for the Sotho, Tsanya and Venda, the University College for Coloureds at

Belleville in the western Cape, and the Indian College in Durban. By its emphasis on the use of African (and Indian) languages for instruction, as well as by planning these universities to serve as the cultural centres for the tribes/nations whose students they were to accommodate, the government of South Africa has forged an effective instrument for the furtherance of its wider *apartheid* policies.

So far as white-dominated southern Africa generally is concerned, however, it seems true to say that educational facilities for all the races are better and more numerous than elsewhere in the continent; that expenditure on all races is increasing; that the totals devoted to African education are growing faster than those devoted to white education; but that *per capita* expenditure on white pupils is considerably greater than on black. Bearing in mind the retention of political power in the hands of whites in these regions, coupled with the expressed intention that those who contribute most in terms of taxation to the available resources must receive most of the benefits from such taxation, one must conclude that these trends will continue so long as the balance of political power remains undisturbed.

Elsewhere, in black Africa, the role of the university in the educational system as a whole has come under intense discussion. When independence came, there were only four universities in the whole of British West and East Africa; Fourah Bay in Sierra Leone, with its special relationship with the University of Durham, and Legon in Ghana, Ibadan in Nigeria and Makerere in Uganda, all three of which enjoyed a special relationship with the University of London. Independence both caused these special ties to be broken, so that individual curricula could grow to suit local needs and the award of local degrees with a currency value of their own, and also caused a great growth in the numbers of universities. Africa has experienced the same kind of questioning and student unrest that has recently swept the rest of the world, and for many of the same reasons. L. C. B. Gower (*op. cit.*) writing in 1967 was still able to claim that the problem was

'to maintain academic freedom and to prevent undue interference from governments which tend to think that he who pays the piper calls the tune, and that a university is just another public corporation to be used for purposes of political patronage and influence . . . few [African leaders] would be prepared to recognize that one of the supporting roles of the academic élite is to offer objective criticism of the political élite, especially where other sources of criticism, such as the press or a parliamentary opposition, have been silenced.'

Five years later these words seem to amount to a counsel of perfection that it would be naive to expect African governments to heed. With the universities and the academic élites of the metropolitan power themselves questioning old and established values of academic life, it would be idle to pretend that the Africans are not entitled to do likewise and to come up with the answers to suit their own cases.

Since independence, African universities have already undergone great changes; they have also become to some extent the political pawns of their governments. The independence of Legon in Ghana was gravely undermined during the Nkrumah regime. The growth of regional tensions in Nigeria resulted in regional views prevailing also in university staffing, to the detriment of accepted academic values. Regional tensions, too, broke up the University of East Africa in 1970, when Makerere, Nairobi and Dar-es-Salaam went their separate ways in pursuit of the individual governments' aims.

What are these aims? Above all, to use universities as a tool in nation-making. Seretse Khama, speaking as chancellor of the University of Botswana, Lesotho and Swaziland at the graduation ceremony in August 1970, spoke of the difficulty in achieving a good relationship between the university and the political authorities. It was, he said, essential to have adequate machinery for consulation and involvement in development plans; there must also be a general understanding of the role to be played by the university, and a basic agreement with its philosophy. It must adopt an investment approach to education, rather than purely the consumer approach as practised in the west. The university must provide not merely top grade personnel, but intermediate manpower; commercial studies and sub-degree level training and an emphasis on adult education should also form part of the university's wares. Milton Obote of Uganda, speaking in October 1970 at the inaugural ceremony of the University of Uganda, said:

'on behalf of the people of Uganda I now dedicate this University today to the advancement of the African revolution. . . . Uganda is going through a revolution towards a socialist state. This fact by itself presupposes that the University must also change its direction. . . . The national policy realises that a highly educated and trained manpower is essential for social services, industrial development and scientific research. . . .'

Even more radical have been Nyerere's aims. Speaking in August 1970, like Obote at the inauguration of his country's university from what had been merely the Dar-es-Salaam college of the University of East Africa, he said one should not consider the university purely as one part of some international body, nor as an introspective intellectual centre; true, a university was 'an institution of higher learning', but it had three major functions. It must transmit advanced knowledge from one generation to the next; it should provide a centre from which to try to advance the frontiers of knowledge; and above all it had to provide for the high-level manpower needs of the country. Priorities might vary, but all were linked in the end:

'Our nation has decided to divert development resources from other potential uses because we expect to benefit by doing so . . . the aim of the University of Dar-es-Salaam must be service to the needs of a developing socialist Tanzania. . . . The University of Dar-es-Salaam has not been founded to turn out intellectual apes whether of the Right or the Left. We are training for a socialist, self-respecting and self-reliant Tanzania.'

8 The Politics of Economics

Faced with the need to fashion the economies of their countries, African governments meet a political problem that it is particularly difficult for them either to resolve or to bypass. The coming of independence shattered that pre-*uhuru* unity and cohesion of the indigenous people that flourished in the common battle against the colonial power, and the lines of conflict have had to be redrawn – no longer between expatriate civil servants and those they administered, but between governments and those they govern. In a sense, of course, the lines of conflict have remained the same and all that has changed is the obligation to put the case; whereas the colonial power could rely on paternalist compulsion, African governments now find themselves obliged to explain, persuade, cajole their own people before (occasionally) resorting to compulsion.

Thus governments, needing in the interests of orderly and speedy economic development to find common cause with those trends and concerns that dominate their economies, run the risk of compromising their own political acceptability to their own people by seeming to lack sympathy with the natural desires of poor and ignorant people. If government is concerned to find, mix and bake the ingredients for the national cake, the people all want a far bigger slice of it; and it is this conflict between the long- and the short-term views that is the chief source of the domestic dissensions over matters economic to be found in Africa today.

Where most of the African countries differ from the developed world is not in the fact of their dependence upon it – after all, all countries of the world depend upon all the others for raw materials, markets, capital and technology – but in the extent of their dependence, the fact that it is not reciprocal, and the narrow limits within which it is focused. Whether this state of affairs is detrimental to developing countries' interests, whether it is inevitable, whether it can be modified or abolished are all propositions that have been argued elsewhere, plentifully. It is not, therefore, proposed to argue here either the ethics or the efficacy of the system that has resulted in so much of the power to influence African countries falling into alien hands, but rather to point out some of the political strains accruing to African countries by reason of their dependence. This, in turn, points to the rationale behind the measures to which many of them have resorted in an attempt to control their own destinies, and, perhaps more important, to be seen to be doing so by their own people.

These vulnerable economies

With the exception only of South Africa, these are all vulnerable economies, based upon the development and export of few products, of necessity the import of very many, and a lack of indigenous skills with which to diversify the economy. The accompanying table (see p. 158) shows those countries which depend upon only one, two or three major export commodities. They comprise no less than eight of the countries with which we are concerned, and the extent of their dependence varies from the 97 per cent dependence of Gambia upon groundnuts, to the 75 per cent dependence of Malawi upon tea, tobacco and oilseeds. This dependence means that in theory, if not always in practice, these countries can easily be crippled by adverse climatic or disease factors, or held to ransom by alterations in the terms of trade, international commodity pricing structures, or a shift in marketing organization. To alter this dependence and to diversify the economy is almost always one of the prime stated objectives of the countries' development plans; the best ways of achieving it are a subject of dispute among governments, economists and ordinary people alike.[1] One school of thought holds that development and growth can only come from inside a country; others maintain that aid, investment and foreign participation are essential. Whether agriculture is an essential base for industrial development or whether it is merely the poor relation of industry, is likewise unresolved.

What is certain is that the sheer amount of personal disturbance and disruption involved must be very great, and affect to its core the type of tribally-structured society to which most

Table 9

The Dependent Economies

Countries dependent upon:

1 Major Export Commodity

Gambia	groundnuts, etc.	97%
Zambia	copper	93%
Zanzibar	cloves	86%
Ghana	cocoa	69%

2 Major Export Commodities

Sierra Leone	diamonds, iron ore	85%
Uganda	coffee, cotton	77%

3 Major Export Commodities

Nigeria	petroleum, oilseeds, cocoa	78%
Malawi	tea, tobacco, oilseeds	75%

Source: UN *Yearbook of International Trade Statistics,*
United Nations, New York, 1967.

Africans, still, belong. The accompanying table of the origin of gross domestic product demonstrates the extent to which Africans are still dependent upon the land. The majority of populations still live in rural areas, scratching out a subsistence livelihood and increasingly turning to cash crops to produce a surplus which they can then sell to gain the wherewithal to meet their needs – for tools, education and medicine, and for such consumer articles as bicycles and transistor radios. In seven out of the nine countries listed, agriculture, forestry and fishing is the sector from which comes the largest contribution to gross domestic product. The exceptions are South Africa – where mining, manufacturing, transport commerce and utilities, and the trade and finance categories are all sizable, and indicate a sophisticated, fairly-balanced economy – and Zambia, where mining accounts for a large preponderance of national wealth. In Rhodesia, too, the agriculture sector is fairly balanced by development in other sectors. Mining accounts for much, comparatively speaking, of the activity in Sierra Leone, South Africa and Zambia; the size of the latter country's mining sector indicates not just the importance of mining to her economy, but the way in which agriculture has been outdistanced. A comparison of these two figures with those

Table 10

Origin of Gross Domestic Product (Where Figures are Available) Expressed as % of Total GDP, 1967

Country	Agriculture, Forestry and Fishing	Mining	Manufacturing	Construction	Transport, Commerce and Utilities	Trade and Finance	Pub. Admin. and Defence	Other Services
Kenya	34.5	0.4	11.0	5.1	10.4	13.8	5.7	19.1
Malawi	50.9	0.1	8.1	4.6	9.0	10.2	7.3	9.8
Nigeria	55.5	5.1	6.1	5.2	4.7	13.5	3.4	6.5
Rhodesia	19.2	6.1	18.8	5.1	11.8	14.9	5.2	18.9
Sierra Leone	31.3	19.2	6.3	3.6	8.5	15.9	5.2	10.0
South Africa	11.6	12.2	20.9	3.9	12.1	17.2	8.8†	13.3
Tanganyika	51.7	2.7	5.5	3.8	5.8	13.7	*	16.8
Uganda	57.8	2.5	7.8	2.1	4.8	10.0	4.0	11.0
Zambia	7.2	40.4‡	11.0†	7.4	6.5	14.1	4.5	8.9

* included in 'other services'
† includes all government services
‡ smelting and refining of metals included in mining.

Source: AID *Economic Data Book*, Africa, USAID, Washington DC, Feb. 1970.

for South Africa, which are close to each other, argues the relative efficiency of the South African agricultural sector which, despite the large size of that country's mining effort, contributes nearly as much to gross domestic product. Only the South African economy, and perhaps that of Rhodesia, can be described as reasonably diversified.

What are the likely consequences of attempts to diversify? Many are known already, and can easily be itemized by economists; a quest for capital, the negotiation of loans, the consequent and longlasting strain on balance of payments accounts which the paying-back of loans entails. The attempts at import substitution, at export to neighbouring or far-distant countries, at the encouragement of new crops or bigger production of old ones, the search for mineral wealth and fair commodity prices and markets – all these are well-known. What is not so well-known, perhaps, are some of the consequences locally. For each new loan higher levels of taxation (or deficits, bringing other problems in their wake) become necessary, each new industry requires goods, services, skills and cash which are thus diverted from elsewhere, every man newly employed requires training, every man not so employed whose legitimate hopes are dashed is a potential disruptive influence on society. The political order is affected by all these factors, and its stability set at risk by most of them. Growth and opportunity bring also challenge and defeat; the idea that a magical panacea, such as the sudden stabilization of prices or discovery of untold mineral wealth, exists is fallacious and harmful.

If domestic trade factors can bring such problems, so also do the volume and direction of trade. An indication of the growth of foreign trade is given in the accompanying table. It shows that most of the countries concerned have, not surprisingly, maintained a growth in volume of trade. Ghanaian exports dropped in 1965 while imports increased sizably, an indication of the Nkrumah development philosophy that was corrected by 1968 and resulted in a favourable trade balance. Kenya's persistent adverse balance has been greatly compensated by tourism as a foreign currency earner; Malawi's dependence on aid is evident from her trade figures. The effects of sanctions on Rhodesia show in the abrupt turnabout of her trade balances after 1965. It is evident that whatever is gained from a rise in the values of goods exported is counterbalanced by the rise in imports that commonly occurs in economies undergoing major development schemes. During the take-off stage, at any rate, future savings on foreign exchange are largely discounted by current losses. Although such losses should not continue in later years except as a result of still further industrialization, it does not follow that local manufacture results in an absolute saving of costs; indeed, such measures as tariff protection and import licensing, resorted to in order to make the local product sell, indicate that local production is in many cases uneconomic. This is not to argue that there is no case for local manufacture; merely that its advantages are not necessarily economic ones, and that its disadvantages repay careful study.

Table 11

Foreign Trade (us $m)

Country	1962	1965	1968
Botswana	Included in South Africa		
Gambia			
Exports	10	14	n.a.
Imports	13	16	n.a.
Balance	−3	−2	n.a.
Ghana			
Exports	323	318	335
Imports	334	448	307
Balance	−11	−130	+28
Kenya			
Exports	174	227	250
Imports	215	282	356
Balance	−41	−55	−106
Lesotho	Included in South Africa		
Malawi			
Exports	n.a.	40	48
Imports	n.a.	64	80
Balance	n.a.	−24	−32

Table 11—contd.

Country	1962	1965	1968
Nigeria			
Exports	472	751	590
Imports	569	772	536
Balance	−97	−21	+54
Rhodesia			
Exports	n.a.	442	256
Imports	n.a.	378	327
Balance	n.a.	+64	−71
Sierra Leone			
Exports	58	88	96
Imports	85	108	91
Balance	−27	−20	+5
South Africa†			
Exports	2,041	2,603	3,235
Imports	1,552	2,699	2,891
Balance	+489	−96	+344
South-West Africa	Included in South Africa		
Swaziland	Included in South Africa		
Tanzania			
Exports	157	192	240
Imports	144	188	256
Balance	+13	+4	−16
Uganda			
Exports	134	206	216
Imports	95	161	162
Balance	+39	+45	+54
Zambia			
Exports	n.a.	532	762
Imports	n.a.	332	515
Balance	n.a.	+200	+247

† figures for South Africa include Botswana, Lesotho, South-West Africa and Swaziland.

Source: AID *Economic Data Book,* Africa, USAID Washington DC, Feb. 1970

The direction of trade patterns, the destination of African exports and the source of imports (as given in the accompanying table) has a certain significance in the political context. Trade with the communist bloc, although it has increased quite substantially since independence, does not appear to have reached significant proportions; Ghana and Nigeria, the two countries whose trade with the Soviet bloc is the largest, still do proportionately little trade with the area. It should also be emphasized that a certain amount of the trade that now passes directly between Africa and the communist countries, and hence shows up on the trade figures, in former years travelled to the same destinations by devious routes because of the existence of marketing arrangements with other countries. Ghanaian cocoa is a case in point.

It is true that trade with the UK has declined and is still declining; but it still remains large, both absolutely and proportionally. Trade with the USA is increasing and will probably continue to do so; EEC trade is sizable, and as association agreements are concluded with the European Community will continue to grow. Inter-African trade is still small, both absolutely and relatively, mainly because of the colonial patterns of transportation from interior to coast. Those countries most involved in inter-African trade are swayed by special factors. Thus, the countries of the East African Community – Kenya, Uganda and Tanzania – are contained in a formal trade area and some of their trade figures are distorted by the overwhelming part played by Kenya. Malawi, which is landlocked, conducts significant amounts of trade with her neighbours, and she and Zambia are the only two black African countries to carry on trade of any size with South Africa – again, because of geographical considerations.

The general pattern seems fairly clear. Diminishing trade with the UK and South Africa, increasing trade with the USA, EEC, the communist bloc and with each other appears to be the general trend. One should remember that trade patterns, like much else, are subject to two influences – what may be called the push/pull syndrome. On the one hand are the impulses of the African countries towards trade, conditioned by such factors as the existence of trade agreements, the trend of commodity prices, trade ties of the past, and pure sentiment; on the other hand, these impulses may be stopped overnight by the actions of other

Table 12

Direction of Foreign Trade (US $m.)

I Destination of Exports

Country	Year	Total	Africa	USA	UK	S. Africa	EEC	Communist Bloc	Others
Botswana				included in South Africa					
Gambia	1967	22	0.1		—	9.0	—	7.3	—	5.1
Ghana	1968	332	2.0	58.7	90.1	—	86.4	20.6	73.8
Kenya	1968	250	96.9	11.8	44.5	—	32.9	3.9	60.1
Lesotho				included in South Africa					
Malawi	1968	48	11.3	2.0	20.7	2.1	4.4	—	9.7
Nigeria	1968	591	10.6	49.1	174.2	0.2	212.5	27.9	116.5
Rhodesia	1967	57	20.1	6.6	0.4	—	19.6	—	10.4
Sierra Leone	1968	95	0.7	2.8	64.3	0.3	20.8	—	6.8
South Africa	1968	2,110	348.7	146.2	666.5	—	371.1	1.7	608.8
South-West Africa				included in South Africa					
Swaziland				included in South Africa					
Tanzania	1968	241	42.8	13.1	54.4	—	30.5	11.6	88.8
Uganda	1968	216	38.0	45.9	42.5	—	17.3	7.3	64.7
Zambia	1968	762	26.2	15.1	223.9	16.5	243.8	10.0	242.5

Source: AID *Economic Data Book*, Africa, USAID, Washington DC, Feb. 1970.

Table 12 – contd.

II Source of Imports

Country	Year	Total	Africa	USA	UK	S. Africa	EEC	Communist Bloc	Others
Botswana						included in South Africa			
Gambia	1967	15	0.6	0.6	7.9	—	1.8	—	1.5
Ghana	1968	308	8.9	58.8	84.9	—	62.7	20.0	59.2
Kenya	1968	357	37.5	22.2	101.0	—	66.1	9.5	97.0
Lesotho						included in South Africa			
Malawi	1968	70	24.8	3.9	21.5	7.7	2.6	0.3	13.3
Nigeria	1968	540	8.9	62.4	167.7	—	149.2	33.1	98.7
Rhodesia	1967	62	6.9	3.8	2.7	—	24.3	—	10.5
Sierra Leone	1968	91	2.6	8.6	25.5	—	17.2	8.6	17.0
South Africa	1968	2,638	168.6	465.9	629.3	—	646.1	9.2	545.3
South-West Africa						included in South Africa			
Swaziland						included in South Africa			
Tanzania	1968	257	42.6	11.8	59.3	—	52.3	18.1	54.1
Uganda	1968	162	40.0	5.4	41.0	—	29.5	7.0	25.9
Zambia	1968	456	159.8	46.6	106.5	114.1	57.7	5.7	54.4

Source: AID Economic Data Book, Africa, USAID, Washington DC, Feb. 1970.

nations. Thus, US balance of payments difficulties may cause her to cut aid or reduce imports or insist upon increasing exports or tying aid to purchases of American goods; or British action in joining the EEC may compel African countries to seek other outlets for their produce and, therefore, other sources for their imports. One man's surplus is always another man's deficit, somewhere.

How much, then, and how critically, can one judge African countries to be dependent on overseas countries in trade matters? As mentioned earlier, it is not so much the fact of dependence as the extent to which it is concentrated on one, or a few, overseas countries that is critical. From this point of view it is clear that African countries' dependence is becoming more diffused over numbers of other countries; this trend is one that will continue, given a charitable interpretation of regional trading agreements. This does not, however, necessarily lessen domestic political stress as demands for changes in trading partners can arise from purely whimsical popular fancy, or as a result of manipulation from government itself for its own political ends – as when Uganda's General Amin ordered out Israeli personnel at short notice, in response to neighbouring Arab countries' requests.

It is a mistake to deduce a political commitment from a bunch of trade figures. Simply because Tanzania trades with China is no indication that she wishes to, particularly, merely that Chinese aid in building the Tan-Zam railroad must be repaid in some way. Malawi's trade with South Africa is not evidence of approval of the latter's *apartheid*, but rather of the existence of historical and geographical barriers to trade elsewhere. And even if the amount of trade the ex-British countries still conduct with the former colonial power is still large, it should not be deduced that ties of sentiment overcome the pull of convenience; as time goes by, increasingly the reverse will be true.

The special cases

The dependence of African countries on one or more commodities has been listed earlier. It is often argued that the existence of large commercial concerns, historical left-overs from colonial days, compromise the newly-won independence of African countries; that these large concerns, either singly or in concert, with each other and/or with the British government or, it may be, with the CIA, act to control the economies of these small countries where they operate; and that these small vulnerable economies are politically dependent upon them. We should look at the case histories of diamonds in Sierra Leone, petroleum in Nigeria and copper in Zambia to see if these assertions are true.

THE DIAMONDS OF SIERRA LEONE : The growth and development of the diamond industry of Sierra Leone[2] affords a particularly valuable insight into government/industry relations in tropical Africa, because it shows very clearly the difficulties of dealing with the pressures that bear upon an African government from its own people, opposition political parties, the demands of the economy, and the various, sometimes opposed, needs of a highly sophisticated and closely international industry – and one which has always been closely associated, moreover, with South African financial circles.

The diamond drama started in 1952 when Sierra Leone Selection Trust (SLST), a subsidiary of Chester Beatty's Consolidated African Selection Trust (CAST) of the Rhodesian copper belt, began systematic mining in its Sierra Leone leases. Although the colonial power still ruled in Freetown, African-controlled independence was clearly foreshadowed and SLST, therefore, was concerned to create and maintain a *modus vivendi* with indigenous politicians. The then minister for mines was Siaka Stevens, later to be prime minister, and under his pilotage a bill was passed through Leg. Co. Its main provisions called for a higher rate of taxation of the profits of SLST, and the government for its part attempted to curb the very considerable amount of illicit diamond digging that was taking place. In this, the Act was unsuccessful and both illicit digging and smuggling increased. To combat these, licences for private digging were issued from February 1956 onwards; government, unable to beat the system, was trying to turn it to advantage.

Control of the industry as well as a fair share of the proceeds could, it was hoped, still be achieved through marketing arrangements, then as always essential to the orderly conduct of the world's diamond industry. Accordingly, all diamonds mined in Sierra Leone were to be sold to the Diamond Corporation of

Sierra Leone (DCSL), an offshoot of the great South African mining finance house of de Beers, through whose Central Selling Organization (CSO) in London world diamond sales have for many years been conducted. This arrangement was successful for about three years, in that it stabilized prices and, hence, export proceeds to the government through the 1957–8 recession in diamonds; but by August 1959 smuggling was again so serious a threat to government receipts and also to the industry itself that a Government Diamond Office (GDO) was set up, to take over marketing from DCSL. The management of this remained in the hands of the Diamond Corporation, but control was vested in an executive board to which the government appointed three members and the Diamond Corporation two, and which drew up the price list for diamonds.

Up to this point the government's dilemma had been relatively uncomplicated. It had secured for itself reasonable participation in, and control of, this lucrative trade. It had managed to surmount the undoubted political liability posed by the existence of an industry that offered untold, undreamt-of wealth to those with sharp eyes and the luck to pocket a lump of dirty glass, yet which sought to deny to that individual the right to sell his windfall and realize his good luck on the grounds that he would therefore jeopardize the functioning of an entire (and foreign-based, and essentially South African-dominated) industry.

All parties concerned – government, and the diamond companies – were at pains to identify themselves as closely as possible with the people of Sierra Leone. Thus, DCSL appointed Mr A. J. Momoh, CBE, chairman of the Public Service Commission, to a directorship in June 1961; the board of SLST for its part secured the services of Dr Davidson Nicol, principal of the then university college of Sierra Leone, in August the same year. Also in August 1961 the Diamond Corporation was replaced as managing agent of GDO by a new company, Diamond Corporation West Africa Ltd (DICORWAF), seemingly on the supposition that a British company registered in London would be more acceptable to public opinion in Sierra Leone than the former South African company which was registered in Kimberley even though the lines of responsibility and control still went back to Johannesburg. Government itself, which had long and rather unfairly suffered under fire from opposition accusations of being unduly influenced by overseas commercial interests, was strengthened at independence by the appointment of a new minister of mines, Mr A. J. Demby; he came from Baoma chiefdom which happened to fall within one of the richest diamond areas in the country, and no doubt it was thought he could sway local opinion in favour of the coincidental interests of government and the diamond companies.

Despite these carefully laid plans, harmony was now wrecked by the dispute that broke out between CAST and DICORWAF concerning the prices offered for SLST diamonds which, the latter suspected and later confirmed, were too low. The negotiations for a new five-year contract that had started in 1960 were broken off in July 1961, and in August the same year CAST contracted to sell for two years to Harry Winston, the New York diamond merchant, at prices above those offered by DICORWAF. This was essentially a domestic brawl within the diamond-merchanting houses; CAST and the de Beers' interests behind the Diamond Corporation, although closely interlocked with each others' interests in southern Africa, pursued trade rivalry within diamond circles. One of the immediate results was to the benefit of Harry Winston, a comparative newcomer to the diamond world who had been shut out of diamond-buying circles by de Beers' practice of selling directly only to old-established merchants and who was anxious to break into the diamond world and also to disrupt de Beers.

Into this domestic brawl the government of Sierra Leone was bound to enter for, while it stood to gain extra revenue from its share of the higher prices offered by Winston, it feared a deterioration in world demand for diamonds if CAST in selling to Winston disregarded the quota restrictions upon which diamond values depended. It also sensed a real threat to Sierra Leonean diggers' receipts for the diamonds they would continue to sell through the GDO. The government accordingly passed an Act in January 1962 to ensure that all Sierra Leone diamonds were sold to the GDO, but such were SLST fears that the Diamond Corporation representation on the GDO would place it at de Beers' mercy that it locked up its production and refused to sell, to anybody, for sixteen months – until a compromise was reached in July 1962. This permitted SLST to sell at least half of its production to the Diamond Corporation, but the rest might go to any licensed purchaser – of whom Winston was one.

The main interest of this story lies in the revelation of an identity of fundamental interests not, as might first be supposed, between government and common people, but between government and international industrial interests – interests, moreover, easily detected as South African orientated. This exposed the government to very real risks – it found it impossible, for example, to prevent illicit digging and smuggling by undertaking adequate policing on behalf of the diamond companies, for this, whatever its long-term effects on the economy, could in the short-term appear only to benefit foreign diamond interests at the expense of Sierra Leone citizens. Again, its support for the Diamond Corporation, while quite explicable for economic reasons, could have attracted radical criticisms for offering aid to one of the bastions of South African hegemony. Much, in this context, clearly turns upon whom a given action is supposed to benefit. This fact explains the moves in December 1969 to nationalize 51 per cent of the country's mining companies, including SLST, by March 1970. The government already possessed *de facto* power over SLST, and the only advantage of *de jure* strength also lay in the moral strength its majority ownership of the companies would give it, in the eyes of ordinary people. It is clear that the greater the government's stake in foreign-based industry and commerce, the stronger the long-term position of that industry and commerce, for the greater is the effective power of government to regulate not just industry, but people in the interests of industry.

THE PETROLEUM INDUSTRY OF NIGERIA : The development of the oil production and export industry in Nigeria, which began in 1957 and has proceeded apace ever since, is worth scrutiny both because it represents the impact of this major international industry upon a developing country, and also because it provides a large new source of capital and of economic development for Nigeria.

The growth of oil production in Nigeria has been swift. In 1958[3] the value of total exports of traditional commodities was £N131.8 million, crude oil exports amounted to £N1 million and represented 0.8 per cent of total domestic exports. Corresponding figures for 1962 were £N147.3 million, £N16.7 million and 10.2 per cent; and those for 1966 were £N186.7 million, £N92.0 million and 33 per cent.

This growth has had profound economic effects. Firstly, the diversification of the economy meant that the agricultural and forestry element in the country's exports has fallen from 90 per cent in 1956 to 75 per cent in 1964. It has helped to level the fluctuations in export earnings, because of the stability in prices that is the hallmark of oligopoly in the integrated oil companies. It has resulted in a considerable saving on foreign exchange in the long-term, while in the short term increased spending on goods and services has had a considerable spin-off effect on the economy generally. It has also had the effect of increasing Nigeria's trading links with Europe other than the UK, which until 1965 took more than half Nigeria's production of crude oil; Federal Germany, for instance, which first imported oil from Nigeria in 1962, was by 1966 taking 15.7 per cent of Nigerian production.

No less resounding have been the political effects of the discovery of oil in marketable quantities in Nigeria, although they have not been as predictable and straightforward as might have been supposed. So far as internal politics are concerned, the great economic advantages of discovery of the product have been counter-balanced by the political difficulties of sharing the benefits among the inhabitants of the country as a whole. The oilfields themselves, situated in the south-central portion of the country and off-shore, have re-emphasized the superiority of the south and east as nationwide sources of energy in contrast to the huge areas of the north and west which are devoid of them, save for the Niger hydroelectric scheme, and suggest that unequal economic growth may result. So, too, the problems of sharing revenues equitably as between the regions of Nigeria and the federal government itself have been very great; the tendency has been to retain 50 per cent of royalties for the state wherein oil has been found, and slightly to reduce the federal government's portion of royalties in favour of other regions. Throughout the Biafran Civil War the question of oil revenues, both as to quantity and as to allocation, remained of prime importance; and the presence of the oil itself constituted a major factor in the declaration of secession.

Externally, as regards Nigerian relations with the rest of the continent of Africa, the development of the oil industry has not had the marked effects that one might expect. It has not significantly altered the balance of foreign policy, nor has it played a part in influencing the progress or otherwise of pan-Africanism or of an African Common Market. In 1966 Nigeria exported only 2 per cent of her oil production to the rest of Africa. In part this was because the African market for oil remains so small in world terms. It is also the case that other sources of oil, North Africa and the Persian Gulf for instance, are more convenient and cheaper sources of supply for North and West African states and for the East African countries. Government policy bars the sale of oil to the lucrative market of South Africa, and to refineries in Portuguese Mozambique. Pure market considerations also play a part; thus one should note that while Nigerian oil is mainly of the heavy and medium grades, which suit the British and other European markets for heating purposes, it is the lighter grades of North African oil that furnish the prime necessities of tropical Africa.

Other market considerations influence independently concluded sales agreements, such as that of Ghana at least one of whose main marketing companies, MOBIL, is closely involved as purchaser of Libyan oil, so that Ghana can take very little of the Nigerian oil. It is worth noting, however, that the Nigerian government's share of oil profits, as agreed with the oil companies, can be revised upwards if the shareholders of a company operating in Nigeria conclude a contract or recognize a law in another African country under which that country's share of profits is higher than Nigeria's; therefore, Nigerian petroleum receipts are tied closely to values obtained for oil from Libya and Algeria, which have in turn aligned themselves with the extremely forceful demands of the Arab Middle East producers.

To summarize, it is probably reasonable to concede that the development of the oil industry has conferred great benefits upon Nigeria. But it must also be stressed that it has brought great problems in its train, some of which are by no means permanently resolved. There is a tendency to seek simple spectacular remedies for the economic ills of African countries, tied as they are to the vagaries of mining and agricultural export earnings on world markets; remedies which would result in increased and far more regular levels of earnings. So far as one can generalize from the particular, the Nigerian experience with oil revenues would seem to reinforce the theories of those who argue that the abilities of African countries to absorb development funds, from whatever sources, and put them to productive use are as critical a factor in national prosperity as the actual level of those funds themselves. Political will is as vital an ingredient as economic planning.

THE COPPER OF ZAMBIA: The story of the British South Africa Company (BSACO) whose claims to the mineral rights of Zambia were judged illegally founded and which received a paltry £4 million compensation for them as a result, is a classic example of the lack of coordination of policies between the great mining houses, and also of the jealousies existing between them. It is clear, too, that the British government just before the time of Zambia's independence was basically unsympathetic to the BSACO's claims. A recent publication on the nationalization of the coper industry in Zambia[4] arives at some very interesting conclusions as to the roles played by the mining companies and by government itself.

Zambia is the world's third largest copper producer, after the USA and USSR, accounting for some 14 per cent of world production – about the same as Chile. The main operating companies were the Anglo-American Group (AA), run by Ernest Oppenheimer from Johannesburg, of de Beers' diamonds, and Rhodesia Selection Trust (RST) controlled by Chester Beatty, who also controlled CAST and SLST. In the early 1960s, in the heyday of the Central African Federation, the policies of RST were judged more liberal towards Africans; but by the end of the 1960s AA had adapted to the change in conditions quite well, in spite of their South African base, and it is thought that the AA managers were young men, not particularly swayed by the past, who had been sent to Lusaka with a mandate to cooperate with the new, African, regime.

Links between the mining houses have always been close, and the extent of their shareholding and representation on each others' boards of directors frequently gives rise to speculation that control of the houses is, in fact, centralized and that they work in harmony. The story of diamonds in Sierra Leone would not support this theory, and Faber and Potter (*op. cit.*) dispute the general thesis that a supra-national big business social system is developing. They demonstrate that the interlocking of AA and

RST through the board of Mufulira mine is not designed to avoid competition, but arose through historical accident as a member of AA held rights at a place where RST wanted to explore. Although there are various connections between the two groups, there is little co-ownership (apart from Mufulira) and cooperation seems to extend only to common and shared action in arenas of mutual interest. AA has minority representation on some boards of RST's subsidiaries, but they are firmly controlled by the RST main board on which AA has no representative. Controlling shareholders of the main units on the copperbelt are reasonably distinct in identity, also in nationality, and these units function separately; nevertheless, as Faber and Potter point out, to Africans all overseas dominated companies look similar and the similarity is reinforced when, under stress, the companies tend to react in a similar fashion to each other.

African groupings

It seems then that the idea that African nations are dominated by the large economic interests is untrue, or true only so far as all countries, even the largest and most developed, have to come to terms with them. The prime attribute of independence, which is domestic and external sovereignty, enables African countries to order and regulate economic concerns in their countries, even the largest; and the idea that these concerns present a united front to African countries is a mistaken one.

It could well be, however, that African countries could use this technique themselves to better their terms of trade and regulate produce and commodity prices in their favour. So far, progress along these lines has been notoriously slow, partly because the African countries themselves are at odds – about trade and commerce no less than about other matters – and also because to make a united front effective would require the cooperation also of underdeveloped countries elsewhere, such as those in South America, with which solidarity of relationship has not so far developed. Nevertheless, certain trade groupings do exist in Africa which might be extended into a wider alliance, to the benefit of all.

SOUTHERN AFRICAN CUSTOMS AGREEMENT: This was signed in

Pretoria in December 1969 by representatives of the governments of South Africa, Lesotho, Swaziland and Botswana; it replaced the old customs union of 1910 which linked the territories economically, and provided for each country's share of the common customs revenue to be allocated by a formula which would allow more of the customs proceeds to the credit of the three developing countries than was previously the case.

Many of the features of the old customs union were retained in the new agreement. Thus, the unit of currency, the Rand, was retained, together with the unity of the customs area as a whole; the free interchange of goods manufactured in the area was kept; payments were still to be made by South Africa to her three partners in the customs area; and the three partners would still conform to South African tariff laws and rates, and to such other regulatory arrangements as the Republic might promulgate.

In several important particulars, however, the new agreement offered the developing countries very much improved conditions over those of the 1910 union. In the first place, the actual amounts receivable were to be greater than in the past; and in the second place they would be distributed according to a formula that took account of each country's production and consumption of the goods concerned. Thus, an overall decline in goods imported or consumed in the area as a whole, brought about by South African quota regulations, need not result in a decline in customs receipts in any one country whose economic position was strong enough to continue high levels of consumption of the goods concerned. Again, special protection has been afforded to infant industries in Botswana, Lesotho and Swaziland, and the three states can specify industries of major importance to their economies so as to ensure that subsequent tariff changes shall not act to their detriment. Member states may not impose any quantitative restrictions or duties on goods produced in the customs area, nor may they impose inter-territorial duties nor transport tariffs on goods travelling between the member states. In general, all duties, tariffs and rebates must be identical, throughout the area; and provision is made for a far higher degree of consultation between South Africa and the three other member states on such matters as any amendment of customs rates, than was previously the case; although it is clear that South Africa still retains the controlling voice in any consultations.

Undoubtedly, the successful conclusion of this agreement has done much already to rectify imbalances and injustices within the South African customs orbit. It will result in larger payments to the three developing countries than in the past, and it will go far to put their infant industrial sections of their economies on their feet. Equally, there is no doubt that the agreement will immensely strengthen the customs area, dominated as it is by South Africa, and will remove a powerful source of friction as between the three countries and their powerful neighbour. It is of course possible that fresh, or renewed, strains will arise in the conduct of the Customs Agreement between South Africa and the three territories so closely bound up with her, just as it is likely that the agreement will provide the forum for the expression of differences between the three small countries themselves. When negotiating with South Africa in the late 1960's they achieved a common front, which may well be jeopardized in future years when the apportionment of customs revenues meets criticisms. But given South Africa's present will to secure détente with her black neighbours, it is probable that the political effects of the Customs Agreement will be either to split the three dependent territories from each other, or to set them collectively apart from their neighbours to the north, rather than to set them at odds either singly or acting together against South Africa.

THE EAST AFRICAN COMMUNITY : The basis for the unity of trade policies in East Africa was founded upon British colonial policy throughout the period of British rule, which always envisaged not only economic integration but centralized political and social institutions as well. Although this complete union was never achieved, the present day East African Community is founded upon the framework that was begun in colonial days. During and even after the attainment of independence by Tanganyika the idea of eventual federation was never forsaken, and the stated readiness of Nyerere to work actively toward regional cohesion was a major factor in the independence negotiations, and served at the time as one of the major arguments in favour of granting self-government to all three territories. These hopes, however, were never realized, and seem today to be even further from fulfilment than they were in 1961.

When independence was attained in 1961, the East African Common Services Organization (EACSO) became the central organization, but no provision was made to integrate either economic planning or taxation and monetary policies in the three countries. The resultant trading imbalances were adjusted by the Kampala Agreement of 1964, which attempted to secure the relocation of certain industries and sought to protect infant industries in Uganda and Tanganyika from competition from Kenya, and also recommended the creation of a distributable pool of revenue among the three countries.

This formula did in fact ease some of Tanganyika's and Uganda's fiscal problems, but the industrial and trading imbalance in favour of Kenya that was so marked a result of colonial days persisted. In general the agreement was poorly implemented, and by 1965 EACSO seemed to be in danger of breaking up altogether. In that year Kenya's exports of manufactured goods to Uganda and Tanzania amounted to four times the value of her imports from the two countries, who were clearly suffering from an almost intractable internal balance of payments problem. The industrial licensing system set up did not succeed in diverting any substantial amount of industry from Nairobi, mainly because the ultimate power of decision as to the location of new industry lay not with the East African Community but with the projected investors who were, naturally, concerned to place capital as advantageously as possible. Overall plans for the direction of industry and for its relocation were not proceeded with, and in practice Kenya continued to secure the majority of new investment while enjoying the fruits of the development of past years.

By 1965 also, very considerable political differences of opinion had arisen between the respective governments of the East African countries. The 1961 sentiment in favour of federation had persisted through 1963, and in June of that year the three governments had agreed to establish federation by the end of the year, calling upon the British government to relinquish all control over Kenya so as to ensure the scheme was implemented. Yet by May 1964 pro-federation pressures were no longer discernible. According to the author of a work on the East African Community[5] the chief impediment lay with Uganda, which objected to the surrender of sovereignty that would be involved in true federation and to the disappearance of its authority over such matters as citizenship and foreign affairs. Uganda also cited the charter of the OAU and in particular the clause concerning the moment when a pan-African, continental government could assume the full direction of African affairs untrammelled by any previous, partial federations; and claimed that her own still federal constitution would compel her constituent states to enter East African Federation as independent units. Uganda's claims saved the convictions of Kenya and Tanganyika from being put to the test, and so during 1964 East African gestures towards Federation were confined to a series of moves to strengthen the structure of EACSO.

Tanzania and Uganda now began to apply quotas to their imports from Kenya in an attempt to right their balance of payments problems, and this action coupled with continuing trade imbalances resulted in the setting up of a commission of enquiry headed by the Danish Professor Kjeld Philip (a former minister of trade and finance), whose report became the basis for the Treaty for East African Economic Cooperation that came into effect in December 1967.

Many of the old organs and procedures of EACSO were retained by the new Community, but one major innovation was the imposition of a transfer tax, by which those members of the East African common market with an overall deficit on their intra-Market trade (i.e. Uganda and Tanzania) can impose a tax on their imports from those countries with which they are in deficit (i.e. in the main, Kenya).

While the operations of this transfer tax did much to counterbalance the effects of inter-state trade (details of which are given in the accompanying table), certain difficulties remained. A major one lay in the fact that customs duties form an important part of revenue sources in countries where income and other taxes are bound to produce little revenue, so the pressures to introduce transfer tax on all possible categories of imported goods are very great. The tax itself is supposed to be phased out by 1982, with no arrangements for its successor; and while it undoubtedly protects local industry it does little to stimulate new industrial investment.

The institutional framework of the Community organization should also be considered. The Secretariat was lodged in Arusha,

Table 13

Inter-State Trade in the East African Community (£000s)

KENYA

Countries	Imports				Exports			
	1966	1967	1968	1969	1966	1967	1968	1969
Tanzania*	3,806	3,288	3,692	4,018	13,282	11,382	13,069	12,848
Uganda	7,317	10,165	8,650	7,803	15,619	14,796	13,265	15,949
TOTAL	11,123	13,453	12,342	11,821	28,901	26,178	26,334	28,797

TANZANIA*

	Imports				Exports			
	1966	1967	1968	1969	1966	1967	1968	1969
Kenya	13,282	11,382	13,069	12,848	3,806	3,288	3,692	4,018
Uganda	3,120	2,432	2,029	1,713	842	750	855	1,177
TOTAL	16,402	13,814	15,098	14,561	4,648	4,038	4,547	5,195

UGANDA

	Imports				Exports			
	1966	1967	1968	1969	1966	1967	1968	1969
Kenya	15,619	14,796	13,265	15,949	7,317	10,165	8,650	7,803
Tanzania*	842	750	855	1,177	3,120	2,432	2,029	1,713
TOTAL	16,461	15,546	14,120	17,126	10,437	12,597	10,679	9,516

* excluding Zanzibar up to 1967

Source: *Africa South of the Sahara*, Europa Publications Ltd, London, 1971.

Tanzania, in deference to claims that development had hitherto favoured Nairobi over other centres of population in East Africa. The accompanying diagram outlines the structure of the organization itself. The three Community ministers are effectively ministers-without-portfolio at home, one from each of the three countries and without cabinet responsibilities – supposedly so as to enable them to function without undue pressures from their own governments. They are the direct links between the Community and their own presidents, however, and are bound to remain in close relationship with members of their own home governments because on all the five councils of the Community they all serve, together with either one or three other members of the cabinet of each of the three countries. Community ministers are each responsible to the Legislative Assembly for the conduct of one of the three fields into which council activity is directed, *viz* common market and economic affairs, communications and research, and finance and administration. The councils themselves are consultative and advisory in character only; they have no binding powers at all. Nor, for that matter, has the Legislative Assembly itself, whose enactments require the assent of the Authority before they become Community law; as this consent must be unanimous, it is clear that each of the three East African heads of state wields a power of veto over Community legislation.

The Community, then, does not possess sovereign powers; it is more of a regulatory and administering agency, dependent for its survival upon the goodwill of the territorial governments. Yet it is more than just that. It is the focus for the administration of a wide range of common services, and also provides a skeletal organization for possible expansion into a far more dynamic, possibly sovereign, body. It is the symbol if nothing else of the economic unity of the area and of a market of 32 million people; it helps to attract the capital and skills and sources of development aid that the whole area needs. It has several times been the staging area for dissenting opinion, perhaps most notably in 1971 when, following the rise to power of General Amin in Uganda, the government of Tanzania refused to recognize the new military government's nominations to Community posts. This dispute would have taken place anyway, even had the Community not existed; and it would be better for it to be fought out

Table 14
The East African Community

THE AUTHORITY
3 Presidents

LEGISLATIVE ASSEMBLY

3 Community ministers
3 Deputy ministers
27 Appointed members
Chairman of assembly
Secretary-general
Counsel to community

Community Services Orgs.

Industrial Council

Development Bank

Central Secretariat

5 Councils

Common Market
Communications
Ec. Consultative
and Planning
Finance
Research and Social

4 Statutory Corpns.

Posts and Tele-
communications
Railways
Harbours
Airways

3 Tribunals

Court of Appeal
Common Market
Industrial Court

in Arusha among the tight-lipped civil servants than publicly and resoundingly in Dar-es-Salaam, or in military terms on the Tanzania/Uganda border as in the latter part of 1972. Within the framework of the Community there still exist powerful pressures towards compromise. It may inspire dissension, but it also provides the forum for agreement. This fact may well be one of the most powerful justifications for its continued survival.

THE EUROPEAN COMMON MARKET : Because of the fragility of the bonds internal to the African continent that have so far been forged to keep the African states together, it may well turn out that it is through their association with the EEC that African countries are enabled to present a common front to the rest of the world. The recent history of the association of the EEC with the ex-British African countries indicates a growing relationship based on self-interest, and has largely overtaken the intense antagonism felt in the earlier 1960s towards the idea of the EEC, reliance upon which, it was felt by ex-British states (very much contrary to the views held by most of the ex-French states), indicated the perpetuation of neocolonialism.

Opposition to African membership or association with the EEC was led by Nkrumah's Ghana, and the first of the West African countries to show solid interest in association with the EEC was Nigeria, partly, no doubt, to demonstrate her independence and dislike of Ghanaian policies. The Yaoundé Agreement in July 1963 between the eighteen former French African and Malagasy states and the six European members of the EEC, which became operative in June 1964 and conferred associate membership of the Community for five years, was not wholly agreeable to Nigeria which felt that such an agreement compromised her politically non-aligned stance and would link her in world eyes with Britain, NATO and the American alliance; nevertheless, she requested the opening of negotiations with the Community in June 1964. In October the same year the Common Market Council of Ministers in Brussels signed yet another mandate for opening discussions on associated status, this time submitted on behalf of the three East African countries of Kenya, Uganda and Tanzania. By January 1965 Zambia was expressing interest.

The common thread that ran through all the ensuing negotiations was the need for some sort of purely trading link with the

EEC without the implications of political involvement. By March 1965 the East African countries had been offered associate status on terms similar to those granted to the ex-French Yaoundé countries, with the exception that quotas were set upon coffee and clove exports to the EEC – no doubt in deference to the interests of the ex-French territories. Nigeria experienced more difficulty, her spokesmen complaining in 1965 that because her trade was split evenly between the EEC, Great Britain and the rest of the world, the number of concessions she could make to Europe without damaging her other economic interests was limited. There is no doubt that at this time Nigeria's negotiating position was hampered, both because of Anglo-French strains and the breakdown of the British application to join the Common Market and also because Nigeria had broken off diplomatic relations with France in 1961, following French atom bomb tests in the Sahara.

The final round of negotiations between Nigeria and the EEC was concluded in July 1965. It was agreed that the EEC would offer Nigerian exports, with the exception of four commodities, the same position as those occupied by the eighteen Yaoundé states. Upon cocoa, plywood, groundnuts and palm products, however, the Community proposed to impose quotas, which would be enlarged by 3 per cent each year until the agreement ended in 1969. In return, Nigeria agreed to give the Community a tariff preference of 2 per cent on a list of twenty-six imported products. In addition it was agreed that the EEC would raise its import quotas by 6 per cent a year if Nigeria would agree to increase its tariff preferential margins for EEC goods by 5 per cent. In addition, Nigeria was not to discriminate against goods from the Six; and was to accord most favoured nation treatment to those countries of the EEC that did not already receive it.

To these terms the UK was opposed, in part because they constituted in her view, a violation of GATT. In addition, Britain claimed, Nigeria should not be required to establish a series of preferential tariffs, because this would constitute a retrograde step away from her previous policy of maintaining an open door trade policy. Again, although Britain herself allowed preferences to goods entering Britain from underdeveloped countries, she did not in turn always demand reciprocal preferences from developing countries – which was what France, in effect, was doing, by implication unethically. It seems that British protests over the

EEC terms accorded to Nigeria in 1965 stemmed from the UK's domestic and international needs to make a rejoinder to the French success in denying membership of the Common Market to Britain. It is also the case that Britain was concerned to demonstrate her broad support for Nigeria, regarded as the 'strong man' of Africa and the best hope, in 1965, of countering Ghanaian intransigence. Whether these objections made much difference to the scope of the Nigerian agreement when it was finally concluded, is doubtful; what is most interesting about the history of these negotiations is the extent to which Nigerian trading interests became the subject of renewed great power bickerings. It may be that the territorial scramble for Africa in the late nineteenth century has been overtaken by the present-day trading scramble. At stake, as before, are European powers' vested interests; only the stage has changed, from Africa to Europe.

Measures to lessen dependence

As well as attempting to lessen their economic vulnerability by forming trade groupings among themselves or by participating in overseas trade alliances, African countries have embarked upon a series of measures designed to lead towards growing self-sufficiency in as many areas of their economies as possible. Although they may appear haphazard as they are reported and unpredictable in their efforts, these measures can in fact be interpreted as coherent programmes in two main fields. One of them is in the field of legislation to control industry; the other is concerned with the regulation of people, and in particular people whose origins are alien to the areas in which they are now to be found.

LEGISLATION FOR INDUSTRY: Industry over the major part of the African continent is now subject to a bewildering variety of controls, of a nature that is rarely encountered in the USA but is more familiar in the more regulated industrial society of Great Britain. Even before a factory goes up or a trading organization is founded, the would-be enterprise has to submit to rigorous government direction of almost every aspect of its functioning. Such matters as the actual location of a factory, the numbers and makeup of those it will employ, the origins of raw materials and/ or readymade components and the destination of the finished product are the subject of much horsetrading between government and industrialist. It is usual, too, to find restrictions placed upon the granting of bank credits; banks may be forbidden to lend money to non-citizens, so that any person or organization wishing to set up is forced to do so by the actual importation of cash from abroad. On the other hand, credit is often available from local banks or other lending agencies to citizens, on somewhat easier terms than can be obtained elsewhere.

Even after business is established, governments go to great lengths to regulate its progress or to change the regulations already set up. By such means as ensuring local participation in the equity of a company, local membership of boards of directors or, perhaps, by stipulating that the local population at large shall enjoy amenities such as hospitals and schools originally designed only for employees, governments spread the benefits of big business as widely as possible – or bring indirect pressure on business itself to achieve this. Restrictions upon the types of goods that may be imported, insistence upon a large local content in goods assembled locally, and a general readiness to alter the circumstances by which profits may be remitted overseas are all ways in which African countries attempt to tip the balance in favour of their own budgets and developmental interests.

Perhaps the best known tool of governments is nationalization, either wholly or in part, of the largest businesses, or those which appear to be the most lucrative, or those active in fields where Africans seem best suited to take over. Typically, a 51 per cent share in the ownership of mining, banking, insurance or allied financial businesses is taken over by governments although the amount of the take-over may be varied, as is the means by which it is financed. The growing tendency is for the take-over of businesses to be financed not by cash payment but out of future profits; the advantages of this method to governments with ailing economies are obvious, as are its disadvantages to the original owners or shareholders in the business concerned. Another sector of the economy which African governments are prone to enter is the import/export business, in particular by setting up government corporations or trading organizations at first in competition with the individuals or companies already engaged in this business, later ousting them completely.

The motives of governments in carrying out these policies are complex, and it is useless to expect them to be confined purely to balance sheet considerations. Economically it is not always in the best interests of the African countries to manufacture locally, although it may well be politically to their advantage to do so. It is often the case, for instance, that while local interests are satisfied by an increase in numbers of people employed, wages paid and ancillary services provided, wider interests are compromised by the high cost of the articles thus produced – especially when compared with the notional cost, less import duty, of similar goods imported from abroad. Efforts are always made to justify governmental action on financial grounds and here the short-term and the long-term view of what constitutes the right course of action by no means coincide. In some countries, such as Tanzania, the justification sought is the achievement of true African socialism which *ipso facto* rules out any privileged classes occupying niches in the economy; it is better for all people to share equally the burdens of poverty than that some should profit at the expense of others. In other cases, the association of indigenous government with the ownership of an industry or a mining complex or with the marketing of primary produce can enable unpopular but necessary measures to be taken – as when the Ghanaian government undertook drastic measures to curb the spread of swollen shoot disease among the cocoa crop – which could not be enforced by a colonial government, or by expatriate business interests, without causing grave unrest.

THE CONTROL OF PEOPLES : Other motives of governments are more purely political, in that to bow to popular demand or to seek to distract people from their legitimate grievances by inviting attention to other matters are methods adopted by all governments at some time to secure their political support. Other chapters of this book have glanced at some aspects of what is called Africanization; that is, the attempts of governments to ensure that Africans hold the highest positions in the civil service and the army, predominate in legal and academic life and the other professions, and occupy the major portion of cultivable land. In South Africa the entire apparatus of *apartheid* has grown up so as to regulate every aspect of the lives of the black majority; where they live, where they are employed, whether they are employed at all or despatched to the Bantustans, their rights to education, training and association are all controlled in the interests of ensuring the privileged position of the whites at the top of the social pyramid. Both Africanization and *apartheid* can only operate to the detriment of the minority of voters, or those with no votes at all, who are unable to influence those in control of the government.

This dogmatically racial approach to the control of peoples is usually disguised in black-controlled Africa where, indeed, many Africans are probably genuine when they deny that they want to rid themselves of the presence or effective functioning of either the Asians, or the Europeans, on purely racial grounds. The difficulty is a complex one in the countries of East and Central Africa where, for instance, Kenya's population of slightly over 9 million included some 49,000 Europeans and 183,000 Asians and Uganda's 6.8 million included, until General Amin's moves in the latter part of 1972 to evict the Asians, some 11,000 Europeans and 77,400 Asians. Numerically these alien peoples, whether or not they hold citizenship of the country in which they live, are not large and they form but a small proportion of the total population; they do, however, occupy a disproportionately large sector of the economy. On the whole, the Europeans pose fewer problems to African governments because they have dwindled in numbers since independence and because they are generally concentrated in areas and fields of activity that are not in direct competition with African aspirations (always excepting farming, which is dealt with elsewhere in this book). In addition, colonial rule devolved upon Africans with good grace, so that black-white relationships have remained relaxed.

The position of the Asians has been far less fortunate. Even in colonial days they were the butt of both black and white, who accused them of undue profiteering at the expense of the Africans. Since independence they have lacked the voice of a strong overseas government to speak for them, and their numbers, far from lessening, have appeared to increase – probably because of their dominance of the retail and wholesale trades, which ensures that the Africans are very much aware of their presence while remaining isolated from them socially. Their cohesion and strong sense of family and religious ties, coupled with their undoubted business acumen and ability to outperform both white and black business concerns, likewise serves to alienate them from the mass of the population. Given the option at independence, in most cases, of assuming the citizenship of the country in which they found themselves or of retaining their (sometimes dubious) claims to Indian or Pakistani or British citizenship, many of the Asians temporized – understandably enough perhaps, in view of the insecurity and feeling of impermanence which even then they experienced. Lacking the secure 'home base' of the white population yet fearing, with good reason, to trust themselves wholly to the goodwill of future African governments, they attempted to hedge their bets, building up family ties and nesteggs of cash and property wherever they could outside Africa and attempting to prolong the options they received to choose local or British citizenship.

The problem of the Asians was thrown into particular relief by the actions of General Amin's regime in Uganda. It was quite true that the vast majority of wholesale and retail trade was conducted by the Asians, and that the country's major industrial enterprises – textiles, and sugar refining – were controlled by Asians; and it is also the case that considerable sums of money were 'bled' out of the country to foreign bank accounts. Whether these factors were the causes or the results of Asian insecurity is now irrelevant. What was relevant was the situation of Uganda after the departure of the Asians. There is no doubt that many Uganda Africans felt their future would be brighter with the elimination of Asian competition in trade; equally there is no doubt that many Uganda Africans resented the loss of jobs in hitherto Asian businesses.

What happened to the Asians in Uganda will almost certainly happen to the Asians elsewhere in black-controlled Africa; it may also happen to the Europeans in the countries of former European settlement, although the process may be more gradual because the political strains on African governments are less acute – as well as being in part taken up by measures to nationalize foreign-owned businesses. Most observers feel that the assumption of local citizenship by Europeans or Asians will only delay, not prevent, the process of Africanization of the jobs carried on by these 'paper citizens', as they have become known. The complexity of controls over business life, the permits needed to trade, to operate a shop, to run a tourist business, to carry on any form of activity whatsoever, whether paid or unpaid – all these serve to deter expatriate business activity and may well be the fore-runners of more studied measures to block non-indigenous enter-prise. It should be noted that reports of Amin's measures against Asians indicated that even those who obtained Uganda citizen-ship were not spared; and, despite official denials, the non-indigenous communities elsewhere in Africa generally feel that in time the same treatment will be meted out to them.

It is tempting to see these problems purely in racial terms, because of the publicity given to black governments' measures against the brown and white minorities in their midst and to the governments in southern Africa in their efforts to contain the non-white majorities in their countries. It is quite true that in conditions of extreme tension, social and political cohesion tends to take place along racial lines. It is equally true that the same tensions can be observed at work where there are no obviously racial antagonisms; the Nigerian Civil War and the widespread suspicion of the Ibo people which sparked off the massacres of the Ibos living in the north is evidence of this.

Nor is the problem confined to societies where unbalanced or militaristic men hold supreme power, as the example of Ghana under Dr K. A. Busia in 1969 shows. Dr Busia was appointed by the colonial government to the post of assistant district commis-sioner as early as 1942; Oxford graduate, scholar, politician (leader after 1951 of the Ghana Congress Party, which opposed, without success, Nkrumah's CPP), leader of the Opposition to the CPP in Legislative Assembly days before independence, he be-came prime minister in 1969 when civilian government was re-stored. The alien population of the country was then estimated at no less than 2 million out of the 6.7 million in the country as a whole, and over half of them were said to be Nigerians. Govern-ment faced heavy unemployment, a constricted economy, infla-tion and a huge shortage of foreign exchange; smuggling was rife, and it was claimed that 80 per cent of all prisoners were alien. This conjunction of economic pressures and unsubstan-tiated rumour pressurized government into action. It was decided to enforce the 1963 Aliens Act, as amended in 1968, which re-quired a person claiming Ghanaian citizenship to have at least one parent born in Ghana. In July 1969 all embassies in Ghana were requested to register their citizens in Ghana; it appears that not all embassies heeded this request, and in December the Ghanaian government accordingly gave all aliens a fortnight in which to get registered, or leave the country. An enormous upheaval followed, during which it is estimated 35,000 people returned to Niger, 100,000 to Togo, 50 to 100,000 to Upper Volta and untold thousands to the Ivory Coast. The worst affected were the Nigerians, who were nearly ubiquitous throughout Ghana and in some cases occupied whole villages. It seems that the Ghana government policy was intended to be aimed at the unemployed and criminal elements, and also at certain categories of traders; its ultimate results are not clear, but confronted by numerous protests from neighbouring and nearby countries and by the existence of hordes of homeless refugees making their way to the frontiers it does not appear that Ghana took her policy as far as did General Amin, but relented. It is, nevertheless, interesting to note that although the episode did not, for obvious reasons, rate as a major item of world news, it was born out of the same kind of economic pressures calling for political action, and resulted in action similar to that afterwards carried out in Uganda.

9 Foreign Affairs

The chapter that in works dealing with other countries or parts of the world might be entitled 'foreign policy' has in this book to be called 'foreign affairs'. The reason is partly that we have to deal with a number of very different countries whose aims differ sometimes slightly, sometimes very radically from each other; but mainly because the essential ingredient of a coherent foreign policy, that is continuity of aim, circumstance and the means for carrying it out, are in all cases (except that of South Africa), almost totally lacking. Forms of government as well as of the personnel comprising them change with great rapidity and, according to some observers as well as some of the participants, little rationale. The conduct of foreign affairs, like that of much of the rest of government, is too frequently the province of one man, the head of state, whose preoccupations amid the urgencies of one-party, one-person rule must accordingly be many and fleeting.

It could of course be argued that precisely this factor makes for unity of purpose in home and foreign affairs, and makes the pursuit of a planned foreign policy more easy to attain. Unfortunately this does not seem to be the case in reality because of the difficulties of follow-up and of ensuring that ambassadors in places as far apart as Peking, Moscow, London, Paris and at the UN in New York are properly instructed and that their reports are properly evaluated at home. There are, too, the weaknesses in procedure and administration and the paucity of trained diplomatic staff that render an informed policy, let alone a consistent one or one that really fulfils the aims of a head of state, almost impossible of achievement.

All this does not mean, however, that we cannot discern any sort of common aims among the majority of the states with whose foreign policy we are now concerned. Chief among these, perhaps, is the desire to restore the dignity and standing of black people everywhere in the world; but it is unfortunate that the unifying force to which the strength of this desire might give rise is largely dissipated by the varying means advocated to achieve it, so that the one outstanding issue upon which the black African states might unite to secure success is precisely the one which leads to much dissension among them. Another major aim of the African states is to maximize the economic aid they receive from the richer countries of the world; and this aim again tends to force them apart from each other as they compete for what funds are made available.

Intertwined with this economic aim is the political aim to preserve so far as possible the stance of non-alignment with the great power blocs. This stems partly from a genuine distaste for the great power politics that they have seen practised with such humiliating results in their own continent, partly from fear of becoming entangled in unwelcome and uncharted alliances, and partly because by so doing they have to bear with taunts that they are neocolonialist. They are motivated also by the wish to increase the sources of aid and support available to them, as well as to channel them in certain desired directions; and this in turn leads to efforts, on the whole unsuccessful, to play one power bloc off against another. But non-alignment brings other dilemmas. To what extent any country whose past history has embedded it within the western capitalist system can be considered non-aligned is difficult to decide. Some, such as Nigeria, have taken the view that they could continue a basically pro-western affiliation, with non-alignment taking the form of a few tentative moves toward contact of various types with countries belonging to the western bloc. Other countries, of which Tanzania has been perhaps the chief exemplar, have claimed that the western heritage of colonization has needed redress by a positive move towards the eastern bloc; to her, non-alignment has meant not the preservation of the ante-independence *status quo*, but the active pursuit of eastern bloc sources of aid to counterbalance the colonial past.

Other aims pursued by the African states in the course of their conduct of foreign affairs are more prosaic. As every sovereign country must be, they are concerned to maintain their external boundaries; and as mentioned elsewhere in this book, on the whole these remain inviolate because once one is threatened, the validity of them all must be doubted. They seek to reduce their dependence on any one power by increasing contacts with others, and also they wish, as it were, to 'stand larger' in the world; to wield real influence, even if power eludes them, in local or regional counsels and at the United Nations. And because power does elude them, in the sense that national armies are small, ill-disciplined and too prone to enter the lists of local civilian affairs, and a truly pan-Africanist army and political leadership is lacking, they are forced to turn to other means of exerting influence to achieve their aims. They are, thus, driven increasingly to act in a broader context than the purely national; to attempt to manipulate, for example, the Commonwealth, to forge some form of tenuous continental or racial unity, and to maximize the African voice at the UN. None of this is achieved without sacrifice, and the efficacy of such efforts has increasingly become open to doubt.

This gadfly diplomacy, as it is sometimes called when it scores some minor success, say, in discomforting South African participation in the Olympic Games, will be discussed later. For the time being we will consider, first, some of the motives and policies that underlay foreign interest in Africa. We will then turn to the foreign affairs conducted first by Ghana and then by Nigeria during the late 1950s and early 1960s, the period when a united African voice could, perhaps, have emerged with a positive programme on to the world stage; then we will turn to the other prospects that have arisen in the latter half of the decade of the 1960s, from the affairs of South Africa and of the Arab states in the north of the continent, for the evolution of some form of continental unity of action, if not of structure.

The view from outside

It is trite but necessary to stress that the degree of foreign relationships between countries depend upon both, or all, parties concerned and not just one; so that in considering African foreign relations one must pay due regard to the motives of those with whom they sought or maintained contact.

Independence brought about a great increase in the dealings of the African countries with the rest of the world, partly because Britain, in relinquishing her hold, both left open opportunities for other relationships and also removed some of the obstacles she had placed in their way (Egypt, with which Britain had severed diplomatic relations following the Suez venture and which was not, in consequence, one of the countries invited to the independence celebrations in Accra in 1957, is a case in point). The ending of the colonial era also widened and increased opportunities for foreign relationships, as distinct merely from shifting them from Britain to other of the great, and not so great, powers. Hence the end of the 1950s saw growing interest in Africa from the USA, the USSR, China, and others of the eastern bloc as well as those countries such as Canada, France and Federal Germany whose political affiliations were not such as to agitate unduly those in the western capitals who feared the continuance of an Africa painted red on the map.

United States interest in Africa remained minimal until Ghanaian independence was clearly imminent. Then, in 1956, a semi-autonomous Office of African Affairs was set up, consisting of two branches, one for North Africa and the other for Africa south of the Sahara, headed by a deputy assistant secretary of state for African affairs. In 1958 Congress authorized a separate Bureau of African Affairs with its own assistant secretary of state; and in 1961 the Kennedy administration appointed G. Mennen Williams as assistant secretary. Diplomatic representation increased in the African capitals, and so, for a while, did the sums allocated to Africa as part of the US foreign aid programme. In the four years 1953–7, under the Mutual Security Act, loans and grants came to $120.3 million; in 1958 alone, they totalled $82.4 million; in 1960, $169.7 million; and in 1962, $315.0 million.[1] The motives for US involvement in Africa at all are by no means urgent. It is the view of one of the foremost American writers on US policy in Africa that the US vented its anti-colonial spleen on Britain's conduct in India and the Far East generally,[2] and that her willingness to be involved in Africa stemmed more from the vestiges of the Dulles cold-war era in wishing to deny the area to overwhelming communist influence. There was, too, a feeling in the early days of independence that the interests of the African countries and of the USA itself were less in conflict than later proved the case. At all events, for a while the US interest waxed, then from 1962 waned as the consciousness grew that the US, while conducting a moderate amount of trade with Africa, was by no means dependent upon the continent for raw materials, and that growing economic perils coupled with difficulties nearer home in Central and South America as well as in East Asia imposed a different set of national priorities upon Washington.

Communist interest in the African continent began with the realization, in 1956 after the start of the Khruschev era, that the apparent failure of colonialism in Africa opened up possibilities for the substitution of communism; in certain circumstances, it was felt, the advent of African nationalism need not be antagonistic to the establishment of communist regimes, given time and the requisite softening-up processes. In the Soviet Union itself, African studies received a tremendous fillip when in 1957 academic work was coordinated under government supervision; the Academy of Sciences was an active participant, money and research staffs were made available, and by the end of 1959 an Africa Institute had been set up in Moscow. Diplomatic efforts included the prompt recognition of new states, and wherever possible sizable diplomatic and consular staffs were despatched to embassies in the new countries. At the end of 1958 the Foreign Ministry gained an African Department, and personal visits, including those by Khruschev himself, the despatch and welcoming of delegations, and the encouragement of student and casual visitors, became an important means of furthering the communist cause. Nevertheless, in spite of all this, there were several setbacks. As early as 1963, instances of discrimination against Africans in Moscow became widely known, and communist attempts to infiltrate African political and trade union circles met with little success. No doubt this was in part due to the inherent difficulties in trying to reconcile Marxist principles with tribal customs; but the jealousies of African governments in retaining power, so hardly and recently won, in their own hands, coupled with the fact that trade union movements almost without exception posed a threat to the political order even when western orientated, let alone when owing allegiance to the communist order, meant that communist inspired influence was deeply mistrusted by African governments.[3]

The early 1960s exposed other difficulties in the way of communist domination of the African continent. Little trade or aid between Russia and Africa took place until 1960, when the Russian trade imbalance (in that she purchased produce from

Africa) was righted by the export of heavy capital goods in return. Aid was closely connected with trade, and it was a frequent practice to negotiate trade, aid and technical cooperation agreements at the same time. Usually aid was in the form of credits, repayable at $2\frac{1}{2}$ per cent over twelve years in local goods or services. Outright grants of money were rare, but took place occasionally for such things as radio stations or hospitals. In general the theory was that aid credits were to develop significant sectors of African economies, but it is sometimes argued that Russian sponsored projects were not as carefully costed or evaluated as the American ones so that actual benefits from them did not conform with expectations. Ghana had signed two sets of trade and aid agreements with Moscow, in August 1960 and November 1961, and Nigerian contact with Moscow began in June 1961 when the mission led by the Nigerian minister of finance was investigating the market for Nigerian produce, in return for which imports of Russian capital goods would take place.

Meanwhile, considerable competition was being experienced from the rest of the communist bloc; for so long compelled to act as suppliers for the Russian market, from which in return they could obtain little in the way of consumer goods and nothing in the form of foreign currency, Czechoslovakia, Poland, the German Democratic Republic, Hungary, Bulgaria and Roumania all had their own legitimate economic reasons for wishing to build up trade with the African continent. In fact, despite their efforts, the main bulk of their overseas trade was concentrated on South America rather than Africa; but the notion that the communist trade, aid and diplomatic onslaught on the African countries in the 1950s and 1960s was either purposely concerted, or motivated purely by political considerations, is wrongly held. An element of considerable competition arose, both as between the satellites themselves, and between the satellites and the USSR.

This competition has been overshadowed by the developing relationship between the USSR and China, and the significance it has borne for African development. It had been the April 1955 Bandung Conference of Afro-Asian states that first brought China into contact with the Africans, and shut the Russians out as not being Asian; and it is probable that this factor of colour, of the non-whiteness of the Chinese and, indeed, the treatment of those of Chinese extraction by the South African authorities, that first forged the elements of Sino-African friendship. The Chinese approach was simple and singlehearted, and took the form of a militantly anti-imperialist backing for the nationalist movements. It early supported the radical FLN of Algeria, and when in the autumn of 1959 Khrushchev's visit to the US and the general detente led China to stigmatize Russia as a betrayer of the revolutionary cause, she also accused Russia of faltering in the anti-colonialist cause. Rivalry developed between the USSR and China in Kenya, where intrigue over military aid and a school for political affairs took place, and with the commitment to build the Tan-Zam railway, so as to lessen the dependence of Zambia upon Rhodesia and other colonialist entities for the import and export of essential goods, the presence of Chinese planners and technicians in Africa was secured. Those who have witnessed the extent of the effort of the Chinese on the railway, their dedication and their discipline and apparent disregard of many of the capitalist procedures and taboos that have made comparable western projects so expensive and irrelevant to current African needs, may feel that Chinese attitudes of self-help and their regard for the needs of society offer much to Africa today.

Growing disunity

In the face of these conflicting approaches from outside, the African countries' responses have, since the early days of independence, tended to be conducted on a pragmatic basis; that is, so far from pursuing their own initiatives in foreign affairs, they have had to frame their actions and declarations in accordance with events that have been out of their control and beyond their power to influence. In the early days it was different, as the experiences of Ghana and Nigeria demonstrate. These countries are interesting to us partly because Ghana was the first African country to gain independence, which she entered with sizable foreign exchange reserves and, perhaps more important, much goodwill from the rest of the world; and because Nigeria, constitutionally only three years behind, was incomparably the largest in terms of population and the richest in resources of all the ex-British states. If any of these black African countries could have exerted the influence that can occasionally make up for lack of power to command a respectful hearing and achieve some if not all of aims sought, it should have been either or both of these two countries. Yet they were to fail; and their successors in gaining independence fared no better.

The options open to Nkrumah in 1957, for example, were wide, and they contrasted oddly with the conventionally held view outside Ghana that, in fact, little change need be expected in attitudes in Accra. Indeed, for quite a while Ghanaian foreign affairs pursued a familiar path, aided no doubt by the fact that many British remained as governmental advisers and in the top civil service posts, that the military command remained in British hands and, for economic as well as personal reasons, Nkrumah's closest adviser at the time was the Australian, Sir Robert Jackson, whose brief continued to be to find money, if not from Britain then from America, to construct the Volta Dam and the accompanying aluminium smelter. Ghanaian behaviour at the Commonwealth Conference of 1957 was nothing if not self-effacing, and the actual growth of Ghanaian diplomatic contacts with non-western countries did not take place for two to three years after independence – and then tended toward closer relationships with other African countries rather than with those of the eastern bloc. Even the first conference of independent African states, held in Accra in 1958, had none of the divisiveness that arose when its successor meeting was held in Addis Ababa in 1960; in 1958, for instance, little was heard of Nkrumah's later insistence on a pan-African political union, and because Nigeria was not yet independent and therefore did not attend the meeting, the jealousy that later bedevilled relations between and within the two countries was not yet obvious.

Nevertheless the seeds of trouble were there. Ghana's pursuit of African unity and the rapid steps taken towards personal and idiosyncratic rule by Nkrumah (apparently influenced by the example of Tubman's Liberia), earned her not only the suspicion of the western powers whose approach to law and order deplored the tyrannical devices of government that had been introduced in Ghana. 1960 was also the year that the Commonwealth Conference, in the wake of the Sharpeville shootings, first found itself preoccupied with African affairs; 1960 was also the year of the Second Pan-Africanist Conference of Addis Ababa, where occurred the fundamental fission between the radicals and the moderates of the African states which still handicaps the successor Organization of African Unity (OAU).

1960 was, finally, the year when Nigeria became independent and sought her rightful place in African, as well as world, affairs; and from the beginning she opposed many of the ideals which Nkrumah by that time was voicing. Nigeria's own voice in foreign affairs was, from the first, a moderate one, envisaging a continuing pro-British, pro-Commonwealth and pro-western stance even if cautious investigation of other contacts took place. It was also a *loud* voice, by African standards; for Nigeria is the largest single African state by area and by population, and by resources (with the exception of South Africa). It was also a largely very Muslim state, as we have already noted in examining some of the political and military struggles for power, and when in 1961 the federal government attempted to negotiate with Israel for aid the Northern Region's government's objections ensured the cessation of the negotiations.

Nigeria, then, seemed in 1960 to have been admirably placed to have carved out for herself a leadership of the African continent that was based partly on influence and the wise counsels of her then leaders, partly on power stemming from her national resources, and partly on the very pertinent fact that, with the national balance of political power residing in the hands of Muslim northerners, she represented the unity of interest between Arab/Muslim and African that true pan-Africanism demanded. Soon after independence, however, the Nigerian federal government's pro-western stance fell victim to party politics. At the general election of 1959 all the three main political parties had followed roughly the same pro-western line; but by March 1960 reports that Nigeria was about to sign a defence pact with Britain were exploited by the Action Group and Chief Awolowo, whose political ambitions (as detailed earlier) obliged him to find a valid issue on which to oppose the government he hoped to displace. By the end of 1960, these and other diffuse fears of Nigerians in political and other walks of life had brought about quite a significant shift in the federal government's stated foreign attitudes; while they made it clear that Nigeria would continue to work with the UN and with the Commonwealth, much of her previously pro-western stance was modified into something closer to non-alignment, and the defence pact with Britain perished.

None of this, it is true, need necessarily have been detrimental either to Nigerian interests in the African continent, or to the more general, and collective, influence or power that could have been wielded by the African continent as a whole. The 1960s were Africa's decade when the great majority of the ex-British colonies gained their independence; but it was also the decade in which occurred the Congo crisis following the abdication of Belgian power in Central Africa. Detailed stories of this episode are legion, and even if they do conflict with each other the main lines of the story are well enough known (see chapter 6 on the military for some aspects of it). It is the results of the Congo crisis that concern us here, for, whatever its effect upon whites the world over, they were no less traumatic to black Africans. For the first time their fundamental differences of outlook were exposed, not just to the world as well as to themselves, but in terms of willingness to consider taking arms against each other; the practical limitations of their power became obvious; the possibility of a measure of re-colonization became very real; neo-colonialism in the interests of big business became a no longer imaginary nightmare but a reality; and African unity became exposed as an illusion as great, perhaps, as that of the unity of Europe. As important, perhaps, was the effect of the Congo upon the relationships between African countries and the great (and not so great) powers, and the United Nations. One cannot quite believe in the extent of Thomas Kanza's naiveté[4] when he relates how, in the Security Council debates on the Congo, he suddenly realized that to the great powers the Congo and the UN itself were merely vehicles for great-power manoeuvrings; but it is certainly true that the Congo episode dissipated much goodwill between Africa and the rest of the world, as well as disseminating a greater sense of reality. From this time on, the African states have been judged more dispassionately and with fewer guilty overtones from the ex-colonial powers than was the case before, and shortly after, 1960.

The later crises

The later foreign affairs crises of the African states have served to emphasize the differences between them rather than their opportunities for common action. The question of the recognition of Biafra in its attempt to secede from the Nigerian federation, attitudes adopted towards Rhodesia and UDI, and the arms sales to South Africa and the 'dialogue' conducted with South Africa itself have all tended to thrust African states into a series of conflicting attitudes.

Four countries only recognized Biafra – Ivory Coast and Gabon of the ex-French territories, and Tanzania and Zambia of the ex-British ones. Ivory Coast acted as it did mainly for reasons of President Houphouet-Boigny's personal philosophy that large federations were simply not viable in Africa; and Gabon's President Bongo claimed to act on purely humanitarian grounds (his capital, Libreville, becoming one of the main airports used for the passage of supplies to the rebel territory). The reasons given by the Tanzanian president for his act of recognition display deep thought on the problem. Nyerere conceded the need for African unity, but only if it coexisted with the general consent of the people involved. 'States, and governments,' he said 'exist for men and for the service of man. They exist for the citizen's protection. . . .' If the mass of Tanzanians withdrew their consent to the Union, Nyerere himself would have worked hard, he said, to maintain unity and prevent secession, but could not possibly deny his people their right to secede if they really wished to. The Biafrans felt they could not live securely in the Federation of Nigeria and wished to govern themselves. Tanzania still hoped unity could be preserved in Nigeria, but it could only be achieved by the Nigerians themselves. After having watched civil war for nearly a year, it seemed to Nyerere that 'by refusing to recognize the existence of Biafra we were tacitly supporting a war against the people of Eastern Nigeria – and a war conducted in the name of unity. We could not continue doing this any longer'. Nyerere's action was followed by that of Kaunda of Zambia, to whom he was very close. The Zambians sent a goodwill mission to Biafra in March 1969, and called for an international ban on arms to Nigeria; force, Kaunda maintained, did no good, only negotiation could settle matters.

The position of the African states since Rhodesian UDI in November 1965 has changed considerably. Their first reaction was to press the United Kingdom to take steps, including immediate military action, to end the rebellion. Pressure was exerted through the OAU (of which more detail is given on p. 210), but in the end only Ghana and Tanzania of the ex-British territories were willing to go so far as to break off diplomatic relations with Britain, on her refusal to deploy force. None left the Commonwealth over this issue. In the following January (1966) a Commonwealth heads of government meeting was held in Lagos, at which the British prime minister was called to account for British handling of the Rhodesia crisis. Two factors in the situation now emerged, and have dominated thinking on the problem ever since. First, while the British government's views on the matter differ widely from those of the African states, nevertheless the position of each is understood by the other and, however plain the speaking, so far no fundamental breach has occurred. The second factor is that the African states themselves are divided on the issue. This division centres around Tanzania and Zambia, on the one hand, whose political affinities have led to the adoption of a militant stance, and on the other hand upon Malawi, whose practical dependence on both Rhodesia and South Africa has led her to adopt an apparently more compliant attitude. This should not be taken to imply that President Banda is any the less committed to African majority rule in southern Africa than are his more extreme colleagues to his west and north; it merely indicates that the needs of his country, as well, perhaps, as his political perceptions, drive him to adopt a less extreme attitude. It has resulted, however, in strained relationships between Malawi and many of the ex-British territories in Africa.

Problems posed by South Africa have also led to wide divisions of opinion, both as between the other African states themselves and between Africa and Britain. The two most recent major crises have been those over the supply of British arms to South Africa, and the whole matter of 'dialogue' – whether, as some ex-French countries as well as some of the ex-British ones maintain, the process of breaking down *apartheid* can be hastened by contact, rather than rigid quarantine, imposed upon South Africa.

Arms for South Africa became a live issue with the advent of a Conservative government in Britain in June 1970, which proposed to reverse the preceding Labour government's policy not to supply arms to South Africa. Discussions on this matter figured largely in the Commonwealth Conference held in January 1971 (see p. 217) and this had been preceded by a determined effort by the African states, in the form of a delegation to Britain led by Zambia's President Kaunda, to stop the sales. The British case was, that much as it deplored *apartheid* and although it had no intention of supplying arms for offensive use by South Africa, nevertheless the government had to stand by a legal obligation incurred earlier over British rights to use the South African naval base at Simonstown. It also had British commercial interests in mind, and the undoubted fact that, should Britain fail to supply arms, the South Africans would have no difficulty in obtaining what was needed from other sources, in particular, from the French.

Dialogue, a means of achieving an end to *apartheid* by peaceful contact between black- and white-controlled Africa, has had as its prime exponent President Houphouet-Boigny of the Ivory Coast, who expressed the philosophy that threats and the fear of violence would merely increase *apartheid* measures instead of bringing about their mitigation and eventual abolition. African reactions to this philosophy have varied widely. The then president of Ghana, Dr K. A. Busia, expressed the cautious view that dialogue was another weapon, not incompatible with sustained armed pressures on the southern African regimes, that might prove effective. Gambia, Nigeria, Uganda took a rigid anti-dialogue line; Kenya stressed that if dialogue were founded upon the principles of the Lusaka Manifesto then it was worth trying; Lesotho favoured quiet diplomacy; Zambia claimed that no negotiation with South Africa could succeed unless it were conducted on the basis of human equality; Malawi favoured it, and has sent an ambassador (thus far, a white Malawian) to represent it in South Africa.

African states' diplomatic reactions, then, to any proposal or crisis are varied to suit the underlying circumstances, be they political/philosophical, economic, or geographic, of the state concerned. It does not seem that the factor of once having been British influences decisions taken, except in so far as it may assist communication and the adoption of joint lines of action which could not be so easily achieved with any of the ex-French territories. One can expect a common starting point in the consideration of proposals, in that government ministers are advised by civil servants whose administrative procedures are still to a certain extent anglicized, even if the personnel is not; but beyond that, it is difficult to see that the quality of African-ness achieves any more of a united front in the face of differing national interests, than does the fact of European-ness impose identical action upon, say, France and Italy.

Challenge from south and north

Before going on to consider the opportunities open to African states by their membership of organs of collective action, it is interesting to view the forces at the opposing poles of the continent. South Africa alone of the ex-British states has both the principles and the means to pursue them that make a cohesive foreign policy possible; and the Arab states, despite the eagerness with which they seek to identify themselves with the aspirations of the black African states, offer religious unity, a degree of racial cohesion, and the economic resources that may one day enable them to unite to act in concert.

To South Africa the decade of the sixties was no less momentous than it was to the newly independent countries. The Sharpeville incident in 1960 was followed by South Africa ceasing to be a member of the Commonwealth in 1961. Politically isolated, conscious of world hostility and economically exposed by the flight of capital from the country during the early period of insecurity, the South African government pursued two main aims; to counter its isolated position both inside and outside Africa, and to revive its economy.

A major bastion of South African policy has, accordingly, been the winning over of friends in the continent itself – this 'good-neighbourliness' being one side of the coin, the reverse of which, 'dialogue' (emanating from the black African countries themselves), is discussed later. This essentially outgoing policy was first formulated by Dr Verwoerd and later taken up by his successor, Prime Minister Vorster; it began with the establishment of good relations with the three former High Commission territories (Botswana, Lesotho and Swaziland), and it continued with overtures to other black African countries, especially those whose economies, like Zambia and Katanga, held striking potential. The exchange of diplomats and the provision of financial and technical aid were mooted; in the end the militant states declined the offers, but Malawi has been outstanding in her acceptance of them and in the diplomatic and financial ties she has evolved with South Africa.

The rapprochement between white and black Africa caused its own anguish within South Africa, where the simmering political feud between the two wings of the Nationalist party, the *verkramptes* (men of narrow and inflexible attitudes) and the *verligtes* (the 'enlightened', less exclusive ones) came to the boil, and although a clear victory for the *verligtes* followed, the issue will continue to be fought. Meanwhile, the 'good-neighbour' policy tended to wither away; the Botswana government in particular maintained its reservations against too close a relationship, and Malawi continued to be alone in her support for it.

This did not matter greatly to South Africa, partly because the policy had served its propaganda purpose in persuading countries outside Africa that the Republic's policies were more humane and productive of peace than had originally been thought possible, and partly because South African relations with the rest of the world became more cordial. Those with Britain remained fairly close, and the advent of a Conservative government in 1970 reversed the previous Labour government's compliance with the UN Security Council embargo on arms sales to South Africa. The practical effects of the embargo had anyway been nullified by the readiness of the French to disregard it, and South African relations with both France and Portugal became cordial. A combination of factors, such as the carry over of the Kennedy-style liberals in the US State Department and the need to placate domestic negro opinion, required US administrations to take a guarded view of South African policies; and opposing financial interests concerned with the role of gold in the world's monetary system have served to emphasize the differences in the essential interests of the USA and South Africa. Nevertheless, relations between the two countries remain on a reasonably friendly level.

At the moment of writing, therefore, it appears that South African foreign policy during the 1960s has been successful. It is undoubtedly the case that the country is very much less isolated in 1972 than it was in 1962; although some opinion outside the country remains inflexibly opposed to *apartheid* doctrines, it is broadly true that this has been countered by the approaches made to, and relationships forged with, foreign countries such as Portugal, France and Germany. These in their turn have helped to stimulate the economy, and in this connection it is especially interesting to note the increasing part played by Japanese interests. Their honorary 'white' status in South Africa together with their own national self-confidence suggest that in the Japanese, the South Africans have found a major industrialized power with whom even closer bonds will be forged.

The Arab states too can, perhaps, claim that the 1960s saw a major advance in their influence, and it is worth examining just what relationship they bear to the African states to their south. Despite professions of Arab-African unity, it is at any rate arguable that the Arabs are more concerned with garnering all possible allies in their conflict with Israel than merely with cementing a somewhat altruistic friendship with the Africans. It is tempting to project ahead for, perhaps, fifty years and consider current relations in the African continent in the context of Arab, rather than African, foreign policy. It may well be that the spasmodic movements we are witnessing at the present will evolve into a pattern at which we can only guess. It is perfectly possible that, denied the advance of Arab influence in the Middle East by Israeli intransigence, the Arabs may turn south upon the splintered societies of Africa. There is little more to stop them now, than there was in the days of the Arab incursions under Othman Dan Fodio into West Africa that established the great emirates of northern Nigeria.

It is true that Arab society and Muslim influence tends to wane in the nationalistic countries of East Africa, and it is also true that in the early years of the decade Cairo was outplayed by Accra in the pan-African leadership stakes. To a certain extent this Arab-African rivalry has been camouflaged by the role played by the Emperor of Ethiopia, that doyen of the rulers of Africa, in pan-African affairs, and by the deference accorded to him. The rivalry, however, still exists, and will continue to do so after any change of regime in Ethiopia. Current (at this 1972 time of writing) moves in Uganda, where Israelis, Asians and British are being removed and replaced by Arab influence, are indicative of the likely trend of events. Arab unity is growing in the face of Israeli intransigence and western oil interests, and Arab resources are enormously augmented by oil revenues. The desert has historically been a pathway rather than a barrier to human intercourse; the 1960s may, in retrospect, turn out to have been the Arabs', rather than the Africans', decade.

Collective efforts – the OAU

No study of African foreign affairs, however brief, could omit the efforts made to achieve national, continental or racial ends by collective efforts – for example, through joint action in the OAU, by influencing or manipulating the Commonwealth, and by lobbying at the United Nations.

The OAU was born of the first of the pan-African Congresses to be held actually on African soil, at Accra in 1958. It was attended by all the African countries then already independent, namely Ghana, Liberia, Egypt, Tunisia, Libya, Sudan, Morocco and the United Arab Republic. On the whole it was a non-contentious affair, chiefly remarkable, perhaps, for the rivalry that developed between Ghana and Egypt for leadership of the organization and for the efforts of Egypt, frustrated by Liberia, to raise the issue of Israel. One of its shortcomings may have been that no form of central secretariat was set up, despite the well argued case for one made by Ghana's leading civil servant of the time, A. L. Adu; on the other hand it is equally arguable that to have evolved one at that time might have hampered the later accession to the Organization of the other African states about to become independent. At all events it provided a starting point for African unity that invoked comparisons with Bandung for Asia in 1955, and inspired Nkrumah to make the first of many journeyings around Africa, seeking contacts and support – and leadership of the Organization for himself.

By 1960 enough interest had been generated, and African states been liberated, for a second Congress to be held at Addis Ababa. This was almost unmitigated disaster for the cause of African unity; despite all efforts at accommodation, the meeting degenerated into a series of factions that spawned, in turn, their own sub-groups during the following year. First the Brazzaville Group of all the ex-French states save Guinea and Mali formed a group in December 1960; this later turned into the Union of African and Malagasy States. This was, on the whole, a moderate grouping, and its rival the Casablanca Group formed in January 1961 comprised Morocco, Ghana, Guinea, Mali, the UAR, Libya and the provisional government of Algeria. Then the Monrovia Group, formed to reconcile the differences between the Brazzaville Group, the Casablanca Group and other moderate countries, was formed in May 1961; its membership consisted of the Brazzaville members together with Liberia, Nigeria, Somalia, Sierra Leone, Togo, Ethiopia, Libya with Tunisia as an observer member. Its first conference at Lagos failed, however, to achieve reconciliation, which was not in fact achieved until the heads of African governments, meeting in Addis Ababa in 1963, formed the OAU.

The first full session of the meeting of heads of African governments belonging to the OAU took place in Cairo in July 1964; the membership of thirty-five included Malawi, about to become independent. In its closing communique the OAU claimed that the Assembly had 'considered ways and means of consolidating inter-African cooperation in all fields of endeavour leading to the goal of African solidarity and unity'. Addis Ababa was to be the headquarters of the organization which would meet once a year, and specialized commissions were set up to deal with educational and cultural matters; economic and social issues; health and nutrition; scientific and technical research; defence; legal matters; and transport and communications. Decolonization proved a major preoccupation of the Assembly, which demanded a boycott of South African trade, condemned Rhodesia and Portugal, and recommended the setting up of a liberation committee, to be maintained as composed of nine member-states who would contribute the necessary funds for the time being until an equitable scale could be determined. Diallo Telli, the permanent representative of Guinea to the UN, was to be administrative secretary-general of the Organization, and was to be assisted by a Kenyan, Algerian, Nigerian and one other deputy to be announced later.

In view of the Organization's later vicissitudes, it is worth noting the comments made upon it at the time of its founding. The Ghanaians saw it as a means of uniting governments, but were critical of the puny scale of the freedom fighting envisaged. Ethiopia saw the Organization as providing a means of settling border difficulties. Guinea saw it as a step to continental unity, Mauretania and Tanzania as a way to rapprochement between the Arab and the African states, and Senegal called for action, not speeches. Nigeria conceded the practical usefulness of the

Organization in its ability to settle disputes, but was doubtful of surrendering sovereignty to it, and Somalia, engaged with Ethiopia and Kenya in border disputes, also conceded its efficacy. Cairo was insistent on the essential harmony needed if the Organization was to work; Kenya claimed that South Africa was the most important issue and demanded an oil boycott; and Uganda expressed concern for the fate of the then High Commission territories about to become independent although embedded in South Africa. Malawi made a plea to avoid self-glorification, Zambia stressed the needs of the common man, and Sierra Leone reinforced the calls for sanctions against southern Africa.

In view of these very differing views as to the fundamental nature of the Organization and the importance attached to it by the individual member countries, it is not very surprising that subsequent meetings have proved acrimonious and action difficult to achieve. The summit meeting in Accra in October 1965 proved particularly contentious from the start, for Nkrumah had to fight off efforts to hold the conference in Cairo, while alleging that the Afro-Malagasy group of countries formed 'the American group of states in Africa'. Some extremely statesmanlike work from both Azikiwe and Balewa of Nigeria persuaded the quarrelling countries to meet, after all, in Accra; a major dispute broke out about whether to admit Tshombe of the Congo, and a member of Afro-Malagasy, to OAU meetings; and there were repeated accusations of Ghanaian subversion from the Ivory Coast, Niger and Upper Volta, all of whom claimed that Nkrumah was sheltering enemies of their regimes. Both Kenya and Nigeria pleaded that the cause of African unity should not receive the setback that a refusal to meet in Accra would imply, and in the end, of the thirty-six member states, only eight refused to attend; Chad, Gabon and Malagasy, which said they were unable to come, and the Ivory Coast, Niger, Togo, Upper Volta and Dahomey which claimed they were unable to attend because Ghana would not cooperate in expelling dissidents from the refuge they had sought in Ghana.

None of this represented a promising start, and the secretary-general's report was equally depressing; it mentioned a confusion between the functions of the specialized agencies and duplication of effort, while the budget was nearly $2 million in debt, because twenty-four of the member states had either not contributed at all, or were in arrears. Nkrumah's pleas for continental unity *now*, and for the establishment of an organization to implement this, were countered, successfully, by the Nigerian motion which advocated a slow start with the gradual creation of a few common services.

The Rhodesian UDI brought about a meeting of the OAU foreign ministers in December 1965, at Accra, where again concerted agreement was difficult to achieve. A committee of five (the UAR, Nigeria, Kenya, Tanzania and Zambia) was set up to coordinate the military aid to be sent to aid the freedom fighters in Rhodesia. Debate then ensued on the line to be taken with Britain; a conference spokesman claimed that all nations represented at the conference would break off diplomatic relations with Britain if UDI were not crushed, militarily, by 15 December (Libya, Tunisia and Kenya dissented from this). In the end, nine countries broke off relations with Britain (Algeria, the Congo Republic, Guinea, Mali, Mauretania, Sudan, Ghana, the UAR and Tanzania), amid grumbles from the ex-French states which claimed it was illogical for the ex-British countries to be fierce in discussion while lacking in action; Sudan, too, drew attention to the absurdity of holding such discussions in the capital of a country (Ghana) which was still a member of the Commonwealth.

The 1966 OAU summit meeting was held at Addis Ababa in October 1966, at which the Emperor of Ethiopia pressed for action against Rhodesia and also for Ghana and Guinea to settle their differences (this, following the deposition of Nkrumah and his subsequent support from Guinean quarters). The Emperor's plea for unity and solidarity was countered by some violent exchanges over the actions of the liberation committee; Tunisia in particular was critical of the actions of the Tanzanian Kambona, who headed the liberation committee, on the grounds of the high costs of the committee, alleged mismanagement of funds and wrong choice of beneficiaries, and on the fact that no proper accounts were being kept. The budget was passed only with extreme difficulty; and of the thirty-eight member-states of the OAU, only eighteen paid their contributions in full.

The 1967 OAU summit meeting was held at Kinshasa, in what is now Zaire (ex-Belgian Congo). The Emperor of Ethiopia again pointed to the need to find solutions to problems, not merely to talk about them, and stressed the necessity of stopping the Nigerian

Civil War: 'political crises have so much plagued our Continent,' he said, 'that our economic and social development programmes are in serious danger'. Nevertheless the dissensions continued; as the liberation committee's session began, delegates of the UAR and Algeria walked out because the Israeli ambassador, together with other members of the diplomatic corps, attended; and the summit itself proceeded to criticize Malawi, which was not attending the meeting, for her soft policy toward South Africa and Rhodesia. Of the more constructive proposals that were carried, the OAU committed itself by resolution to work with the UN to secure Israeli withdrawal from UAR territory; and Zambian mediation settled the border dispute between Kenya and Somalia. A mission of six was appointed to proceed to Lagos to press for the end of the Civil War, but the four who finally journeyed to Lagos on 23 November achieved nothing. Finally, this meeting was addressed by U Thant, the UN secretary-general, who urged the OAU to use its good offices to prevent border disputes and warned the delegates that the UN itself was no substitute for efforts by the African states themselves to achieve their aims.

The 1968 meeting of the OAU summit was held in Algiers in September, and seems to have been rather muted in character; its resolutions criticized the NATO powers and condemned the actions of France, Portugal and the UK while calling for support for UN efforts to enforce sanctions against Rhodesia. It attempted to establish that aggression by Rhodesia and southern Africa against any one African state would be construed as aggression against all African states. The real fireworks, as so often, had taken place in the deliberations of the liberation committee, which had met in July and attempted to allocate aid as between competing candidates for liberation movements throughout Africa, and had in particular demanded the withdrawal of aid from the Pan-African Congress of South Africa (PAC), which was considered to be inefficient and unrepresentative, until the split in its leadership had been healed.

By 1969 the liberation committee itself was thought ripe for radical reorganization. A seventeen-nation organization based in Dar-es-Salaam, it was again criticized for its inefficiency and misuse of funds, and also for its relationship with some of the dissident parties and individuals that were plaguing the existence of the legitimately-controlled black African states nearby; but the matter of its reorganization was thought so complicated that the matter was referred back to an eight-nation committee, due to report in 1970. Meanwhile, the OAU summit itself was held in Addis Ababa in 1969; it was continuingly critical of southern Africa and castigated the western nations and Japan for co-operating with South Africa, and renewed its condemnation of Israel for aggression against the Arab states. Again, it called for a ceasefire in Nigeria; the four African countries which had recognized Biafra diplomatically abstained from voting on this resolution.

The 1970 meeting of the OAU was held in September at Addis Ababa, lasting only three days; Mauritius was the only member-state to send no delegation, and the meeting generally was remarkable for the extent to which it mended many of the old quarrels. In particular, Nigeria was publicly reconciled with Tanzania, Zambia, Ivory Coast and Gabon which had all recognized the rebel state of Biafra. On the other hand, discussions on the sale of arms to South Africa by Britain and on decolonization in general emphasized the fact that eight of the states present (including Malawi and Lesotho, of the ex-British states) disagreed with the majority 'hard' line on these subjects.

In 1971 the main crisis of the OAU concerned the legitimacy or otherwise of the new regime in Uganda headed by General Amin; the first Council of Ministers meeting held in February reached deadlock in the matter, and despite some intensive negotiations by the Nigerian prime minister, General Gowon, the resumed Council of Ministers meeting, closely followed by that of the heads of state in Addis Ababa in June, were neither of them attended by Uganda delegates. The other great debate lay over whether or not to conduct meaningful 'dialogue' with southern Africa, a procedure first broached by the Ivory Coast the previous year and which had inspired, in turn, the Lusaka manifesto calling for unity, non-alignment and the liberation of southern Africa. In the end 'dialogue' was rejected by the members present, but unsatisfactorily, for the twenty-seven votes in favour of rejection had to be balanced against four which favoured dialogue, two abstentions, three members who refused to vote, and four absentees from the meeting. The resolution that was carried repeated the principles of the OAU charter, supported the Lusaka manifesto and claimed that any dialogue to take place should be that between the minority regimes and those they ruled. Another important resolution, while continuing to support Egypt against Israel, for the first time forsook a purely UN approach to the matter and pledged an African initiative – thus appearing to link black and Arab Africa more closely.

Some of these very serious rifts appeared healed by the time the 1972 summit meeting took place, this time at Rabat in June. There was a welcome absence of divisive crises, and both the presence of General Amin and the absence of bickering about 'dialogue' removed two major difficulties from the consideration of more important matters. Several disputes were settled, notably those between Libya and Chad, Congo (Brazzaville) and Zaire, northern and southern Sudan, and Guinea and Senegal, while the formal ending of the frontier dispute between Morocco and Algiers was also achieved. Most important of all, perhaps, Diallo Telli was replaced as administrative secretary-general of the OAU by a Cameroonian, Mr Ekangaki (who is fluent in both English and French). Telli had long been identified with a particular brand of talk that resulted in few deeds, and had, in consequence, lost the confidence of members and notably of Ethiopia, Zaire and Nigeria. 1972, again, was the first year in which representatives of the liberation committee were allowed to participate in the proceedings of the Council of Ministers; its budget was doubled, and it seemed likely that its activities and those responsible for its day-to-day running might be brought into the mainstream of OAU activity and, perhaps, supervision.

After a decade or so, it is not wholly easy to sum up the achievements of the OAU. Certainly the Organization itself has reached the stage of realizing that merely to survive is not enough. It has undoubtedly been held together very largely by one man, the Emperor of Ethiopia; the succession to him is not clear. The OAU has not proved effective as a device for settling internal political questions, but then no world agency ever has; but it has been successful in reconciling personal differences, and boundary questions. There have been (at the time of writing) no signs that the much talked about military high command for Africa will come about, but that would certainly be a logical development, coupled with rumoured attacks on Portuguese colonialism rather than on South Africa, as presenting a more diffuse target and greater chance of success. On other, less spectacular fronts (such as the other specialized agencies set up at the first Addis Ababa meeting), little is heard.

The Commonwealth

Whatever may prove to be the final judgment on the OAU, it does seem that African countries' membership of the Commonwealth and attendance at its heads of governments meetings have been of little practical benefit to their avowed aims – although, of course, other benefits such as the flow of information and a certain amount of domestic *kudos* for politicians have certainly proved useful. The black African presence at Commonwealth conferences was first felt in July 1957 in London, when Prime Minister Nkrumah of Ghana was bid welcome to a meeting designed to heal the stresses put upon the Commonwealth by the Suez crisis. Stress was laid upon the weaknesses of the UN, and of the need to build it up; disarmament was touched upon; Chinese influence was noted as a growing issue which one day would have to be dealt with; in short, the tone of the meeting was easy and straight-forward and only once did dissension between individual members of the Commonwealth (India and Pakistan) come to the surface. With the benefits of hindsight one finds it remarkable that the comparative lack of development capital available for the poorer from the richer nations passed with no comment; on the other hand, some concern was expressed at the implications of the proposed free trade area in Europe, and an examination of the situation was called for.

The next Commonwealth conference was held in London in May 1960, and again Ghana was the only black African nation to be represented; membership was now ten, consisting of the original five white members with India, Ceylon, Malaya and Pakistan together with Ghana. This was the meeting that, shocked by the Sharpeville shootings, assented to the retention of Ghana within the Commonwealth even though she was now a republic; this meeting could still talk about *apartheid* with its chief prac-titioner, but, as the *Sunday Times* report had it, it was 'probably the first at which African problems dominated its thought', and the first at which the problems of race loomed so large. On the negative side, the conference failed to take up the idea, emanating from Ceylon, of setting up a Commonwealth Court to hear appeals connected with human rights issues, and little concern was expressed about Commonwealth/Europe trade.

The March 1961 conference saw the disappearance of South Africa from the Commonwealth, following her decision not to pursue the question of continued membership as a republic in the face of determined probings from the Malayan prime minister. For the first time it was suggested that Commonwealth conferences might take place elsewhere than in London, and Ottawa became prime candidate for the next meeting; otherwise, the discussion placed priority upon disarmament, with the plight of the Congo also mentioned.

The next Commonwealth conference was, in fact, again held in London, in September 1962, and by this time its multiracial character and greatly increased membership was much in evidence. The loss of South Africa had been balanced by the accessions of Nigeria, Cyprus and, since the last conference, those of Sierra Leone, Tanganyika, Jamaica, and Trinidad and Tobago. International affairs were reviewed, as was progress toward disarmament, but the major part of the discussion centred upon the British application to join the European Common Market. To all arguments that what would benefit Britain would benefit also the Commonwealth, the newer countries only repeated their fears of the immediate effects of Britain's entry upon the primary commodities upon which their economies depended, and which might no longer receive preferential treatment; this fundamental clash of national interests was not resolved.

The Commonwealth conference of July 1964, again held in London, saw eighteen governments represented. Race relations was a major issue, hope for general and progressive disarmament was expressed as was support for the UN, concern over events in Cyprus, and alarm over the deteriorating relationship between India and Pakistan. The British government statement on the progress of the remaining dependencies led to the expression of concern over Southern Rhodesia and to the condemnation of *apartheid* and Portuguese policy in Africa. This conference also prompted efforts, in which the Africans played a leading part, to strengthen the structure of the Commonwealth by setting up a Commonwealth Secretariat. This, it was hoped, would improve communications among Commonwealth members while lessening the influence of the Commonwealth Relations Offiice of the British government, which normally undertook such work. The necessity of funds for development projects, administrative training and education was stressed, and there was firm support for a medical conference and also for the Commonwealth Parliamentary Association. In addition, the setting up of a Commonwealth Foundation was urged, to administer funds to help with the interchange of professional personnel.

The next conference, held in London in June 1965, contained twenty-one members. Disarmament occupied a major session, and a mission was set up to make contact with the parties to the fighting in Vietnam. Tension between Malaysia and Indonesia, the situation in Cyprus, policies of the Portuguese and South Africans and events in the Caribbean all came in for their share of comment; the (by now) customary British statement on the remaining dependencies was listened to, and a major debate took place on economic affairs and development. Reports submitted on the Commonwealth Foundation and the Commonwealth Secretariat were accepted, and the Canadian, Arnold Smith, became the first head of the Secretariat. Australia and Britain had been keen to whittle down the initiatory powers of the Secretariat, and Australia, Malawi and India viewed it as a purely functional office; Ghana, Canada and Sierra Leone, on the other hand, sought to endow it with a more authoritarian role but did not succeed in this.

In January 1966 came the Commonwealth meeting convened in Lagos, specifically to discuss the crisis brought about by the Rhodesian UDI; firmly and adroitly handled by the British prime minister, the African countries gained little that was practical from this debate. Indeed, the events of the meeting were to be overshadowed by the Nigerian military coup that took place so soon afterwards and was to do so much to destroy the notion of the effectiveness of possible African intervention. At the main 1966 Commonwealth conference, held in September in London, twenty-two heads of government or their deputies attended and Rhodesia supplied the major element in the discussion. While sanctions were to be tightened up, the special difficulties of Zambia and Malawi (as Rhodesia's neighbours) were recognized. Otherwise, the familiar topics were discussed; disarmament, the non-self-governing dependencies, world economic affairs, and international relations – where there was cause for congratulation in the restoration of diplomatic relations between Pakistan and Malaysia, and at the end of the confrontation between the latter and Indonesia.

The next Commonwealth meeting did not take place until January 1969, and was again held in London. By now the membership had risen to twenty-nine, and clearly any idea that the old form of Commonwealth consultation in small, intimate and rather informal surroundings survived, was ended. The range of usual subjects was discussed; the Middle East, Czechoslovakia, China, south-east Asia and Guyana crises were all discussed, but the lion's share of the talk, and probably of African feeling, was devoted to Rhodesia and the *Fearless* proposals. It is clear that a great gulf existed between the British government, and those other members of the Commonwealth in favour of far stronger measures to bring the Rhodesian government down.

Two years later, in January 1971, the next Commonwealth heads of government meeting was held in Singapore. Thirty-one members attended, and again it was the problems of southern Africa that dominated the proceedings. A Commonwealth Declaration was issued, (with overtones of the Statute of Westminster) that among other matters stigmatized racial prejudice as a 'dangerous sickness threatening the healthy development of the human race', and racial discrimination as 'an unmitigated evil of society'. The British entry into the EEC and world economic affairs in general were mentioned, but there was lengthy discussion on Rhodesia, the operation of sanctions and of the rights and wrongs of the British arms deals with South Africa. A study group, on the security of the Indian Ocean was set up, consisting of representatives of Australia, Britain, Canada, India, Jamaica, Kenya, Malaysia and Nigeria, but this proved very shortlived when Britain decided that her legal obligations required the supply of certain weapons, for defensive purposes only, to South Africa. This was the meeting at which the British prime minister, speaking in the Westminster parliament, felt more time could usefully have been given to discussion of other events and places; and the general criticism made of the conference as a whole was that the recently grown practice of delivering lengthy set-piece speeches, designed as much for home consumption as for consideration by the other prime ministers actually at the conference, reduced the whole affair to little more than a talking-shop.

This seems a fair criticism, but whether it is the cause or the effect or will, indeed, have any effect at all on the functioning of the Commonwealth, is far from clear. What does emerge is the fact that the Commonwealth's value to the black African states in their struggle to obtain freedom for their brothers in southern Africa, is severely circumscribed. Its meetings obtain publicity, and grievances aired there obtain a large audience. But neither the Commonwealth as a body on its own, nor as an influence on other institutions such as the United Nations, will secure an abatement of the policies pursued in Salisbury or Pretoria. Indeed, it seems more likely that assiduous devotion to Commonwealth meetings is nugatory; for, as the British prime minister made clear, the insistence upon discussing African affairs to the exclusion of what he felt were more important matters in the world context is self-defeating in its purpose.

The United Nations

African states have set great store by their membership of the UN. All the ex-British states (excepting, of course, South Africa, which was a founder-member) became members very soon indeed, usually within the month after independence; and only Gambia, which delayed for over a year, failed to follow up admission closely by establishing a diplomatic mission in New York. These UN missions have had a significance lacking for the older established countries, partly because they have been one of the first, and most visible, of the signs of sovereignty, and partly, perhaps, because the UN has been invested by the African countries with a significance that has not been accorded to it by, say, the older countries who have seen the rise and demise of the ideals of the old League of Nations. The equality of votes cast in the General Assembly appeared to offer prospects of obtaining real leverage on the world's problems; and on the more practical plane, simply because of shortage of trained diplomatic personnel and money the African missions at the UN serve as a kind of general ambassadorship to most of the rest of the world, with whom they are otherwise unable to carry on active diplomatic relations.

The functions of the missions accredited to the UN were fourfold. They formulated policy; designed and executed tactics to implement it; collected and reported information; and indulged in much, much propaganda. On the whole their missions remained small, with those of Ghana, Nigeria and Kenya tending to be the largest (reaching double figures by 1967). Because of this they have had to concentrate upon one or two only of the topics that occupy un deliberations; and because of their own recent history and enduring will to liberate their brothers still under domination, the subjects upon which they have concentrated have been colonialism and economic development, and to a certain extent, human rights. The extent to which they have, in the past decade or so, forced their own preoccupations upon the rest of the un is quite remarkable, and has come about because of their efficient caucus system. The African group was formed after the 1958 Accra Conference of Independent African States, and merged with the Asian group (many of whose aims and sympathies they shared). In 1959 the Asian-African group at the un comprised 35.4 per cent of un membership. By 1968 the Afro-Asian group comprised 52 per cent of membership; the actual change in name of the group occurred in 1960, when the independent African nations outnumbered the Asians.[5] The African countries themselves formed, in 1958, an organization called the Informal Permanent Machinery, composed of a co-ordinating body (which met every month) and a Secretariat of four from different states by rota, to whom might be added observers from any of the African states not, at the moment, numbered among the four.

Organizationally, the Afro-Asians early made themselves felt. They agitated to increase the number of limited membership organs (which, at the un's birth, consisted of the Security Council, the Economic and Social Council (ecosoc), and the Trusteeship Council); and they secured the formation of, for example, the Committee on South-West Africa. Their membership of this and other committees enabled them constantly to keep the issues upon which they were interested before the un and the world at large. They also managed to secure representation upon the un Secretariat, and with the 1965 un Charter amendments to the three older organs, secured also membership of the Security Council, ecosoc and the Trusteeship Council. They had, however, few bargaining counters with which they could actually make their wishes heeded. One such was their ability to try to play the great powers off against each other; another was the ability to muster large numbers of votes in the Assembly.

The actual achievements of the African countries are very arguable. They scored an early success when, in 1960, the UN General Assembly adopted a draft Declaration on Colonialism and, at the succeeding session, established a Special Committee to examine the implementation of the Declaration. This as applied to the predicaments of Rhodesia, South Africa, South-West Africa and so on resulted in a fairly clear and predictable pattern of events. Special sub-committees, committees on *apartheid* and the like would be formed, composed, typically, of representatives from a number of the smaller countries (many of them belonging to the ex-colonial, underdeveloped states), and one or two from the larger, developed countries. Extreme demands would be tabled in the UN General Assembly and punitive action sought; debate would ensue and was usually followed by a veto in the Security Council. Attempts to rush proposals through without prior consultation with, or passing information to, those of the developed nations who had an interest in the matters under debate led to the almost complete separation of developed from underdeveloped countries. One tactic used has, it seems, been scotched; that of securing the membership of one of the great western powers upon lesser committees so that it would be forced to be associated with the findings of the committee. These powers have increasingly refused to be so involved and in at least one case (concerning the establishment in 1966 of a 'group of experts' to examine whether *apartheid* threatened international peace) this has resulted in the proposed action not taking place at all.

Concerning development, again, early promise has petered out. The United Nations Commission on Trade and Development (UNCTAD) suffered, initially, the opposition of the western powers. By 1962 they had been persuaded to acquiesce in its establishment, and the first UNCTAD meeting in 1964 secured some advantages for the undeveloped countries as well as, for the first time, ensuring that the developed world accepted the problem as one that concerned all. But the second UNCTAD, in New Delhi in 1968, and more particularly the third in South America in 1972 saw extreme and strident demands made upon the developed nations which can only be judged as self-defeating. On the other hand, the decade of the 1960s saw a great increase in the amount of funds channelled through the UN in less controversial ways, for use, for instance, in programmes of technical assistance or for the World Health Organization.

In summary, it is probably true that the African countries have derived some benefit from their UN membership. They have certainly imposed their urgencies and priorities over the preoccupations of many of the other countries; they have mobilized opinion, publicized events and secured pronouncements and resolutions in the General Assembly where, before, these were lacking; they have swept a number of nasty items out of the hidey-holes they formerly inhabited, into the glare of world scrutiny. It is difficult to believe that, were another Sharpeville to occur this year, UN reactions would not be very much more forcible than they were in 1960. Over development they cannot be said to have succeeded; human rights issues have interested them only so far as they have related to racial issues, or colonialism, and certainly not with regard to their own internal affairs. Their influence over policy pronouncements has been sizable; over action, negligible. It is difficult to avoid the conclusion that, as well as lacking actual power to enforce action and moral influence to take its place, they have overplayed their hand. In the UN arena and in general world opinion the extravagance of their demands and the language in which they have been framed – no matter how legitimate their case – have forfeited them much-needed goodwill. Gadfly tactics certainly secure results, but they are rarely those desired, and never predictable.

Notes

Chapter 2: Constitutions: The Setting-Up

1 David C. Mulford, *Zambia, The Politics of Independence, 1957–1964*, Oxford University Press, 1967.

Chapter 4: Constitutions: The Breaking-down

1 For an outstanding account, see Claire Palley, *The Constitutional History and Law of Southern Rhodesia*, 1885–1965, Clarendon Press, Oxford, 1965.

2 See W. J. W. McCartney, 'The Parliaments of Botswana, Lesotho and Swaziland', *The Parliamentarian*, April 1969, vol. I no. 2, General Council of the Commonwealth Parliamentary Association, London, 1969.

3 Monica Wilson and Leonard Thompson (eds), *The Oxford History of South Africa*, vols. I and II, Clarendon Press, Oxford, 1971.

Chapter 5: What of the Safeguards?

1 S. A. de Smith, 'Westminster's Export Models: The Legal Framework of Responsible Government', *Journal of Commonwealth Studies*, vol. I, no. I, Nov. 1961, Leicester University Press.

2 My thanks are due to Mr Patrick M. Morton, of New College, Oxford, for allowing me to read an advance draft of his 1972 B. Phil. thesis on the Tanzanian Ombudsman Commission.

3 John P. Mackintosh, *Nigerian Government and Politics*, Allen & Unwin, London, 1966.

4 Chief Anthony Enahoro, *Fugitive Offender*, Cassell's, London, 1965.

5 Ruth First, *South-West Africa*, Penguin, Harmondsworth, London, 1963.

6   For detailed comment on this judgment, see especially eds. Ronald Segal and Ruth First, *South-West Africa: Travesty of Trust,* Deutsch, London, 1967; and for another view of this contentious and important case, see the South African Department of Information's *Ethiopia and Liberia versus South Africa,* Pretoria, 1966.

7   Sir Dingle Foot, 'A Commonwealth of Law', *Round Table,* vol. LXX, no. 240, London, 1970.

8   See R. J. Symonds, *The British and Their Successors,* Faber, London, 1966.

9   A. L. Adu, *The Civil Service in New African States,* Allen & Unwin, London, 1965.

10 D. J. Murray (ed.), *Studies in Nigerian Administration,* Hutchinson Educational, London, 1970.

11 See E. L. Sommerlad, *The Press in Developing Countries,* Sydney University Press, 1966.

12 Rosalynde Ainslie, *The Press in Africa,* Gollancz, London, 1966.

13 See Theodore Bull, *Rhodesian Perspective,* Michael Joseph, London, 1967.

14 L. C. B. Gower, *Independent Africa, The Challenge to the Legal Profession,* Harvard University Press, Cambridge, Mass., 1967.

15 S. Andreski, *The African Predicament,* Michael Joseph, London, 1968.

16 R. Wraith and E. Simpkins, *Corruption in Developing Countries,* Allen & Unwin, London, 1963.

Chapter 6: The Military

1   See Robin Luckham, *The Nigerian Military 1960–67,* Cambridge University Press, 1971, for a very illuminating account of the relationship between military and civilian authority in Nigeria.

2   Major-General H. T. Alexander, *African Tightrope,* Pall Mall, London, 1965.

3   A. A. Afrifa, *The Ghana Coup,* Cass, London, 1966.

4   See W. Gutteridge, *The Military in African Politics,* Methuen, London, 1969.

5   See Claude S. Phillips, Jr, *The Development of Nigerian Foreign Policy,* Northwestern University Press, USA, 1964, for a very full account of this episode.

6   See John Gittings, *The Role of the Chinese Army,* Oxford University Press/RIIA, London, 1967.

7   For a very good account of the Nigerian civil war see John de St Jorre, *The Nigerian Civil War,* Hodder and Stoughton, London, 1972.

8   Ruth First, *The Barrel of a Gun,* Allen Lane, London, 1970.

9   See, in particular, Catherine Hoskyns, *The Congo Since Independence,* Oxford University Press/RIIA, London, 1965.

Chapter 7: Politics and the Man on the Shamba, or Land, Labour and Learning

1   Swahili for cultivated field; corresponds closely to smallholding.

2   Cherry Gertzel, *The Politics of Independent Kenya,* Heinemann, London, 1970.

3   Quoted from Francis Wilson, 'Farming, 1866–1966', *Oxford History of South Africa,* Monica Wilson and Leonard Thompson (eds), Clarendon Press, Oxford, 1971.

4   Ioan Davies, *African Trade Unions,* Penguin, Harmondsworth, 1966.

5   F. A. Wells and A. W. Warmington, *Studies in Industrialization, Nigeria and the Cameroons,* Oxford University Press for NISER, London, 1962.

6   T. M. Yesufu, *An Introduction to Industrial Relations in Nigeria,* Oxford University Press for NISER, London, 1962.

7   Clements Kadalie, *My Life and the ICU,* Cass, London, 1970.

8   *Ibid.,* introduction by Stanley Trapido.

9   See Wogu Ananaba, *The Trade Union Movement in Nigeria,* Hurst, London, 1969.

10   William Tordoff, *Government and Politics in Tanzania,* East African Publishing House, Nairobi, 1967.

11   Clement K. Lubembe, *The Inside of Labour Movement in Kenya,* Equatorial Publishers, Nairobi, 1968.

12   Roger Scott, *The Development of Trade Unions in Uganda,* East Africa Publishing House, Nairobi, 1966.

13   David R. Smock, *Conflict and Control in an African Trade Union,* Hoover Institution Press, Stanford, California, 1969.

14   The figures in the three paragraphs following are based on Economic Commission for Africa, *Summaries of Economic Data,* UN, New York, 1970.

Chapter 8: The Politics of Economics

1   For interesting, if as yet unfashionable, views on this see the work of P. T. Bauer, in particular, *Dissent on Development*, Weidenfeld and Nicolson, London, 1972.

2   See H. L. van der Laan, *The Sierra Leone Diamonds*, Oxford University Press for Fourah Bay College, London, 1965.

3   See L. H. Schatzl, *Petroleum in Nigeria*, Oxford University Press for Nigerian Institute of Social and Economic Research, Ibadan, 1969.

4   See M. L. O. Faber and J. G. Potter, *Towards Economic Independence*, Cambridge University Press, 1971.

5   Ingrid Doimi di Delupis, *The East African Community and the Common Market*, Longman, London, 1970.

Chapter 9: Foreign Affairs

1   AID, *Special Report Prepared for the House Foreign Affairs Committee*, March, 1966.

2   Rupert Emerson, *African and United States Policy*, Prentice-Hall, New York, 1967.

3   For a good account of communist interest in the African continent during this period, see Zbigniew Brzezinski (ed.), *Africa and the Communist World*, Oxford University Press, London, 1964.

4   Thomas Kanza, *Conflict in the Congo*, Penguin, Harmondsworth, 1972.

5   See David A. Kay, *The New Nations in the United Nations*, Columbia University Press, New York, 1970.

Further Reading

See the books cited in the text for detailed information and comment on individual chapters of this book.

To comment on the contemporary African scene requires access to a good press-cuttings library. In particular, the correspondents of the *Times*, the *Financial Times*, the *Guardian* and the *Daily Telegraph*, among the London dailies, provide good news coverage and stimulating comment. The weekly journal *West Africa* (London) is outstanding.

The following periodicals repay study :

The Journal of Modern African Studies, Cambridge University Press (quarterly).

African Affairs, Royal African Society, Oxford University Press (quarterly).

Africa, International African Institute, Oxford University Press (quarterly).

Journal of Commonwealth Political Studies, Leicester University Press (three times yearly).

Journal of Development Studies, Cass, London (quarterly).

Africa Confidential, Africa Confidential, London (by subscription only, fortnightly).

Africa Contemporary Record, Rex Collings, London (yearly from 1968–9).

Otherwise, the list is long. Some of the publications that would be most helpful to the general reader wishing to know more about the details or the background of African politics, are :

David E. Apter, *The Political Kingdom in Uganda*, Princeton University Press, 1967.

Dennis Austin, *Britain and South Africa*, Oxford University Press for RHA, 1966.

Henry Bienen, *Tanzania, Party Transformation and Economic Development* (expanded edition), Princeton University Press, 1970.

Ian Brownlie (ed.), *Basic Documents on African Affairs*, Clarendon Press, Oxford, 1971.

Gwendolen M. Carter (ed.), *African One-Party States*, Cornell University Press, New York, 1962.

Lionel Cliffe and John S. Saul (eds), *Socialism in Tanzania*, vol. I, *Politics*, East African Publishing House, Dar-es-Salaam, 1972.

Michael Crowder, *The Story of Nigeria*, Faber, London, 1962.

Michael Crowder, *West Africa Under Colonial Rule*, Hutchinson, London, 1968.

K. O. Dike, *Trade and Politics in the Niger Delta*, Clarendon Press, Oxford, 1956.

René Dumont, *False Start in Africa*, Deutsch, London, 1966.

Rupert Emerson, *Africa and United States Policy*, Prentice-Hall, Englewood Cliffs, 1967.

Cherry Gertzel, *The Politics of Independent Kenya* 1963–8, East African Publishing House, Nairobi, 1970.

Cherry Gertzel, Maure Goldschmidt and Donald Rothchild (eds), *Government and Politics in Kenya*, East African Publishing House, Nairobi, 1969.

W. K. Hancock, *Smuts, The Sanguine Years*, and *Smuts, The Fields of Force*, Cambridge University Press, 1962 and 1968.

A. J. Hanna, *The Story of the Rhodesias and Nyasaland,* Faber, London, 1965.

John Hatch, *A History of Post-War Africa*, Deutsch, London. 1965.

A. J. Hughes, *East Africa* (revised ed.), Penguin, Harmondsworth, 1969.

Guy Hunter, *The New Societies of Tropical Africa*, Oxford University Press for IRR, 1962.

Harold Ingrams, *Uganda*, HMSO, London, 1960.

Griff Jones, *Britain and Nyasaland*, Allen & Unwin, London, 1964.

John de St. Jorre, *The Nigerian Civil War*, Hodder & Stoughton, London, 1972.

Patrick Keatley, *The Politics of Partnership*, Penguin, Harmondsworth, 1963.

A. H. M. Kirk-Greene, *Crisis and Conflict in Nigeria*, vols I and II, Oxford University Press, 1970 and 1971.

Colin Legum, *Africa, A Handbook*, Anthony Blond, London, 1965.

Colin Legum, *Pan-Africanism* (revised ed.), Praeger, New York, 1965.

Colin Leys, *European Politics in Southern Rhodesia*, Clarendon Press, Oxford, 1959.

P. C. Lloyd, *The New Élites of Tropical Africa*, Oxford University Press for IAI, 1966.

J. G. Lockhart and C. M. Woodhouse, *Rhodes*, Hodder & Stoughton, London, 1963.

D. A. Low, *Buganda in Modern History*, Weidenfeld & Nicolson, London, 1971.

D. A. Low and R. Cranford Pratt (eds), *Buganda and British Overrule 1900–1955*, Oxford University Press for EAISR, 1960.

John P. Mackintosh, *Nigerian Government and Politics*, Allen & Unwin, London, 1966.

J. S. Mangat, *A History of the Asians in East Africa*, Clarendon Press, Oxford, 1969.

Philip Mason, *The Birth of a Dilemma*, Oxford University Press for IRR, 1958.

Ali A. Mazrui, *Towards a Pax Africana*, Weidenfeld & Nicolson, London, 1967.

Tom Mboya, *Freedom and After*, Deutsch, London, 1963.

Vernon McKay, *Africa in World Politics*, Harper & Row, New York, 1963.

D. J. Murray, *The Governmental System in Southern Rhodesia*, Clarendon Press, Oxford, 1970.

Kwame Nkrumah, *Autobiography*, Nelson, Edinburgh, 1957.

Julius K. Nyerere, *Freedom and Unity*, Oxford University Press, 1967.

Julius K. Nyerere, *Freedom and Socialism*, Oxford University Press, 1968.

Julius K. Nyerere, *Ujamaa, Essays on Socialism*, Oxford University Press, 1968.

Roland Oliver and Gervase Mathew with Alison Smith (eds), *History of East Africa*, vols I and II, Oxford University Press, 1963 and 1968.

Claire Palley, *The Constitutional History and Law of Southern Rhodesia, 1888–1965*, Clarendon Press, Oxford, 1966.

Ronald Segal, *Political Africa*, Stevens, London, 1961.

George W. Shepherd Jr, *The Politics of African Nationalism*, Praeger, New York, 1962.

M. G. Smith, *Government in Zazzau*, Oxford University Press for IAI, 1960.

Paul Streeten, *The Frontiers of Development Studies*, Macmillan, London, 1972.

L. M. Thompson, *The Unification of South Africa 1902–1910*, Clarendon Press, Oxford, 1960.

Immanuel Wallerstein, *Africa, The Politics of Unity*, Pall Mall, London, 1968.

Sir Roy Welensky, *400 Days*, Collins, London, 1964.

Monica Wilson and Leonard Thompson (eds), *The Oxford History of South Africa*, vols I and II, Clarendon Press, Oxford, 1969 and 1971.

Index